D0400679

Connecting Past and Present

Concepts and Models for Service-Learning in **History**

Ira Harkavy and Bill M. Donovan, volume editors

Edward Zlotkowski, series editor

STERLING, VIRGINIA

Originally published by AAHE

Connecting Past and Present: Concepts and Models for Service-Learning in History
(AAHE's Series on Service-Learning in the Disciplines)
Ira Harkavy and Bill M. Donovan, *volume editors*
Edward Zlotkowski, *series editor*

About This Publication

This volume is part of AAHE's Series on Service-Learning in the Disciplines. Copyright © 2000 American Association for Higher Education. Copyright © 2005 Stylus Publishing, LLC. All rights reserved. Printed in the United States of America. For information about additional copies of this publication or other AAHE or Stylus publications, contact:

Stylus Publishing, LLC.
22883 Quicksilver Drive
Sterling, VA 20166-2102
Tel.: 1-800-232-0223 / Fax: 703-661-1547
www.Styluspub.com

ISBN 1-56377-020-2
ISBN (set) 1-56377-005-9

Contents

Part 3
Case Studies: Latin-American and European History

Appendix

About This Series

by Edward Zlotkowski

The following volume, *Connecting Past and Present: Concepts and Models for Service-Learning in History*, represents the 16th in a series of monographs on service-learning and the academic disciplines. Ever since the early 1990s, educators interested in reconnecting higher education not only with neighboring communities but also with the American tradition of education for service have recognized the critical importance of winning faculty support for this work. Faculty, however, tend to define themselves and their responsibilities largely in terms of the academic disciplines/interdisciplinary areas in which they have been trained. Hence, the logic of the present series.

The idea for this series first surfaced late in 1994 at a meeting convened by Campus Compact to explore the feasibility of developing a national network of service-learning educators. At that meeting, it quickly became clear that some of those assembled saw the primary value of such a network in its ability to provide concrete resources to faculty working in or wishing to explore service-learning. Out of that meeting there developed, under the auspices of Campus Compact, a new national group of educators called the Invisible College, and it was within the Invisible College that the monograph project was first conceived. Indeed, a review of both the editors and contributors responsible for many of the volumes in this series would reveal significant representation by faculty associated with the Invisible College.

If Campus Compact helped supply the initial financial backing and impulse for the Invisible College and for this series, it was the American Association for Higher Education (AAHE) that made completion of the project feasible. Thanks to its reputation for innovative work, AAHE was not only able to obtain the funding needed to support the project up through actual publication, it was also able to assist in attracting many of the teacher-scholars who participated as writers and editors. AAHE is grateful to the Corporation for National Service–Learn and Serve America for its financial support of the series.

Three individuals in particular deserve to be singled out for their contributions. Sandra Enos, former Campus Compact project director for Integrating Service With Academic Study, was shepherd to the Invisible College project. John Wallace, professor of philosophy at the University of Minnesota, was the driving force behind the creation of the Invisible College. Without his vision and faith in the possibility of such an undertaking, assembling the human resources needed for this series would have been very difficult. Third, AAHE's endorsement — and all that followed in its wake

— was due largely to then AAHE vice president Lou Albert. Lou's enthusiasm for the monograph project and his determination to see it adequately supported have been critical to its success. It is to Sandra, John, and Lou that the monograph series as a whole must be dedicated.

Another individual to whom the series owes a special note of thanks is Teresa E. Antonucci, who, as program manager for AAHE's Service-Learning Project, has helped facilitate much of the communication that has allowed the project to move forward.

The Rationale Behind the Series

A few words should be said at this point about the makeup of both the general series and the individual volumes. Although history may seem a somewhat unusual choice of disciplines with which to link service-learning, "natural fit" has not, in fact, been a determinant factor in deciding which disciplines/interdisciplinary areas the series should include. Far more important have been considerations related to the overall range of disciplines represented. Since experience has shown that there is probably no disciplinary area — from architecture to zoology — where service-learning cannot be fruitfully employed to strengthen students' abilities to become active learners as well as responsible citizens, a primary goal in putting the series together has been to demonstrate this fact. Thus, some rather natural choices for inclusion — disciplines such as anthropology and geography — have been passed over in favor of other, sometimes less obvious selections, such as history. Should the present series of volumes prove useful and well received, we can then consider filling in the many gaps we have left this first time around.

If a concern for variety has helped shape the series as a whole, a concern for legitimacy has been central to the design of the individual volumes. To this end, each volume has been both written by and aimed primarily at academics working in a particular disciplinary/interdisciplinary area. Many individual volumes have, in fact, been produced with the encouragement and active support of relevant discipline-specific national associations.

Furthermore, each volume has been designed to include its own appropriate theoretical, pedagogical, and bibliographical material. Especially with regard to theoretical and bibliographical material, this design has resulted in considerable variation both in quantity and in level of discourse. Thus, for example, a volume such as Accounting contains more introductory and less bibliographical material than does Composition — simply because there is less written on and less familiarity with service-learning in accounting. However, no volume is meant to provide an extended introduction to service-learning *as a generic concept*. For material of this nature, the reader is referred to such texts as Kendall's *Combining Service and Learning: A Resource Book for Community and Public Service* (NSEE 1990) and Jacoby's *Service-Learning in Higher Education* (Jossey-Bass 1996).

February 2000

Introduction

by Ira Harkavy and Bill M. Donovan

The question that animates this volume is: Why connect service-learning to history courses? The authors of its essays answer that question in different ways. Indeed, this volume illustrates and highlights a diversity of historical approaches and interpretations. Nonetheless, the authors tend to agree that they do their jobs better as teachers (and in some cases as researchers) by engaging their students in service-learning.

Service-learning helps history teachers teach history better for a variety of reasons. Primary among them, perhaps, is that service-learning courses at their best tend to focus on pressing real-world problems. Problems such as poverty, poor schooling, hunger, homelessness, urban crises are troubling and compelling. Service-learning — by engaging students in activities designed to help others; to make things better; to contribute to a specified community, school, or agency — adds an immediacy and relevance that increase meaning and student motivation. The complex, interrelated real-world problems of real communities are, of course, historical problems — problems that are profoundly shaped by past events and experience. Students "discover" this through their reading, activity, and reflection, and they also "discover" that historical knowledge is essential for understanding and effective action. Moreover, service-learning engages students in active doing, thus providing an opportunity for them to put their ideals into practice and make a contribution. It provides (to paraphrase Dewey) a starting point for history, a present situation with immediate and pressing problems.[1] In short, service-learning is a powerful catalyst for historical research and scholarship.

Integrating service-learning into history courses also leads to new learnings and insights for faculty members. In other words, it results in "creative surprises," unexpected findings and conclusions.[2] The majority of the authors in this volume emphasize how their thinking and pedagogy changed as a result of their developing and teaching a service-learning course. Historians involved in service-learning courses clearly learn much as they teach. Based on the "reports from the field" that follow, we believe that it is not extravagant to claim that service-learning can help historians better contribute to the core mission of American higher education; namely, to advance, preserve, and transmit knowledge, as well as help produce the well-educated, cultured, truly moral citizens needed to develop and maintain an optimally democratic society.

This volume begins with four essays that provide different takes on history and service-learning. Different takes are highly appropriate for a discipline that has all past human behavior as its beat. One of us, Bill Donovan, makes a case that service-learning advances both higher education and the discipline of history. Focusing on undergraduate education in particular, Donovan argues that service-learning can help undergraduates develop both intellectually and as citizens, connecting "students' outside lives with key historical issues inside the classroom while call[ing] into question the narrow careerism that has become so prevalent on college campuses." Donovan goes on to distinguish service-learning from community service and experiential learning, emphasizing that good service-learning requires deep and sound intellectual grounding within an academic course. He also presents a series of steps that provide an answer to the how-to question — how to integrate service-learning into a history course. He concludes with a call for service-learning to focus on the problems of our cities and for historians to employ service-learning to ensure the vitality of the discipline now and in the future.

The other one of us, Ira Harkavy, has a different goal for his essay. How to integrate service-learning into a history course is not his primary concern. Instead, he sees a service-learning movement that could benefit from the study of history. Criticizing "traditional" service-learning for its too narrow focus, he calls for developing an approach that places an increased emphasis on improving the quality of life in a higher education institution's local community. He suggests that the early history of the American urban research university provides a valuable model that can help inform and improve service-learning.

Harkavy and Donovan both present historical research to make their case. Both of them also identify the problems of the American city as a primary focus for service-learning courses and research projects. Harkavy, in fact, argues that service-learning practitioners/theorists can contribute to knowledge, student learning, citizenship, as well as to solving the problems of the American city if they learn from history and build upon the work of their turn-of-the-century predecessors.

While John Saltmarsh discusses crises in American society, particularly "the crisis of our civic life," his essay takes primary aim at historical teaching and scholarship as currently practiced. Using Emerson's essay "The American Scholar," with its sharp critique of detached, disengaged scholarship as touchstone, Saltmarsh contends that what Emerson prophesied has become an unfortunate reality. Disengagement of historians from the world has, he emphasizes, deep intellectual and personal costs. Both positivist and postmodernist "distancing" (our term, not his) have resulted in poor teaching, irrelevant research, and alienation of faculty members.

Saltmarsh sees teaching a course in American-based community experience as a direct challenge to the dominant views of pedagogy and epistemology held by the history profession. He writes that the "greatest challenge [to the history profession] comes down to the fact that community-based education and scholarship posit engagement and direct relevance as a counterweight to detached objectivity." Saltmarsh describes his own and his students' experiences in a service-learning course in which "the past ceased to be an object and became, instead, a vital, interactive part of their lives."

While Saltmarsh calls for radical change of the profession through service-learning, J. Matthew Gallman argues that service-learning has benefits that can be accomplished with only a slight change in traditional approaches. He does see significant benefits "for students and the community *above and beyond* specifically disciplinary gains," particularly helping students "to think about — and learn about — social justice issues." Nonetheless, in addressing a number of obstacles to service-learning, Gallman indicates how these concerns can be effectively addressed within the dominant paradigm of the profession. He makes a powerful case for a service-learning instructor's knowing the students' service sites well, even "spending time . . . engaged in service alongside his or her students." (This suggestion is, in our judgment, much more radical than Gallman lets on.)

Gallman's major argument is that service-learning enhances the ability of students to use metaphorical analysis — it helps in "training the metaphorical mind." In his view, history as a discipline, given the problem of chronological distance from the actual service activity, requires a metaphorical approach. He calls for placing students "within" the metaphor — "using their experiences to better understand the shifting relationship between the middle classes and people who are poor." Gallman's call for personal engagement finds deep resonance in many of the essays that follow.

Michael Zuckerman's essay opens the second section of the volume. Here, historians focus on their various experiences with integrating service-learning into a specific history course. Zuckerman's essay also leads off four essays by Americanists, followed by essays by scholars whose "terrains" are Latin America, Ancient Athens, and Europe.

Zuckerman's essay provides an excellent transition from the conceptually oriented articles to case studies. His piece is in itself a work of compelling historical writing, as he richly describes the process of his engagement, a process driven by a felt need to act, to try to do something about the appalling conditions of the public schools in his university's (the University of Pennsylvania's) local community.

From the title of his essay, "The Turnerian Frontier," to its conclusion, Zuckerman interlaces his text with allusions to Frederick Jackson Turner's "frontier" thesis. Zuckerman's urban American frontier is both more troubling and more promising than Turner's Western pioneering frontier. It provides opportunities for service, civic engagement, and, most centrally, learning. Zuckerman concludes his essay, and its description of his students' intellectual and personal journeys, as follows:

> When I sent my students off to the Turnerian frontier [the John P. Turner Middle School in West Philadelphia], I was overwhelmed by the ways in which their experience enriched their understanding of America. When I sent them to a nearer frontier [University City High School, a school literally bordering Penn's campus], I was, if anything, even more overwhelmed, and their understanding was, if anything, even more enriched. Their service-learning was, by their lights, immensely satisfying as community service. It was, by mine, even more rewarding as learning.

Zuckerman's essay also chronicles his learning as a result of his experience teaching a service-learning course. Improvisation and on-the-ground, ongoing problem solving characterize his style and approach. Albert Camarillo's piece similarly describes how integrating service-learning into a history course "educated the educator." Among other things, Camarillo describes his learning to think and teach differently and his crossing of disciplinary boundaries in the process of figuring out how to "build a service component into a history course."

For a service-learning practitioner, Camarillo has a long story to tell. Encouraged by colleagues at Stanford's pioneering Haas Center for Public Service, Camarillo piloted a service-learning course that continues more than 10 years later. Camarillo's course focuses on poverty and homelessness in America. Having chosen this topic on the bases of both an intellectual interest and personal concern about a societal problem, Camarillo describes how he worked to relate his professional expertise as a historian of ethnic and racial minorities to the contemporary reality of poverty and homelessness.

As with Zuckerman's, Camarillo's journey begins with his experience and then concentrates on what his students did and learned. Camarillo is motivated by "the meaningful engagement and greater understanding of both historical and contemporary issues" that his students exhibit. He describes the process as follows:

> The factor that supercharges student interest in this topic is the dialectical relationship between the service and the learning. Exposure to homelessness through the service placement inspires students to wrestle intellectually with the required readings and motivates them to participate in discussions in which I often serve merely as moderator rather than discussion leader. At the same time, the service experience challenges students to examine personal and societal values, to pose a variety of questions about American institutions and policies, to think critically, and to understand better the crises faced by fellow citizens who find themselves in temporary

shelters as they try to cope with the devastating effects of poverty. The service makes the students better learners and makes me a better teacher.

John Puckett, a historian and faculty member in Penn's Graduate School of Education, and Elisa von Joeden-Forgey, a graduate student in history, echo Zuckerman's and Camarillo's findings of significant academic and civic learning among their students. They are also similarly concerned with how to make the service-learning and history connection. With a critical eye, they dissect their experience, in particular highlighting problems with the single-semester course format that they initially employed. Impacts on both the college students and the high school students with whom the under-graduates worked were, according to Puckett and Forgey, too limited and ephemeral. They describe significant improvement and "much deeper relationships" once they expanded the course to two semesters.

An academic year-long format might have been particularly necessary for Puckett and Forgey's course, since it involved college and high school students doing local history projects on significant community issues. Puckett and Forgey define this approach as "academically based community service," a type of service-learning that integrates research, teaching, and service and that "puts the hands-on investigation of societal problems at the core of the undergraduate academic program." Using Harry Boyte's illuminating concept of *public work*, Puckett and Forgey view academically based community service as a "powerful form of public work uniquely appropriate for American higher education."

For Beverly W. Jones, service-learning is particularly appropriate for a historically black college or university (HBCU) such as her institution, North Carolina Central University. Her essay, as Harkavy's, makes the case for history; namely, historical knowledge is crucial for effective action in the present. Citing the historical tradition of communalism and service in the African-American community as manifested in mutual aid societies, fraternal orders, churches, and HBCUs, Jones argues that colleges and universities need to play a more central role than ever before in order to improve the conditions of poor blacks living in America's cities.

Jones provides a case study of how North Carolina Central University (NCCU) reclaimed its tradition of service by partnering with poor communities "to improve their quality of life and create means of capacity building." According to Jones, the appointment in 1993 of Julius Chambers as chancellor represents the critical turning point in NCCU's movement back to service. Chambers's efforts spurred a revision of the university's mission to highlight the expectation that "faculty and students . . . engage in scholarly and creative as well as service activities that benefit the larger community." Presidential leadership helped set the stage for service-learning classes taught by Jones and other colleagues that focus on student learning and development, and genuine community improvement.

Bill Donovan's second essay opens a series of four by non-Americanists. Although a historian of Latin American colonial societies, Donovan has taught service-learning courses both in and outside of his primary field. His chapter, in fact, largely focuses on his experiences integrating service-learning into a freshman history survey course. Donovan highlights the significant ongoing assistance he received from Loyola College's Center for Values and Service, one of the many service-learning centers that have developed over the past decade. Most centrally, Donovan's case study of the freshman survey course, as well as his brief discussion of how he integrated service-learning into courses on Latin American history, Western history from late antiquity to the Renaissance, and historical methods, illustrates his argument that service-learning "enhance[s] student understanding of historical issues and processes." Donovan also describes how personally connecting to others through service can help advance student learning:

> One student wrote that the lectures and readings on the killings and destruction in Central America had not really made an impact on her because the statistics were so overwhelming. But after speaking to a young man from Guatemala, who had to flee for his life, she now genuinely understood the tragedy of events there. For her, as for many other students, the human connection of the service project opened her intellectual understanding.

Marshall Eakin, like Donovan, is a Latin American historian. And like Donovan, he emphasizes that making a connection to people and to a site powerfully advances student learning and historical understanding. Eakin helps his students make that connection very far from home in an intensive month-long service-learning course in the Chilean desert. Eakin describes the process of how his course came into being, from an idea developed and proposed by a Vanderbilt student to its actual implementation. The central role of that Vanderbilt undergraduate (she also served as a paid teaching assistant for the course) illustrates how service-learning can provide undergraduates with opportunities for intellectual leadership usually reserved for graduate students.

Although Eakin and his students necessarily confronted logistical issues and learning opportunities different from those encountered in a less intensive service-learning experience at a more familiar and less distant site, they also faced questions that transcend the nature of a site and degree of immersion. While developing the course, Eakin, for example, had concerns about effectively drawing on his training as a historian of Latin America, providing students with a historical perspective on the issues they would confront, and striking "a balance between academic and service work." At the conclusion of the course, Eakin found that a good balance had indeed been achieved. He also concluded, however, that the course would have been stronger had the service work been more historical in nature. This finding resonates with Puckett and Forgey's emphasis on students doing community history. The experience in Chile, with the enormous effort that such an ambitious project entailed, also led Eakin to conclude that Vanderbilt needs to develop a service-learning center as a vehicle for building a more systematic program. Zuckerman, Camarillo, and Donovan would certainly concur with Eakin's finding, since service-learning centers on their campuses have played such central roles in developing and implementing their courses.

Of the courses described in this volume, Eakin's takes us the greatest geographical distance. Ralph Rosen, a professor of classics at Penn, might place his students at a high school adjacent to the university's campus, but he takes them a very long temporal distance indeed. Rosen and his students focus on making connections between antiquity, specifically Ancient Athens, and present-day Philadelphia.

Why would a professor of classics teach a service-learning seminar? For Rosen, the answer is straightforward: Classical studies is important, helping us to better understand and live effectively in the world. A service-learning course in classical studies provides an opportunity to illustrate in practice the significance of classical studies — a significance that cannot be adequately conveyed through mere persuasive rhetoric.

Rosen describes his experience teaching two service-learning seminars: one entitled Community, Neighborhood, and Family in Ancient Athens and Modern Philadelphia; the other, Scandalous Arts in Ancient and Modern Communities. In both these seminars, undergraduate students shared their learning and worked with students from a local high school. Rosen's students, in effect, had the opportunity to teach and to learn through teaching — or to learn through (to use Lee Shulman's wonderful phrase) "professing the liberal arts" (1997: 151). This approach had positive impact on the high school students as well. Rosen writes:

> The students at UCHS [University City High School] were uniformly excited by the visits from Penn. Their teacher told me time and again that her students always eagerly looked forward to the visits from the Penn students. She found that even some of the more uninterested students felt drawn out by the experience of having Penn students visit. To my surprise (because this had not been my experience with the first course), she told me that most of the students were actually interested in the antiquarian aspects of the material; that is, they were amazed at the clear connections to be found between ancient society and our own.

Service-learning, according to Rosen, helped make the case for classical studies to both college and high school students, and even affected his reading of classical texts. Steve Hochstadt, a European historian at Bates College, Lewiston, Maine, finds that service-learning can significantly advance understanding of the Holocaust for his students as well as public school students in communities around Bates. Similar to Rosen, Hochstadt argues that teaching history is a superb way for students to learn history. Summarizing the impact of "professing" history, Hochstadt writes: "Students who teach . . . in local schools can simultaneously serve and learn, performing useful and valued functions for many community members, while deepening their knowledge of a historical subject."

Hochstadt has been leading a Holocaust teaching project at Bates since 1992. Offered to students on a voluntary basis during a short five-week semester, the project stands somewhere between community service and service-learning. Although no credit is given for participation in the project, only students who have previously taken Hochstadt's course on the Holocaust are permitted to be project members. Moreover, students in the project take part in an orientation designed to improve their effectiveness as teachers.

The particular organization of the project notwithstanding, Hochstadt's central conclusion that multiple, often implicit, agendas are achieved through the linkage of service and learning has general applicability. In his case, secondary goals of reducing prejudice, increasing interest in history and raising the intellectual aspirations of public school students, and improving town-gown relations are all significant. His conclusions that some of the many agendas of a service-learning project might be in conflict and that a faculty member needs to be conscious of his or her different purposes and agendas are helpful reminders for both beginning and experienced service-learning practitioners.

More generally, we conclude that the essays in this volume should be enormously helpful to historians and other scholars interested or involved in service-learning teaching and research. The authors not only provide persuasive answers to the "why connect service-learning and history" question, but they also provide powerful strategies for how to make the connection. Their essays give rich description and texture to important organizational issues, including the role of university presidents and service-learning centers. The various discussions of pedagogical approaches, such as doing community history, teaching history to K-12 students, and focusing on pressing urban issues in the higher education institution's locality are particularly instructive.

In our judgment, these contributions are less significant, however, than the creative, active approach to course development and implementation that the authors' work exemplifies. More generally, their essays are the testimonies of "reflective practitioners" able to learn in and from the problems of their profession (Schön 1984).[3] Their practice, including the expression of that practice in their writings, offers a compelling case for service-learning as a powerful pedagogy for advancing learning, citizenship, and service.

We believe that these essays also make a compelling case for the importance of history. Why study history? We, along with many (most?) of the authors in this volume, would answer: to better understand the world in order to help change the world for the better. Service-learning, we would further argue, helps historians better understand the world *as they work* to change it. The essays in this volume certainly do not (indeed, could not) prove that point. They do effectively pose the question and provide a good place to begin to look for answers. To put it another way, a central question for historians is, what are the most effective ways to do history — to study and teach it? We hope this volume contributes to a serious, sustained, and systematic discussion within the profession as to whether and in what ways service-learning can improve the historian's craft (Bloch 1953).

Notes

1. Dewey's actual statement reads: "the true starting point of history is always some present situation with its problems" (1966: 24).

2. For an illuminating discussion of the concept of creative surprises, see William Foote Whyte's (1991) "Social Sciences in the University."

3. Also see Schön's (1995) exceptional article "Knowing-in-Action."

References

Bloch, Marc. (1953). *The Historian's Craft*. New York, NY: Knopf.

Dewey, John. (1966, orig. 1916). *Democracy in Education*. Reprint, New York, NY: Free Press.

Schön, Donald A. (1984). *The Reflective Practitioner*. New York, NY: Basic Books.

——— . (Nov./Dec. 1995). "Knowing-in-Action: The New Scholarship Requires a New Epistemology." *Change* 27(6): 26-34.

Shulman, Lee S. (1997). "Professing the Liberal Arts." In *Education and Democracy: Re-Imagining Liberal Learning in America*, edited by Robert Orrill, pp. 151-173. New York, NY: College Entrance Examination Board.

Whyte, William Foote. (1991). "Social Sciences in the University." *American Behavioral Scientist* 34(5): 618-633.

Service-Learning as a Strategy for Advancing the Contemporary University and the Discipline of History

by Bill M. Donovan

In this volume the editors seek to initiate a discussion about prevailing assumptions of teaching and scholarship. In this chapter I argue that the current definitions of scholarship and teaching are overly restrictive — harmful to American higher education as an institution, and to faculty members in particular. In bringing service-learning to the table, I endorse the concept of problem-focused teaching and scholarship, the tradition of which is firmly grounded in the origins of modern American higher education. Urban institutions especially must undertake a far more active role in stopping the social decay now bordering so many campuses. Yet I do not view service-learning just as a primarily defensive response to academia's critics. Instead, I argue here that service-learning offers enormous intellectual benefits for teaching and research. Instructors who use service-learning regularly affirm that students are more engaged in learning through connecting their lives outside the classroom with the course material presented in it. In becoming better students, they also more clearly see the connections between themselves and off-campus communities. To be sure, service-learning is not appropriate for every history course. But it is highly flexible, and has been profitably utilized in a wide variety of courses.

The following essay puts service-learning within a larger discussion of the purpose of higher education institutions, teaching, and scholarship. Other essays in this volume illustrate what service-learning is in a wide variety of history courses. I accept that my proposals as well as my analysis of the profession will provoke controversy. But the time has come to discuss candidly where American higher education is going and the part that we as historians and educators will play in that journey. We simply can no longer afford to be passive actors believing ourselves secure behind campus walls and tenured status, removed from the crisis within our cities and increasing public hostility to liberal learning. Nor, as too often the case, can we clamor at every public summons to reevaluate aspects of higher education as a threat to institutional and faculty autonomy. We must reconnect our institutions, our discipline, and ourselves to the wider society that supports us with its young men and women, its financial capital, and its faith that intellectual pursuit should be valued. To do so will open up new research and teaching possibilities that can enrich us as a discipline. To retreat from the challenge will further marginalize American intellectual life.

Furthermore, while much of what I say is applicable to many of the sciences and the liberal arts in general,[1] my argument here is specifically directed to my fellow historians. The essential nature of our discipline synthesizes diverse data into coherent representations of how and why events occurred in the past, and the connections of those events to contemporary society. In Dewey's famous words, "the true starting point of history is always some present situation with its problems" (1966: 24). Dewey's aphorism is evident in the rise of such fields as African-American and women's history. Thus, history as a discipline serves naturally as a vehicle for incorporating out-of-classroom experiences into teaching and scholarship.

The Importance of Undergraduate Education

A word needs to be said about the undergraduate focus of my remarks here. Although service-learning has been successfully used in graduate classes, much of the service-learning literature concerns undergraduate teaching and learning. Frank Rhodes, the past president of Cornell University, has emphasized that even at elite research institutions (and surely at other types of colleges and universities as well)

> undergraduate education is fundamental to the existence of the university: it occupies more time, involves more people, consumes more resources, requires more facilities, and generates more revenue than any other activity. Almost everything else the universities do depends upon it. . . . It is through undergraduate education [that] the public encounters the university most directly, and it is on undergraduate education that the health of [universities] will stand or fall. (1994: 181)

The vast majority of our undergraduate students will not pursue graduate work in history, and most of us teach far more nonmajors than majors. Moreover, while many students and parents continue to acknowledge the value of the liberal arts, 50 percent of all undergraduates choose a major in vocational and occupational fields (Jacoby 1994: 9). Classes in history accord such students an invaluable context to aid them in determining their identities as individuals and as members of society at large. It equips them with analytical tools to appraise contemporary social and political issues. One hopes that history helps them to gain a sense of connection to the intellectual achievements of Western and other civilizations.

It is crucially important for American society, as well as higher education, that students leave college not simply knowledgeable in their fields but as individuals who can live responsibly in an increasingly diverse and interdependent world; who are socially responsible, ready to assume an active role in their communities, and have an appreciation for the importance of lifelong learning and the liberal arts.[2] Thus, our task as college educators must be to nurture ethical as well as critical thinking. But in the future doing so will be far from easy, for in part our very ability to do so effectively means that we in the academy must rethink some basic assumptions about teaching and learning. How many of us have actively considered the matter of how students really learn? I offer this question not as an invitation to an endless debate on epistemology, but as a concern that goes to the center of our effectiveness as educators, both in the classroom and in print. CIRP (Cooperative Institutional Research Program) studies indicate that even though demographic characteristics of entering freshmen continue to remain generally constant, their expectations and approaches to learning have significantly changed over time. Increasingly they are involved in formal as well as informal learning outside the traditional faculty-centered classroom.[3] New technologies, particularly the Internet, distant learning, and wired dormitories, are only accelerating this trend. Such changes are leading more and more frequently to students leaving college with a disjointed educational experience.

Without an ability to see their undergraduate education as a coherent process, many students and their parents come to view college as a white-collar trade school and attach little importance to the arts. When neither students nor the general public sees colleges and universities as communities of scholars in touch with the problems and aspirations of the general citizenry, it can come as no surprise that a national audience has emerged for those who criticize the resources appropriated for education and who deride academics as members of a privileged class who do not really work.[4] Service-learning will not, obviously, halt this cottage industry of intellectual bashing. But it does call into question the distorted images of academic life. It can connect students' outside lives with key historical issues inside the classroom while calling into question the narrow careerism that has become so prevalent on college campuses.

But before turning to the aims and methods of service-learning, it is essential to distinguish it from community service and experiential learning in general. Although community service has enjoyed a long relationship with American higher education, it is essentially independent of academic pedagogy. While community service might promote public awareness, it does not promote learning per se. Experiential learning, on the other hand, primarily revolves around internships, which often have no direct connection with texts and lectures. What differentiates service-learning from community service and most internships are the roles assumed in it by faculty and by critical reflection. According to the National and Community Service Act of 1990, *thoughtfully organized service . . . integrated into the students' academic curriculum or provides structured time for students to think, talk, or write . . . enhances what is taught in school by extending student learning beyond the classroom and into the community, and helps to foster the development of a sense of caring for others. (CNS 1994)*[5]

In other words, to be successful, service-learning cannot be simply conceptually tacked on. Instead, it must originate in the classroom, tied to texts and lecture material, and designed to meet the basic educational goals of the course. Students must critically reflect on the relationship between their service and their course materials. Thus, faculty participation becomes crucial, not only in relating the service experience to the course but also in making sure that working with different social, economic, and racial populations does not reinforce stereotypes.

Service that is conceptually nebulous does little to advance learning. Hence, much thought and preparation about themes and texts are essential if service-related experiences are to be successfully applied in the classroom. To be sure, there is a generic civic and moral value imbedded in service experiences, but this generic value should not be allowed to compromise the intellectual rigor and educational goals of the course. The fact that a course utilizes service-learning does not imply that every text and every lecture should be channeled toward social problems. Nor does it imply that already successful lectures or other essential historical information should be jettisoned. Within this volume one will find undergraduate history courses that might not at first glance be identified with public service. The range of historical topics those courses address provides some idea of the intellectual range and organizational options service-learning can support.

Service-Learning Issues and Challenges

As the courses featured in this volume attest, using service-learning is not without its difficulties. It must be thoughtfully integrated into the structure of the course, but consideration must be given to the agencies and communities where students carry out their service work.[6] It is crucial that faculty discuss with site workers the type and length of service most useful to them. The fact that some students are disinclined to do service can result in an adverse experience both for them and for the population with whom they work. Faculty must take care that students act responsibly, show up when they are scheduled, and understand that they are working *with* and not simply *for* others. Programs involving children especially need to be able to count on students showing up.

Furthermore, it is only to be expected that some students will find the service work irrelevant to their understanding of the class material, in much the same manner in which some students find individual texts and assignments pointless. Difficulties of this nature, however, can be overcome by making clear why the service was chosen and how it relates to the course. Still other students will seek to maintain comfortable stereotypes. In these cases, good preorientation sessions together with class discussions in which students explain their experiences and insights often serve to deflate facile generalizations, and, when the instructor takes care, this can be done in a noncontentious fashion.

At some institutions, assistance is available to help faculty create service-learning courses. Community outreach offices can assume much of the load in setting up a service component, dealing with risk and liability issues, and proposing appropriate locations. Campus Compact, a national organization of college and university presidents representing more than 640 institutions, is a valuable resource for syllabi, applicable literature, and referrals to faculty already engaged in service-learning. The Service-Learning Listserv and the Invisible College site on the Internet represent other valuable, electronic resources. Nonetheless, the time and effort necessary to prepare a service-learning course should not be underestimated. Sometimes, faculty-development grants are available, not only to compensate for the time and effort involved, but also to signal an institution's willingness to support new teaching endeavors.[7]

Discussions of service-learning inevitably lead to questions of assessment. Faculty must identify the criteria that confirm successful completion of the service component, with regard to both faculty course objectives and student learning objectives. In light of the grade-centered attitude that many students hold, this means indicating explicitly how much weight the service contributes to the final course grade, and indicating clearly its relevance to the course material. The most common method of determining service-effectiveness has been through the use of surveys. These can be incorporated as separate categories into standard computer-read teaching evaluations, supplemented by qualitative student comments; or separate service-learning evaluations can be used.

In the last few years, quantitative research into the effectiveness of service-learning as a pedagogy has begun to appear. These studies indicate that well thought out service components with clear connections to the course enhance students' class participation and willingness to accept intellectual challenges (Giles and Eyler 1994).[8]

A second and more difficult issue involves assessing the broader goals of promoting civic virtue and social responsibility. Such broader goals are especially important because it is here where the public debate outside the academy tends to focus. How effective is service-learning in helping colleges and universities engage productively with their surrounding communities? As James Robertson Price and John Martello point out:

> To go from service-learning as it is currently practiced to the emergence of an educated citizenry effectively engaged in solving problems requires a big leap, both imaginatively and conceptually. Moreover, it is a leap that the service-learning movement must clarify, explain, and negotiate. If not, what will happen five or ten years from now when students, faculty, administrators, community members, and financial supporters look around and find that our cities and communities are still riddled with massive public problems, and that our citizens are as apparently lacking in civic virtues and skills as ever? (1996: 18)

If, beyond its pedagogical merits, we consider service-learning not as a form of voluntarism but as an act of citizenship, then the chances of reaching some of these larger goals increase. CIRP surveys of incoming freshmen indicate that a rising number of them arrive on college campuses with service experiences, some of which they carried out as a requirement for high school graduation.[9] Hence, using service-based assignments will not come as a complete surprise to them.

Higher Education Reform in Historical Context

American higher education has frequently been the target of critics inside and outside the academy. Commentators from all sides of the political spectrum have produced best-selling jeremiads detailing all that is supposedly wrong with American colleges and universities. But the current assault on the nation's higher education establishment promises to have far more difficult results than those of the past, and poses significantly different challenges than do the faddish intellectual hecklers found on television talk shows and on the pages of *Time, Newsweek,* or *People* magazines. Technological developments together with the fiscal dilemmas that plague every level of education suggest that difficult changes are at hand.

Not surprisingly, a growing chorus of private groups and public officials call for the country's educational establishment to demonstrate some manner of accountability for what it does, and for what it allegedly fails to do. State legislatures and elected officials have already begun to change the face of higher education by assailing flagship campuses and publicly funded institutions. The Ohio Legislature's decision to terminate doctoral history programs at state-supported universities — including private schools receiving state aid — except at the Ohio State University, and Minnesota's efforts to change university tenure policies represent just two recent challenges. James F. Carlin, chairman of the Massachusetts Board of Higher Education, openly proclaims his goal of abolishing tenure, a practice he terms "an absolute scam." Carlin charges that public colleges are "managerially dysfunctional . . . [and] devoid of accountability. . . . [In the future] meaningless research [should be banned]: [indeed,] 50% of research outside the hard sciences is a lot of foolishness" (1997: A5). The fierce debate over the National History Standards, the offensive personal assaults against professional historians involved in the Smithsonian's Enola Gay exhibition, and the attempt to close the Woodrow Wilson Center confirm that our discipline stands on the front line in this educational struggle, whether we like it or not.[10]

The issue, then, is no longer whether our colleges and universities will change, but the direction of the change. Who will lead this process; how will it affect the curriculum and the traditional discipline-based department system? Will change be determined by state and federal legislators, outside administrators, or by the faculty? Rethinking what we consider our mission as teachers, and to some extent, our definition of scholarship, could well be the academy's best instruments for shaping what will happen.

It is today undeniable that urban colleges and universities must reach out to their immediate communities.[11] Their futures depend on the viability of urban economies and surrounding campus neighborhoods. Urban decay heavily influences recruitment and retention of students, faculty, and support services. The notion that university communities can retreat behind campus walls, oblivious to outside problems, carries a tremendous cost, and is unsustainable in the long run. Yet the case for academic engagement with the community does not rest primarily on the urgency of contemporary problems. As Alfred North Whitehead (1929) has rightly pointed out, universities have never been restricted to purely abstract learning. The history of modern American higher education sustains Whitehead's observation.

The original mission of American colleges looked outward to the wider community. Harold T. Shapiro notes: "Unlike many of the great European universities, the first American colleges were not established by independent groups of faculty and students, or by royal initiative, but by private and public communities to serve important civic purposes" (1997: 69). Even the earliest schools, which began as religious institutions, sought to encourage the improvement of civil society. The number of colleges remained modest during the first decades of the new American republic. In large part that limited number denoted social attitudes toward access to higher education, but at the same time, it also reflected the reality that higher education lacked the monopoly on professional accreditation that it now possesses. Furthermore, a great deal of education and intellectual life flourished outside the confines of college campuses. Subscription libraries, literary clubs, debating societies, and civic institutions, the most notable of which was the Lowell Institute, all engaged in educating the public at large. Indeed, well into the 20th century, much of America's foremost intellectual talent operated independent of the higher education establishment.

Traditional liberal arts colleges provided the educated, professional middle class necessary for the rising American republic. Land-grant institutions, of course, owed their creation to the belief that public higher education should serve the public benefit. After the mid-19th century, the number of urban colleges rapidly expanded, most notably Roman Catholic–affiliated colleges such as Catholic University in Washington, DC, which explicitly sought to meet the needs of immigrant students unable to enter secular institutions. Central to their mission, and to the religious who taught in and administered them, was providing social guidance for the benefit of struggling immigrant neighborhoods. Their goal was to instill models of citizenship and social ethics with professional training. Such European immigrant neighborhoods have now almost disappeared as later, American-born generations moved to the suburbs. But the identity and mission statements found in catalogues of religious-affiliated colleges and universities sustain the principal position originally given to social outreach and responsible individual behavior.

The modern American university system came into existence in the period between the 1870s and the end of World War I, and one of the most important developments of that era can be found in the merger of the German university model with the American liberal arts college. That merger ultimately led the social science and liberal arts disciplines toward objective natural science models.[12] These have profoundly affected how we, as academic scholars, define ourselves, perform research and teaching, and how the public perceives us. The research dimension in Daniel Coit Gilman's fusion of German and American university models became increasingly dominant in the post-World War I and II eras. While service is an essential component of both types, their direction and methods fundamentally differ.

Ira Harkavy's (1996) essay on American universities before World War I reminds us that service to the community was originally a central function of research institutions. After the carnage of World War I, however, applied research for social and political reform retreated in the face of a natural science model and an underlying commitment to a "detached and objective study of society" that "allowed no room for an ameliorative approach" (62). The still greater horrors of World War II accelerated the trend toward abstracted research, in which research and teaching per se are not directed at solving problems troubling surrounding communities. The service provided by faculty and academic departments consisted solely of the specialized research they produced, whether it had any particular wider ramifications.

Ironically, although applied technology played an indispensable role in

America's triumph in World War II, that triumph served only to increase the separation of applied and pure sciences into virtually dichotomous entities. As all freshman texts on Western civilization point out, the notion of "pure" as opposed to "applied" science goes back to the Greeks, who separated philosophic inquiry from practical expression.[13] Early modern scientists such as Galileo and Huygens reconnected theoretical and applied sciences as evidenced in Francis Bacon's articulation of science's purpose as the "relief of man's estate." But in reality, Bacon spoke too soon, for technological progress largely developed on a very narrow theoretical base until the second industrial revolution, when emerging chemical, pharmaceutical, and public utilities industries together with public health concerns directly relied on advances in basic science (Stokes 1997: 33-34).

Within the second industrial revolution's intellectual and economic background arose the German research university. For just as industry increasingly required skilled managerial talent, so it demanded skilled engineers and scientists to maintain the pace of economic growth. Thus, part of Germany's contribution to the new economy came from its establishment of universities focused on original research and teaching alongside new technical schools concentrated on applied science for industry. Americans brought this institutional division home with them in creating new universities such as Johns Hopkins and the University of Chicago, and in reconstructing existing schools such as Harvard, Yale, and the University of California. The experience of World War II, particularly in the construction of the atomic bomb, seemed to validate that distinction.

The Challenge of the Present

Two circumstances further molded the character of post–World War II American higher education. First, the GI Bill together with the Cold War stimulated an unprecedented expansion that continued well into the 1970s as baby boomers packed campuses and classrooms. Second, the natural sciences increased enormously in prestige and funding as science and technology came to be viewed as ideological battlegrounds in the struggle between East and West. In response to changing circumstances and funding conditions, many academic departments, history among them, pragmatically appropriated "scientific" terminology and methodologies, some even retitling themselves "social sciences." In pointing this out, I do not wish to suggest that historians simply ignored social issues or became intellectual chameleons to take advantage of funding opportunities. During this same period, historians produced a wealth of meaningful research on topics crucial to American society.

But the research university model's rise to dominance in American higher education has not come without cost. One cost has been a fractionaliza-tion of knowledge in which research, the creation of new knowledge, has become an end rather than a means to an end. Furthermore, the merger of two very different educational traditions has produced a confusion of mis-sion together with a tension felt throughout American higher education. Traditional teaching institutions and liberal arts colleges are now common-ly staffed by faculty who view career goals and professional success largely through the prism of their own specialized discipline and scholarship.[14] College administrators, trustees, and alumni complain of faculty defining themselves primarily as members of an academic department, rather than as part of a greater institution. Such a department-based culture is seen as highly detrimental to institutional mission and identity.

A highly competitive environment for students and funding reinforces this situation as faculty publications increasingly become the chief mecha-nism for achieving national recognition. Academic administrators in faculty reviews exert internal pressure by adopting publications as the primary standard for tenure, promotion, and performance assessment. As a result, other scholarly and professional activities depreciate, thus reinforcing the cycle of faculty energy removed from larger institutional priorities.

But the end of the Cold War has now transformed the environment for American higher education. A thoroughly altered financial climate is the most conspicuous change that has come about. The Department of Education's National Center for Educational Statistics predicts not only increasing college enrollments but also steadily increasing tuition costs to the year 2006. At the same time, federal and state spending for higher edu-cation — a $180-billion enterprise — will remain comparatively stagnant.[15] It is misguided to believe that colleges and universities can raise prices indef-initely, particularly in the face of a growing chorus of voices that say current costs are already too high. How will tuition-driven public and private insti-tutions pay for accelerating costs in technology, infrastructure, and salaries? What will be the long-term consequences with regard to career choices, pur-chasing power, and the ability to send children to college for a generation of college graduates saddled with enormous debts from loans taken for college and graduate study?[16]

Even more challenging, albeit perhaps less evident, is the uncertainty regarding higher education's changing social and ideological role in the United States. The late Bill Readings persuasively argued that the rise of the modern university has been fused to the nation-state through its promoting and pro-tecting the idea of a national culture. But with the idea of a single national cul-ture now in retreat, what will become of this traditional and favored educa-tional role? Concurrently, the essential character of higher education has veered so far away from John Henry Newman's model of the liberal arts university as to be unrecoverable. In Newman's university, institutional identity and authority lay in the faculty (Readings 1996; Rothblatt 1997).[17] During the last three decades, however, the locus of authority has shifted emphatically toward upper-level administrators, who, sometimes with the prodding of trustees, increasingly employ business concepts and criteria in their management practices.

Clearly, insights taken from business can help universities operate more efficiently, but at their heart, universities are not business corporations. Department chairs are not the equivalent of middle mangers; tenured faculty have an independence of action simply not found in the business world. There is much to be said, moreover, for not immediately reacting to every twist of the market. Nonetheless, the use of business standards, with their jargon of "performance indicators," "quality control," and "accountability for cost and benefit," has put higher education on the defensive and by doing so has begun to change the fundamental relationship of academia with the general public.

Perhaps the most obvious expression of this transformation can be seen in the importance administrators and prospective students and their parents attach to ratings of colleges and universities such as those found in *Money* magazine's "Best Buys," *The Princeton Review,* and *U.S. News* and *World Report's* "Top Colleges and Universities." Although such ratings mostly affect regional institutions, even elite universities broadcast favorable rankings to the public.[18] In this ratings game, institutions rise and fall based on ambiguous criteria selected by magazine editors. This brave new world of higher education explicitly defines students and their parents as consumers urged to search for educational bargains, or get their money's worth through tuition discounting. Individual university traditions and missions become subordinate considerations. College recruiters and administrators, in turn, increasingly downplay the concept of a university education as an intellectual and cultural preparation for understanding life, in favor of the strengths their institutions offer with regard to careers. Colleges and universities now market "excellence," which sounds impressive, but essentially stands for nothing.

Tenured faculties serve as a *bête noire* for those advocating market-oriented changes and those who see universities as bastions of elitism. The former views tenure as economically illogical, as impeding rational cost-control and promoting mediocrity by making faculty unaccountable for their job performance. At a time when economic pressures have virtually eliminated white collar job security in the public and the private sectors, why should higher education remain exempt? Conservative critics, on the other hand, blast the academy for engaging in worthless "so-called research" — something they see essentially as "busywork." The professoriate has "betrayed [their] profession. They have scorn for their students and they disdain teaching" (Prewitt 1994: 207-208). Although the veracity of such charges is debatable, television and print media tend to indict most faculty as culpable, thereby adding fuel to the fire of higher education's critics.

In an essay about the difficult choices universities now face, Donald Kennedy, the former president of Stanford University, calls for universities to show greater responsiveness to the pressing needs of society. In doing so he notes "a certain reactive caution in the academy about this notion" (1994: 110-111). Such caution is dangerous in light of the very real pressures on the academy's institutional integrity. As the 21st century begins, colleges and universities cannot deceive themselves that the current economic and social climate is transitory. We must find ways to return the liberal arts and sciences to the center of the debate about how American society can best meet the challenges of this new century.

Service-Learning and a New Mandate for Higher Education

I believe the most obvious place to begin is in our cities. Here metropolitan universities can and should take the lead in proposing solutions to reverse the decline of neighborhoods.

Making the decision to spend fiscal and human resources on public issues will not be easy. Implementing such decisions will encounter even greater difficulty, for at some point curriculum issues will arise. Elite institutions and those with a clear sense of mission will find this least troublesome. The former because elite schools by definition have the freedom to engage in new ventures that institutions with less secure reputations and scarcer resources do not. The latter because many of these institutions have kept community issues as a conscious part of their self-identity. Those institutions that will face the greatest challenge in this regard are those without a readily distinct identity, in particular, those found under the general heading of "comprehensive universities."

It is the comprehensive university where the merger of higher education models has produced the most difficulty. Many private colleges have transformed themselves into comprehensive institutions for purposes ranging from sheer survival to simply becoming more competitive in the education market. These private schools join the 60 percent of public universities also identified under this classification, to constitute a substantial segment of American higher education. Because no archetype defining the successful comprehensive university exists, it is here that faculties most often face bewildering and conflicting signals vis-à-vis institutional goals and professional responsibilities. Randomly selecting five such schools will result in enormous differences in size; student composition; the number, quality, and variety of graduate and undergraduate programs; academic resources; and the size and quality of the faculty. Administrators and admissions officers reiterate that undergraduate teaching is their faculty's primary obligation, but this obligation is broadly defined to include mentoring and student recruitment. In institutions with residential student populations, it also often includes substantial interaction with students outside ordinary working hours. Teaching, especially for non-American historians, is concentrated in survey courses that might or might not be in their subdiscipline, and a typical semester finds such faculty with three or more course preparations. Departmental, university, and community service also make heavy demands on faculty time.

Obviously, service-learning cannot solve the institutional and professional ambiguities inherent in comprehensive universities. Service-learning can, however, be a powerful instrument in reconnecting colleges and universities to their surrounding communities, and by so doing help restore higher education as an important participant in the debate over regional and national problems. In this way, service-learning both complements and enriches traditional scholarly research while enhancing teaching effectiveness.

The greatest challenge to introducing service-learning lies not within this approach itself, but within the academy. As a social sector, we are resistant to change. And yet, much of service-learning's potential hinges on faculty acceptance. It will be tragic if professional historians simply reject service-learning as faddish or incompatible with "historical objectivity" in the classroom. Organizations such as the American Historical Association and the Organization of American Historians must begin focusing on the pedagogical issues raised here as part of the larger question concerning our relationship to the public. Reconnecting our profession, ourselves, and our students to the world beyond our campuses might be the best strategy we have to counter the increasingly shrill attacks made on higher education. Moreover, it might be the only strategy we have that can ensure that a future audience will exist that values the studying and reading of history.

Notes

1. See the other disciplinary volumes in this series for examples.

2. See Reginald Wilson's (1996) perceptive article "Educating for Diversity," particularly his discussion of how white and minority students sharply differ in their perceptions of racism in American society. See also William G. Bowen's (1997) "No Limits."

3. See the annual CIRP study, much of which is usually found in *The Chronicle of Higher Education*. The Harvard study surveying alcohol and drug use among entering freshmen is dismal in its findings. It is unrealistic to claim, as many faculty do, that dealing with such behavior is not part of their job description, since the consequences of antisocial activities are evident in students' intellectual and social performance.

Michael G. Dolence and Donald M. Norris (1995) have written a provocative work on what they see ahead for higher education. Although faculty will find some of its language off-putting, its ideas, as well as the book's high sales among college and university administrators, make it a work worth reading.

4. In this regard, it is telling to note some recent works on the current state of higher education. Cole, Barber, and Graubard's (1994) *The Research University in a Time of Discontent* has a highly distinguished group of academics writing on such topics as "America's Research Universities Under Public Scrutiny," "In Defense of the Research University," and "Can the Research University Adapt to a Changing Future?"

See, too, Sheldon Rothblatt's (1997) *The Modern University and Its Discontents* and Bill Readings's (1996) *The University in Ruins.* Readings makes a very compelling argument on how the university is being ensnared in the discourse of "excellence," which, while seemingly harmless and perhaps even good for higher education, is in essence a techno-bureaucratic approach to education driven by corporate market forces more interested in profit margins than in learning.

5. The four criteria for effective service-learning are: "Students learn and develop through active participation in thoughtfully organized service experiences that meet actual community needs and that are coordinated in collaboration with the school and community; is integrated into the students' academic curriculum or provides structured time for students to think, talk, or write about what they did and saw during the actual service activity; that provides students with opportunities to use newly acquired skills and knowledge in real-life situations in their own communities; and that enhances what is taught in school by extending student learning beyond the classroom and into the community, and helps to foster the development of a sense of caring for others" (CNS 1996).

6. Most colleges and universities have a community service or community outreach office in which faculty can obtain information and support for selecting suitable sites for their classes.

7. My institution has reaffirmed its support of service-learning by making available two full-tuition scholarships, worth more than $18,000 each, grants for students to attend service-learning conferences, together with a package of grants to aid faculty in creating service-learning courses.

8. Dwight Giles has published a series of fundamental works on the theory and practice of service-learning. I would like to thank him for allowing me to read his forthcoming statistical study on service-learning.

9. CIRP is sponsored by UCLA's Higher Education Research Institute and the American Council on Education. Surveys of freshmen began in 1966. Since then, CIRP has introduced follow-up surveys and faculty surveys. The state of Maryland, for example, has instituted a 20-hour community service requirement for its public high school students.

10. The September 1997 issue of *Perspectives* contains one article titled "The Politics of Labels: A New Attack on the Smithsonian," which quotes one critic complaining of . "the staples of cutting edge 'academic' research — smirking irony, cultural relativism, celebration of putative victims, facile attacks on science . . . the cynical debunking of core American beliefs," and another on the "near death experience" of the Woodrow Wilson Center.

11. Thus far, college presidents and trustee bodies have taken the most public role. For example, Tulane University's new president, Scott S. Cowen, said the following in his Sept. 24, 1998, Convocation Address, "Tulane is a university in service to the public. A university truly committed to economic development and to building and renewing the communities in which its people live and work, from those in New Orleans and Louisiana to those in the far reaches of the world where Tulane has a presence. We should use these community experiences to strengthen and differentiate our learning and research efforts." Outreach to the surrounding community is also found in Tulane's mission statement. I would like to thank Vincent Ilustre, service-learning assistant director of Tulane University, for bringing this to my attention.

12. See Peter Novik's *Noble Dream: The "Objectivity Question" and the American Historical Profession* (Cambridge University Press, 1988) for a devastating critique of objectivity in among modern American historians.

13. In revising this essay, I found Donald Stokes's *Pasteur's Quadrant: Basic Science and Other Essays* (Brookings Institution, 1997) highly useful in articulating my ideas far more concisely in this section of the essay.

14. Many of these faculty members, realistically or not, see their stay as temporary before returning to a research university.

15. See, for example, *The Chronicle of Higher Education*, Aug. 29, 1997, pp. 5, 30-36; and "Rationing Higher Education: Why College Isn't for Everyone," *The New York Times*, Aug. 31, 1997, Section E.

16. The information on these questions is vast. For two articles on this topic see "High-Cost Private Colleges Want Congress to Raise Limits on Student Borrowing" and a following article on Wesleyan University, whose 1997 seniors taking loans average $18,000 in debt, in *The Chronicle of Higher Education*, Sept. 5, 1997, pp. A42-A44.

17. Jaroslav Pelikan (1992) replaces the centrality of place Newman gave to teaching with research and publication. It is difficult to believe that Newman would accept Pelikan's argument.

18. For example, in his 1997 open letter to alumni, parents, and friends, the president of Johns Hopkins University cites its *U.S. News & World Report* rankings and its fifth-place finish in *Money*'s "costly but worth it" category as one of the university's "recent outstanding accomplishments."

References

Bowen, William G. (1997). "No Limits." In *The American University: National Treasure or Endangered Species?*, edited by Ronald G. Ehrenberg, pp. 18-42. Ithaca, NY: Cornell University Press.

Carlin, James F. (Dec. 15, 1997). "A Take-No-Prisioners Approach to Changing Public Education in Massachusetts." *The Chronicle of Higher Education*, p. A5.

Cole, Jonathan R., Elinor G. Barber, and Stephen R. Graubard, eds. (1994). *The Research University in a Time of Discontent*. Baltimore, MD: Johns Hopkins University Press.

Corporation for National Service. (1994). "Service-Learning: An Overview." In *Roles for Higher Education*. Washington, DC: Corporation for National Service.

Dewey, John. (1966, orig. 1916). *Democracy in Education*. Reprint, New York, NY: Free Press.

Dolence, Michael G., and Donald M. Norris. (1995). *Transforming Higher Education: A Vision for Learning in the 21st Century*. Ann Arbor, MI: Society for College and University Planning.

Giles, Dwight, and Janet Eyler. (1994). "The Impact of a College Service Laboratory on Students' Personal, Social, and Cognitive Outcomes." *Journal of Adolescence* 17: 327-339.

Harkavy, Ira. (1996). "Back to the Future: From Service-Learning to Strategic Academically-Based Community Service." *Metropolitan Universities* 7(1): 57-70.

Jacoby, R. (1994). *Dogmatic Wisdom: How the Culture Wars Divert Education and Distract America*. New York, NY: Anchor.

Kennedy, Donald. (1994). "Making Choices in the Research University." In *The Research University in a Time of Discontent*, edited by Jonathan R. Cole, Elinor G. Barber, and Stephen R. Graubard. Baltimore, MD: Johns Hopkins University Press.

Prewitt, Kenneth. (1994). "America's Research Universities Under Public Scrutiny." In *The Research University in a Time of Discontent*, edited by Jonathan R. Cole, Elinor G. Barber, and Stephen R. Graubard. Baltimore, MD: John Hopkins University Press.

Price III, James Robertson, and John S. Martello. (Summer 1996). "Naming and Framing Service-Learning: Taxonomy and Four Levels of Value." *Metropolitan Universities* 7(1): 11-23.

Pelikan, Jaroslav. (1992). *The Idea of the University: A Reexamination*. New Haven, CT: Yale University Press.

Rhodes, Frank H.T. (1994). "The Place of Teaching in the Research University." In *The Research University in a Time of Discontent*, edited by Jonathan R. Cole, Elinor G. Barber, and Stephen R. Graubard. Baltimore, MD: Johns Hopkins University Press.

Readings, Bill. (1996). *The University in Ruins*. Cambridge, MA: Harvard University Press.

Rothblatt, Sheldon. (1997). *The Modern University and Its Discontents: The Fate of Newman's Legacy in Britain and America*. Cambridge and New York, NY: Cambridge University Press.

Shapiro, Harold T. (1997). "Cognition, Character, and Culture in Undergraduate Education: Rhetoric and Reality." In *The American University: National Treasure or Endangered Species?*, edited by Ronald G. Ehrenberg. Ithaca, NY: Cornell University Press.

Whitehead, Alfred North. (1929). *The Aims of Education and Other Essays*. New York, NY: Macmillan.

Wilson, Reginald. (1996). "Educating for Diversity." *About Campus* 1(2): 4-9.

Service-Learning, Academically Based Community Service, and the Historic Mission of the American Urban Research University

by Ira Harkavy

Why study history? That question is often the stuff of history survey cours- es. It should, however, be a question addressed when doing any historical research project. For this project, the pertinent question is, why study the late 19th and early 20th-century urban research university? Simply put, my hope is that the study of the early history of the American urban research university might serve as a source of ideas and creative approaches for the service-learning movement. More generally, this essay is based on John Dewey's observation that "the true starting point of history is always some present situation with its problems" (1966: 24). For me, the present situation is a service-learning movement that, in spite of its notable accomplish- ments, should and could do better. Historical research, I assume, can be use- ful in helping to make the present situation better. This brief essay, needless to say, will not prove that assumption. It might perhaps illustrate how his- torical study could be useful to service-learning practitioners/theorists as they develop and advance their work.

Service-Learning and Strategic Academically Based Community Service

The service-learning movement has nearly arrived.[1] Witness this volume and the entire series on service-learning and the disciplines, the extraordi- nary growth of Campus Compact from 12 member institutions in 1985 to 640 colleges and universities in 1999, and the focus on service-learning by influential national higher education associations such as the American Council on Education, Association of American Colleges and Universities, National Association of State Universities and Land-Grant Colleges, and American Association for Higher Education. Although relatively silent on service-learning, the prestigious Association of American Universities, an organization of 60 American and two Canadian research universities, has recently focused on issues of community service and university-community relationships.[2]

This increased acceptance is all to the good. Service-learning is one of a handful of creative, active pedagogies (among them collaborative, peer-assisted, and problem-based learning) that enhance a student's capacity to think critically, problem solve, and function as a citizen in a democratic society.[3] Although all to the good, it is not as good as it could be. The advance of service-learning would, I believe, have better results if service-learning practitioners asked and answered, in a reiterative fashion, this simple question: What are the goals of the service-learning movement?

This is a difficult question indeed, requiring lots of hard thinking and rethinking. It is certainly not meant to be an academic (in the pejorative sense) question. "Know thy goals" is surely a first principle for any movement. "It is," as Francis Bacon stated in 1620, "not possible to run a course aright when the goal itself is not rightly placed" (in Benson 1972: xi).

In my judgment, the service-learning movement has not "rightly placed" the goal. It has largely been concerned with fostering the civic consciousness, moral character, and academic learning of college students. (Needless to say, all very worthy goals.) Providing service to the community has obviously been an important component of the movement. Community problem solving and making a difference in the actual conditions of communities, however, have tended to play minor roles in service-learning programs. The most influential work advocating what might be termed a "trickle-down theory" of service-learning's impact is Benjamin R. Barber's *An Aristocracy of Everyone: The Politics of Education and the Future of America*. In a discussion of mandatory citizen education and community service, Barber writes:

> *To make people serve others may produce desirable behavior, but it does not create responsible and autonomous individuals. To make people participate in educational curricula that can empower them does create such individuals. The ultimate goal is not to serve others, but to learn to be free, which entails being responsible to others [emphasis added]. (1992: 250-251)*

In its classic form, service-learning may function as a pedagogical equivalent of "exploitative" community-based research. Academics, of course, have often studied and written about poor, particularly minority, communities. The residents of these communities have largely been subjects to be studied, providing information that would produce dissertations and articles that someday, somehow would contribute to making things better. Meanwhile, the poor have gotten poorer, and academics have gotten tenure, promoted, and richer.

Similarly, advocates and practitioners of service-learning have tended to agree that the goal of that pedagogy is to educate college students for citizenship. Citizenship is learned by linking classroom experience to a service experience that is at best seen as doing some good for the community. The real beneficiaries are, however, the deliverers, not the recipients, of the service. Someday, somehow when we have effectively educated a critical mass of the "best and the brightest" for citizenship, things would be made better. Meanwhile, the causes of our societal problems have remained untouched, the distance between the haves and have nots has widened, and universities have continued to largely function as institutions engaged in symbolic actions rather than institutions producing knowledge for (to use Bacon's phrase) the "relief of man's estate." [4]

Urban colleges and universities are in a unique position to "rightly place the goal" and "run [the] . . . course aright" by going beyond traditional service-learning (and its inherent limitations) to strategic academically based community service, in which contributing to the well-being of people in the community (both in the here and now and in the future) is a primary goal. It is service rooted in and intrinsically tied to teaching and research, and it aims to bring about structural community improvement (e.g., effective public schools, neighborhood economic development, strong community organizations) rather than simply to alleviate individual misery (e.g., feeding the hungry, sheltering the homeless, tutoring the "slow learner"). Strategic academically based community service requires a comprehensive institutional response that engages the broad range of resources of the urban college or university (including the talents, abilities, and energy of undergraduates involved in traditional service and service-learning activities) to solve a strategic problem of our time — the problem of creating democratic, local, cosmopolitan communities.

Why will urban "higher eds" go beyond service-learning to strategic academically based community service? Most centrally, they will increasingly have no choice. The need for communities rooted in face-to-face relationships and exemplifying humanistic values is most acute in the American city. The problems of the American city have increasingly become the problems of the urban college and university. Since they cannot move (as more mobile institutions have done), there is no escape from the issues of poverty, crime, and physical deterioration that are at the gates of urban higher educational institutions. The choice is to hold on to a mythic image of the university on the hill and suffer for it, or to become proactively, seriously, fully, effectively engaged. Summarily stated, the future of the urban university and that of the American city are intertwined.

Urban research universities in particular will move to strategic academically based community service because it is consonant with their historic mission and the words and actions of their founders and early leaders. In 1876, Daniel Coit Gilman, in his inaugural address as the first president of Johns Hopkins, America's first modern research university, expressed the hope that universities should "make for less misery among the poor, less ignorance in the schools, less bigotry in the temple, less suffering in the hospital, less fraud in business, less folly in politics" (in Long 1992: 184). Judged against Gilman's criteria, the performance of the American research university over the past 124 years has not been, to put it very mildly, adequate. More to the point, the abiding belief in the democratic purposes of the American research university echoed throughout higher education at the turn of the 20th century. For example, in 1908, Harvard's president, Charles Eliot, wrote:

> At bottom most of the American institutions of higher education are filled with the democratic spirit of serviceableness. Teachers and students alike are profoundly moved by the desire to serve the democratic community. . . . All the colleges boast of the serviceable men they have trained, and regard the serviceable patriot as their ideal product. This is a thoroughly democratic conception of their function. (in Vesey 1970: 119)

University presidents of the late 19th and early 20th centuries worked to develop the American research university into a major national institution capable of meeting the needs of a rapidly changing and increasingly complex society. Imbued with boundless optimism and a belief that knowledge could change the world for the better, these captains of erudition envisioned universities as leading the way toward a more effective, humane, and democratic society for Americans in general and residents of the city in particular. Progressive academics also viewed the city as their arena for study and action. They seized the opportunity to advance knowledge, teaching, and learning by working to improve the quality of life in American cities experiencing the traumatic effects of industrialization, immigration, large-scale urbanization, and the unprecedented emergence of an international economy.[5]

The Role of SABCS in the Development of the American Urban Research University

The tradition of problem-driven, problem-solving strategic academically based community service (SABCS) is readily identified in the histories of four leading urban universities at the turn of the 20th century: Johns Hopkins, Columbia, the University of Chicago, and the University of Pennsylvania.[6]

Gilman, Hopkins's president, for example, was the guiding force behind the organization of the Charity Organization Society (COS). An organization designed to provide a scientific approach to helping Baltimore's poor, COS studied the causes of poverty, collected useful data, and worked to get at the root causes of destitution. Moreover, a number of Gilman's leading faculty members, such as Herbert Baxter Adams and Richard Ely, had close ties to Levering Hall, the campus YMCA, which was deeply engaged in work with

Baltimore's poor. Students in Adams's and Ely's Department of History, Political Economy and Political Science worked through Levering Hall "to use the city as a laboratory for economic study" (Elfenbein 1996). John Glenn, chair of the executive committee of COS, remarked in 1888 that Hopkins was the first university where social welfare work was "almost a part of the curriculum."[7]

Hopkins may have been the first, but certainly not the only, university to integrate social welfare work as part of the curriculum. More generally, Progressive Era academics viewed cities as extraordinarily appropriate, valuable sites for study and action. The city was the center of significant societal transformation, the center of political corruption, poverty, crime, and cultural conflict, as well as a ready source of data and information. To quote Richard Mayo-Smith of Columbia, the city was "the natural laboratory of social science, just as hospitals are of medical science" (Karl 1974: 31). Simply stated, the city was the logical site for creative faculty and students to effectively integrate theory and practice.[8]

In most cases, Progressive Era university presidents and academics had an expert-driven model of change, founded on the assumption that the expert, with scientific knowledge in hand, would increase efficiency in governmental agencies and design institutions that improve the quality of life for the urban poor and immigrant. The expert's role was to study and assist, but not to learn from the community (Hackney 1986: 145).

Not all turn of the century academics shared that authoritative, elitist conception of the university's role. Seth Low, president of Columbia from 1890 through 1901, promoted a decidedly democratic approach in dealing with New York City and its communities. In his inaugural address, Low stated "the city may be made to a considerable extent, a part of the university." Columbia was also to be part of the city, resulting in a democratic, mutually beneficial relationship between town and gown. In an article "The University and the Workingman," Low wrote that the "working men of American . . . [should know] that at Columbia College . . . the disposition exists to teach the truth . . . without fear or favor, and we ask their aid to enable us to see the truth as is appears to them" (Bender 1987: 282-283).[9]

Low is also notable for his enthusiastic embrace of New York City as the source of Columbia's greatness. He not only brought "the College into closer touch with the community," but also significantly improved Columbia by successfully encouraging faculty and students to focus their intellectual work on helping New York solve its problems (Kurland 1971: 53).

A mediocre institution in the 1870s and 1880s, Columbia was widely viewed as a snobbish school for rich young men. Upon assuming the presidency, Low made his goal clear: "I am desirous," he told an alumnus, "to build Columbia into a great university, worthy of New York" (in Kurland 1971: 55).

He took the occasion of his inaugural address to emphasize that Columbia was not simply *in* New York City, but *of* New York City (Bender 1987: 282). In his inaugural address, Low also echoed Francis Bacon's proposition that the purpose of scholarship is service for the betterment of humanity:

> *Consider for a moment the significance to the college of a great city about it. First of all, it means for everyone of us that there is no such thing as* the world of letters apart from the world of men. *There are such things, undoubtedly, as most unworldly scholars, men oftentimes "of whom the world is not worthy," but such scholars are never made except out of men who see humanity, as in a vision, ever beckoning from behind their books. The scholar without this vision is a pedant. He mistakes learning for an end in itself, instead of seeing that it is only a weapon in a wise man's hands [emphasis added]. (in Cary 1897: 40)*

Low went beyond posing and answering the question "knowledge for what?" He called on students to become engaged directly with the city and its communities and people. Engagement with, and study and action in, New York City, according to Low, would produce educated, prepared, moral students, as well as significant contributions to knowledge:

> . . . the real world is not to be found in books. That [real world] is peopled by men and women of living flesh and blood, and the great city can supply the human quality which the broad-minded man must not suffer himself to lack. *There is a variety of life in this city, a vitality about it, and, withal, a sense of power of which, to my thought, are of inestimable value to the student whose desire it is to become a well-rounded man.* . . . There is but one New York on all of this continent, and, for the purposes of technical and professional training her location in New York supplements the work of Columbia with advantages not elsewhere to be had. So, also, I believe the great city will lend itself readily to the encouragement of profound research. *As there is no solitude like that of a crowd, so there is no inspiration like it [emphasis added]. (in Cary 1897: 40-41)*

Low clearly articulated a morally inspired, instrumental, active approach to research, teaching, and learning. In effect, repudiating Plato's notion of the groves of academe, with its physical and intellectual separation of town and gown, Low linked town and gown, identifying a mutually beneficial, interactive relationship between Columbia and the city as crucial to intellectual and institutional advancement. Low even went so far as to invoke Bacon's standard of progress as the test of inquiry and research. In Low's case, the specific test was Columbia's ability "to influence the life of New York" (in Bender 1987: 284).

Low's presidency was a great success. As one authority has noted:

By 1901, Seth Low had taken a small, dissension ridden college and made it into a great university. He had taken a financially undernourished institution and infused it with great quantities of fresh money, and, by building Columbia a new home [Morningside Heights campus], he had made certain that the university would remain in the City of New York. (Kurland 1971: 60-61)

Low's extraordinary contributions to Columbia and to the practice and theory of community-university partnerships have largely been forgotten. His vision of a cosmopolitan, democratic, civic university was significantly ahead of its time. Moreover, the brevity of his tenure, the 43-year imperious reign of his successor (Nicholas Murray Butler), and the dominance of Plato's aristocratic, scholastic, "liberal" educational theory in American colleges and universities also account for Low's limited impact.

While Low provides a particularly compelling vision of university-city relationships, the University of Chicago in practice had the closet ties to its locality. Work emanating from Hull House, the social settlement founded by Jane Addams and Ellen Starr on Chicago's West Side in 1889, was enormously significant in forming ties between the university and its city. Adopting a multifaceted institutional approach to the social problem of the immigrant groups in the 19th Ward, Hull House residents offered activities along four lines designated by Addams as the social, educational, humanitarian, and civic. In addition to its various residents' programs, Hull House was a site for labor union activities; a forum for social, political, and economic reform; and a center for social science research (Harkavy and Puckett 1994). Regarding its research function, Addams noted, "The settlements antedated by three years the first sociology departments in universities and by 10 years the establishment of the first foundations for social research" (in Costin 1983: 45).

In 1895, Jane Addams and the residents of Hull House published *Hull House Maps and Papers,* a sociological investigation of the neighborhood immediately to the east of Hull House; in Addams's words, it was a record of "certain phases of neighborhood life with which the writers have been familiar" (Addams 1970: viii). Inspired by Charles Booth's *Life and Labor of the People in London,* the Hull House residents compiled detailed maps of demographic and social characteristics, and produced richly descriptive accounts of life and work in a poor immigrant neighborhood. Theirs was not dispassionate scholarship, as evidenced by Florence Kelley's poignant advocacy on behalf of sweatshop laborers, whose

reward of work at their trade is grinding poverty, ending only in death or escape to some more hopeful occupation. Within the trade there has been and can be no improvement in wages while tenement house-manufacture is tolerated. On the contrary, there seems to be no limit to the deterioration now in progress. (in Addams 1970: 41)

It is not surprising that male sociologists at the University of Chicago were closely associated with Hull House, acknowledging that "it was Addams and Hull House who were the leader and leading institution in Chicago in the 1890s, not the University of Chicago" (Deegan 1988: 5). Indeed, *Hull House Maps and Papers* "established the major substantive interests and methodological technique of Chicago Sociology that would define the School for the next forty years" (Deegan 1988: 24).

The Chicago School of Sociology was created in this nexus of "serving society by advancing intellectual inquiry" (Fitzpatrick 1990: 39). In the early years of the Chicago School no invidious distinctions were made between the applied sociology pursued by Jane Addams and the Hull House residents and the academic research of the first generation of University of Chicago sociologists.[10] Indeed, the two groups had a close working relationship, grounded in personal friendships, mutual respect, and shared social philosophy. Four men of the early Chicago School, Albion Small, Charles R. Henderson, Charles Zeublin, and George E. Vincent, were ministers or ministers manqué — intellectual Social Gospelers with strong civic commitments. (The exceptions, with no theological proclivities, were George H. Mead and William I. Thomas.) Like the women of Hull House, the Chicago sociologists were "social activists and social scientists."[11] Action social research, Chicago-style, encompassed scholarly documentation of a social problem and lobbying of politicians and local community groups to obtain action (Bulmer 1984: 45-63, 238, n. 1).

In its early years, the University of Chicago demonstrated that by doing good, a research university could do very well. For William Rainey Harper, Chicago's first president, teaching, research, and service were not only fully compatible, but their effective integration through a focus on the city's problems became, in effect, his primary strategy for developing the university into a major academic center. After its founding in 1892, the university

quickly became an important part of the social ferment in Chicago. The University of Chicago Settlement took its place in the stockyards district in 1894 to work along with Hull House. President Harper served on the Chicago Board of Education, and a large number of his faculty were actively engaged in work with the elementary and secondary schools of Chicago and other sections of Illinois. The faculty also provided members and chairmen for a wide range of organizations and commissions concerned with philanthropy, improved sanitation, slum clearance, cultural developments, waterways, labor legislation, strike settlements, and a host of other activities.

Such practical endeavors were encouraged as fitting for a university, providing a broad field for testing ideas and theories. *[emphasis added]* (Rucker 1969: 9)

Harper made a particularly important intellectual contribution when he identified the university as the strategic institution capable of creating an optimally democratic society. For Harper, the American university had a singular purpose: Its "holy" purpose was to be the "prophet of democracy." Indeed, no other captain of erudition so passionately, so farsightedly, envisioned the university's democratic potential and purpose. Profoundly religious, deeply dedicated to the progressive Social Gospel, Harper conceptualized the university as the holy place designed to fulfill democracy's creed: "the brotherhood, and consequently the equality of man." The university would fulfill that creed through "service for mankind, wherever mankind is, whether within scholastic walls, or without these walls and in the world at large" (Harper 1905: 21, 28-29).[17]

Undoubtedly, the most notable work at Chicago during this period was the development by Dewey and his colleagues of the Chicago School of Philosophy. Hailed by William James as so "wonderful . . . that it deserves the title of a new system of philosophy" (in Rucker 1969: 3-4), the Chicago School emerged from the action-oriented engagement of Dewey and his colleagues in the real-world problems of the city in which they lived and worked. Dewey's Laboratory School at the University of Chicago, moreover, served as the most important vehicle for developing and disseminating the ideas of the philosophy department. Through and beyond Dewey's departure to Columbia in 1904 and Harper's death in 1906, the city's reform movement remained closely tied to the university, with scholars playing key roles in efforts to improve education and politics (Shils 1988).

Chicago academics were by no means unique in involving themselves in city reform movements. In Philadelphia the independent administration of Rudolph Blankenburg received significant assistance from faculty in the University of Pennsylvania's Wharton School. The early Wharton School most fully exemplified an entire college within a wider university devoted to integrating research and teaching with political activity. Endowed in 1881 by Joseph Wharton as the School of Finance and Economy, it quickly developed *in practice* into a "school of political and social science," under the direction of Edmund James. James, a future president of both Northwestern and the University of Illinois, saw Wharton's future as dependent upon its successful involvement with local issues and real-world problems. He created, therefore, a unique organizational innovation — a school devoted to providing a social scientific response to the problems of industrialization (Harkavy and Puckett 1991; Sass 1982: 55-89; Swanson 1966).

James's innovations went beyond his fashioning of the Wharton School's direction. In 1889, he established the American Academy of Political and Social Science as an organization linking academics and leading citizens for the study of societal problems. James and his Wharton colleagues also played key roles in establishing the Municipal League of Philadelphia and the National Municipal League. Like the American Academy, these organizations were predicated on the concept of partnership between academics and reformers. Among the scholars and other leaders who participated in the National Municipal League were Theodore Roosevelt, Herbert Baxter Adams, Richard Ely, Francis A. Walker, Edward L. Godkin, and Daniel Coit Gilman (Sass 1982: 75-78).

James's organizational innovations, institutional alliances, and personal relationships with leading Philadelphians established the bases for Wharton's success. Under his friend and successor, Simon Patten, Wharton arguably became, along with the University of Chicago, one of the two premier centers of American social science between 1900 and the outbreak of World War I. Continuing James's strong urban emphasis, Patten enlisted Wharton undergraduates and graduate students in Philadelphia's Progressive Movement (Hackney 1986: 138). As an eminent scholar, he exemplified that being actively engaged in public affairs could contribute to academic success. Within a few years, however, Patten and like-minded colleagues ran afoul of hostile University of Pennsylvania trustees.

In the 1890s, a number of social scientists had faced serious difficulty because of their reform-oriented writings and activism. The trial of Richard Ely by the Wisconsin Board of Regents and the dismissal of Edward Bemis from the University of Chicago are two of the best known cases. Although Wharton's more comprehensive reform approach might have helped shield individual faculty, the school became quite vulnerable as its campaign for reform went further than local elites wished. Indeed, the Penn trustees fired Simon Patten's close friend and junior colleague Scott Nearing in 1915; two years later, they refused to extend Patten's tenure beyond the age of retirement, as was routinely done for distinguished faculty members. By 1917 and America's entry into World War I, most of Wharton's reform faculty had resigned or been dismissed (Sass 1982: 125-126; Tugwell 1982: 3-70).

World War I closed one chapter and began another in the history of community-urban university relationships. The brutality and horror of that conflict ended the buoyant optimism and faith in human progress and societal improvement that marked the Progressive Era. American academics were not immune to the general disillusion with progress. Indeed, disillusion and despair led many faculty members to retreat into a narrow scientistic approach. Scholarly inquiry directed toward creating a better society was increasingly deemed inappropriate. While faith in the expert and in expert knowledge carried on from the Progressive Era, it separated from its reformist roots (Bulmer and Bulmer 1981: 370; Hackney 1986: 138; Ross 1984: 165-166).

Conclusion

The four historical studies presented above are not designed to evoke images of a paradise lost. Among other things, these efforts tended to be neither democratic nor participatory. More centrally, they failed to become the dominant model for the American university. They were, quite simply, far in advance of their time, particularly given America's engagement in what Robert Nisbet has termed a "Seventy-Five Years War," which finally ended with the end of the Cold War (1988: xi, 1-39). New conditions, however, now prevail. Decades of focusing attention and resources abroad resulted in the neglect of problems at home, creating, in turn, severe and highly visible domestic crises.

These crises are most visible and pressing in our cities. The futures of our cities and the institutions located within them, particularly institutions of higher education, depend on resolving the crises of urban poverty, poor schooling, inefficient bureaucratic delivery of services, collapsing communities, and so on with "all deliberate speed." Universities, more than any other societal institution, have the broad array of intellectual resources needed to take the lead toward finding solutions. For universities to do so, however, they need to do things smarter and better than they have ever done them before.

Service-learning, as too often defined and practiced, is much too weak a reed to get universities from here (internally directed, solipsistic, self-referential institutions) to there (problem-solving, cosmopolitan, civic institutions). To mix metaphors, we need a strong reed that can serve as a powerful lever for moving universities and society forward. Strategic academically based community service may hold promise for producing the structural change needed to markedly reduce the deprivation and (inhuman) human suffering found in our cities. I have suggested that the early history of the American urban research university provides us with a useful example from which to learn and build. For the founders, the mission of the university was to create a better, more democratic city and society through advancing and transmitting knowledge. Even with its limitations, their model might be termed strategic academically based community service, since it integrated research, teaching, and service in order to advance knowledge, promote citizenship, and make fundamental improvements in the lives of people and their communities. Appropriately adapted by service-learning practitioners/theorists to current settings and circumstances, that model can, I believe, help the American urban research university to better fulfill its historic mission through working to create and maintain attractive, highly livable cities that are centers of learning, progress, and democracy.

Notes

1. In a 1996 issue of *Metropolitan Universities* (vol. 7, no. 1) entirely dedicated to service-learning, Deborah Hirsch, the issue editor, begins her excellent introductory essay by stating that "service-learning has arrived." *Nearly* arrived, in my judgment, more accurately reflects the current state of the field and the movement. See Hirsch's (1996) essay as well as a number of other useful articles in that issue.

2. Campus Compact is, in my judgment, the organization most responsible for the growth and development of community service and service-learning across higher education. A compact of college and university presidents, Campus Compact explicitly defines its goal as a commitment to "supporting students in the development of skills and values to promote citizenship through participation in public service" (document, 1997 Campus Compact governing board meeting).

Indications of the increased focus on service-learning by influential national higher education associations include these: the American Council on Education's (ACE) cosponsorship with Florida State University of a June 1998 national conference on "Higher Education and Civic Responsibility," which set an agenda for a new ACE National Forum on Higher Education and Civic Responsibility; the Association of American Colleges and Universities's Program for Health and Higher Education, which has highlighted the potential role of service-learning in effective AIDS education and prevention; the National Association of State Universities and Land-Grant Colleges's Kellogg Commission report on the "Engaged Campus"; and the American Association for Higher Education's sponsorship of this *Series on Service-Learning in the Disciplines* and its appointment of Edward Zlotkowski as a senior associate to edit the series as well as to advance service-learning in general. Since 1996, under the leadership of Tulane University, an ad hoc working group representing 26 Association of American Universities (AAU) institutions have convened to address the role of research universities in serving their local and regional communities. Among the working group's goals is to support federally funded community service programs, strengthen the connections between government agencies that support community service, and address problems related to the administration of community service programs. Moreover, the October 1999 meeting of AAU presidents was significantly devoted to university-community relationships.

3. For an illuminating discussion of "active" pedagogies, see Schneider and Shoenberg 1998.

4. For the citation to Bacon and a useful discussion of his work, see Benson 1978.

5. For an excellent discussion of the concept of "captains of erudition," see Diner 1980.

6. The discussion on Hopkins, Columbia, the University of Chicago, and the University of Pennsylvania is largely derived from Harkavy 1996 and 1999.

7. The quoted phrases are from *Christian Advocate,* New York: April 1889; and Letter from John Glenn to D.C. Gilman, 13 July 1888, Gilman Papers, MS 1 Ferdinand Hamburger, Jr. Archives, Johns Hopkins University, Baltimore, MD.

8. For a discussion of the Progressive Era as a golden age of university-community relationships, see Hackney 1986.

9. For an excellent discussion of Seth Low's Columbia, see Bender 1987, pp. 279-284; also see Harkavy and Benson 1998.

10. As Ella Fitzpatrick indicates, this commitment was also shared by the political science and political economy departments at Chicago: "They stressed the importance of using scholarship to advance both knowledge and civic-mindedness" (1990: 41).

11. The quotation appears in a different context in Fitzpatrick 1990 (p. xv), but research indicates that it aptly describes the first-generation Chicago sociologists. For a discussion of Social Gospel influences in American social science in its formative period, see Link and McCormick 1983, pp. 23-24.

12. For a more extended discussion of Harper's vision of the university as the "prophet of democracy," see Benson and Harkavy 2000.

References

Addams, Jane, and Associates. (1970, orig. 1895). *Residents of Hull House, Hull House Maps and Papers.* Reprint, New York, NY: Arno.

Barber, Benjamin R. (1992). *An Aristocracy of Everyone: The Politics of Education and the Future of America.* New York, NY: Oxford University Press.

Bender, Thomas. (1987). *The New York Intellect: A History of Intellectual Life in New York City, From 1750 to the Beginnings of Our Time.* Baltimore, MD: Johns Hopkins Press.

Benson, Lee. (1972). *Toward the Scientific Study of History.* Philadelphia, PA: J.B. Lippincott.

———. (1978). "Changing Social Science to Change the World: A Discussion Paper." *Social Science History* 2: 427-441.

———, and Ira Harkavy. (2000). "Effectively Integrating the American System of Higher, Secondary, and Primary Education to Develop Civic Responsibility." In *Civic Responsibility and Higher Education,* edited by Thomas Ehrlich, pp. 174-196. Washington, DC: Oryx Press.

Bulmer, Martin. (1984). *The Chicago School of Sociology: Institutionalization, Diversity, and the Rise of Sociological Research.* Chicago, IL: University of Chicago Press.

———, and Joan Bulmer. (1981). "Philanthropy and Social Science in the 1920s: Beardsley Ruml and the Laura Spelman Rockefeller Memorial, 1922-29." *Minerva* 19: 347-407.

Cary, Edward. (1897). "Seth Low: A Character Sketch." *Review of Reviews* 16: 33-42.

Costin, Lela B. (1983). *Two Sisters for Social Justice: A Biography of Grace and Edith Abbott.* Urbana, IL: University of Illinois Press.

Deegan, Mary Jo. (1988). *Jane Addams and the Men of the Chicago School, 1892-1918.* New Brunswick, NJ: Transaction.

Dewey, John. (1966, orig. 1916). *Democracy in Education.* Reprint, New York, NY: Free Press.

Diner, Steven J. (1980). *A City and Its Universities: Public Policy on Chicago, 1892-1919.* Chapel Hill, NC: University of North Carolina Press.

Elfenbein, Jessica. (1996). "To 'Fit Them for Their Fight With the World': The Baltimore YMCA and the Making of a Modern City, 1852-1932." Ph.D. dissertation, University of Delaware.

Fitzpatrick, Ella. (1990). *Endless Crusade: Women Social Scientists and Progressive Reform.* New York, NY: Oxford University Press.

Hackney, Sheldon. (1986). "The University and Its Community: Past and Present." *Annals of the American Academy* 488: 135-147.

Harkavy, Ira. (1996) "Back to the Future: From Service-Learning to Strategic Academically-Based Community Service." *Metropolitan Universities* 7(1): 57-70.

————— . (1999). "School-Community-University Partnership: Effectively Integrating Community Building and Education Reform." *Universities and Community Schools* 6(1-2): 7-24.

————— , and Lee Benson. (1998). "De-Platonizing and Democratizing Education as the Bases of Service Learning." In *Academic Service Learning: A Pedagogy of Action and Reflection,* edited by Robert A. Rhoads and Jeffrey P.F. Howard, pp. 11-20. San Francisco, CA: Jossey-Bass.

Harkavy, Ira, and John L. Puckett. (1991). "The Role of Mediating Structures in University and Community Revitalization: The University of Pennsylvania and West Philadelphia as a Case Study." *Journal of Research and Development in Education* 25(1): 10-23.

————— . (1994). "Lessons From Hull House for the Contemporary Urban University." *Social Service Review* 68(3): 299-321.

Harper, William Rainey. (1905). *The Trend in Higher Education.* Chicago, IL: University of Chicago Press.

Hirsch, Deborah. (1996). "Overview." *Metropolitan Universities* 7(1): 5-9.

Karl, Barry D. (1974). *Charles E. Meriam and the Study of Politics.* Chicago, IL: University of Chicago Press.

Kurland, Gerald. (1971). *Seth Low: The Reformer in an Urban and Industrial Age.* New York, NY: Twayne Publishers.

Link, Arthur S., and Richard L. McCormick. (1983). *Progressivism.* Arlington Heights, IL: Harlan Davidson.

Long, Jr., Edward LeRoy. (1992). *Higher Education as a Moral Enterprise.* Washington, DC: Georgetown University Press.

Nisbet, Robert. (1988). *The Present Age: Progress and Anarchy in Modern America.* New York, NY: Harper and Row.

Ross, Dorothy. (1984). "American Social Science and the Idea of Progress." In *The Authority of Experts,* edited by Thomas L. Haskell, pp. 157-171. Bloomington, IN: Indiana University Press.

Rucker, Darnell. (1969). *The Chicago Pragmatists.* Minneapolis, MN: University of Minnesota Press.

Sass, Steven A. (1982). *The Pragmatic Imagination: A History of the Wharton School, 1881-1981.* Philadelphia, PA: University of Pennsylvania Press.

Schneider, Carol Geary, and Robert Shoenberg. (1998). "Contemporary Understandings of Liberal Education." Academy in Transition discussion paper. Washington, DC: Association of American Colleges and Universities.

Shils, Edward. (1988). "The University the City and the World: Chicago and the University of Chicago." In *The University and the City: From Medieval Origins to the Present,* edited by Thomas Bender, pp. 210-230. New York, NY: Oxford University Press.

Swanson, R.A. (1966). "Edmund James, 1855-1935: A Conservative Progressive in American Higher Education." Ph.D. dissertation, University of Illinois.

Tugwell, Rexford G. (1982). *To the Lesser Heights of Morningside: A Memoir.* Philadelphia, PA: University of Pennsylvania Press.

Vesey, Lawrence R. (1970). *The Emergence of the American University.* Chicago, IL: University of Chicago Press.

Emerson's Prophecy

by John Saltmarsh[1]

Action is with the scholar subordinate, but it is essential. Without it he is not yet a man. Without it thought can never ripen into truth. The preamble of thought, the transition through which it passes from the unconscious to the conscious, is action. Only so much do I know, as I have lived. Instantly we know whose words are loaded with life, and whose not.

— Ralph Waldo Emerson[2]

A Noble Dream and the Scholar's Reality

In my training to become a professional historian of American culture, Emerson's 1837 essay "The American Scholar" was part of the canon. That training, in the late 20th century, is governed by a culture of specialized knowledge and techniques for reaching interpretive conclusions by means of rules of evidence and inference. It adheres to an empiricist conception of historical scholarship through which the historian's task is the rigorous reconstruction of the past through careful examination of the documentary and material record. It is a training that includes internalizing the central, sacred ideal of "objectivity" — "that noble dream" — a creed that seeks to lend scientific legitimacy to scholarship by stressing the historian's role as a neutral and disinterested scholar (Novick 1988). But objectivity, observes Parker Palmer, "keeps us from forging relationships with things of the world. Its modus operandi is simple: when we distance ourselves from something, it becomes an object; when it becomes an object, it no longer has life, it cannot touch or transform us, so our knowledge of the thing remains pure" (1998: 51-52).

I was trained to become the American scholar that Emerson obliquely prophesied — and warned against — a scholar whose intellectual work would be dispassionate and detached, one who resisted connecting thought with action. Emerson's essay issues a call for reform of education that argues, as one biographer notes, for the "superiority of the whole person to the specialist who accepts the divided self as a necessary effect of the division of labor" (Richardson 1995: 264). But consistent with my professional socialization, Emerson's essay was taught only as a document of American literary nationalism, a rejection of American culture as a mere European derivative, and a declaration of American cultural independence. We were not invited to interpret the text as a mirror of our training, to recognize that

Emerson "was not so much interested in separating America from its European past as he was in separating the individual from an incapacitating education" (Richardson 1995: 264). Our training as professional historians demanded that we carefully neglect the essay's central argument and studiously ignore Emerson's admonition that the true scholar would have to remain grounded in the world.

The historian's cult of objectivity lies at the heart of Emerson's fear that the American scholar was becoming a divided self, the whole person giving way to the disconnected specialist, the organic unity of both self and knowledge being dissipated, with knowledge and morals occupying separate stations in the scholar's life. In a contemporary context, and by that I mean specifically within the culture of higher education since the end of World War II, Emerson's prophecy has manifested itself in models of knowledge based on a scientific epistemology emphasizing the detached, rational, analytic observer as the highest judge of truth (Bender 1993). The professional academic's "oath of allegiance" is a formula for disengagement. Within the historical profession in particular, any shift toward engagement or "relevant" scholarship has been met with a defensive fervor and resistance that makes a virtue of irrelevance (Novick 1988: 417).

Hence, even as the 1980s and 1990s saw incursions of postmodernism drive the profession into an epistemological crisis, the mainstream reaction has been retrenchment to a position of even deeper disengagement rather than a reasoned critique that could open the door to a more engaged pedagogy. This reaction has been so strong that a new professional organization has emerged, The Historical Society, to repudiate the relativistic and ideological implications of postmodern theory and techniques, and to express dissatisfaction with postmodernist trends within the traditional professional associations, the American Historical Association and the Organization of American Historians (Keylor 1999). Indeed, so strong is the cult of objectivity that the debate, or crusade, as it more often seems, has been polarized to represent the simplistic extremes of defense of, on the one hand, the virtues of rationality, objectivity, detachment, and respect for documentary evidence and, on the other, the falsity inherent in a framework shaped by biases of race, class, ethnicity, gender, and sexual orientation. This debate reflects the tendency that Richard Rorty (1998) has observed, that the dominance on campus of the extremes of the culture of objectivity and cultural politics has virtually eliminated discussion of the root causes of social problems. The argument has been framed as if there were no legitimate ground for historians who repudiate *both* the relativist implications of postmodernism *and* the profession's deep incapacity to engage the past through the present, to enrich historical understanding for a wider public audience and public purpose, and to make history come alive for students.

In the church of traditional academics, where, as Saul Alinsky once wrote, "The word 'academic' is synonymous with 'irrelevant'" (1969: ix), the teaching of a history course incorporating community-based experience is heresy, pure and simple. And for many, including in all likelihood many of the contributors to this volume, it has often meant distancing themselves from their profession's roots and strictures. The sociology of this distancing has both personal and political dimensions. For some, their professional academic lives have been incomplete because their personal values have been disconnected from their professional lives. They want their teaching to have a purpose, and they recognize that "good teaching cannot be reduced to technique; good teaching comes from the identity and integrity of the teacher" (Palmer 1998: 10). Questions of engagement "are not irrelevant," writes one historian,

> *especially to mid-career academic baby boomers typically ambivalent about turning to the past but increasingly anxious over where we seem to be headed, reluctant to slip into the free fall of disbelief offered by their 30-something postmodernist colleagues — a generation crowding 50 that finds itself, to borrow from Matthew Arnold's "Stanzas From the Grand Chartreuse," "Wandering between two worlds, one dead, / The other powerless to be born." (Cooper 1999: 782)*

As Peter Novick has observed, challenges to the ideal of objectivity are, for historians, "an enormously charged emotional issue: one in which the stakes are very high, much higher than in any disputes over substantive interpretations. For many, what has been at issue is nothing less than the meaning of the venture to which they have devoted their lives" (1988: 11).

For those who see history as a cornerstone of the liberal arts, their role as educators demands that they nurture the growth of human beings who can listen, read, talk, write, problem solve, empathize, and work in a community. Students should have the ability to apply knowledge that leaves the world a better place than they found it. To do so they should be able to make connections — between different bodies of knowledge and experience, and between theory and practice (Cronon 1999). These faculty members recognize that a liberal education requires a reorientation of their professional role that goes beyond engaged methods of teaching and learning and connects education to citizenship, building upon the recognition that democracy is a learned activity and that active participation in community life is a bridge to citizenship (Boyte and Kari 1996; Sullivan 1995). In addition to the content of individual history courses and the professional skills of rules of evidence and methods of interpretation, history as liberal education elevates skills of citizenship — critical thinking, public deliberation, collective action, and community building (Reyes 1998: 36).

Thus, to teach a course in American cultural history that includes community-based experience as an essential part of the primary evidence to be analyzed and interpreted is not simply a matter of redesigning the curriculum. It demands a conceptual shift that goes to the core of the profession, challenging the historian's view of pedagogy, epistemology, and the profession's sacred tenets. It fundamentally challenges the cult of objectivity. Pedagogy is transformed to connect structured student activities in community work with academic study, decentering the teacher as the singular source of knowledge, incorporating a reflective teaching methodology, and shifting the very model of education, to use Freire's distinction, from "banking" to "dialogue" (1970). A connected epistemology recognizes that knowledge creation is a collective act that includes contributions from those outside the academy and students and faculty. Furthermore, it recognizes that truth is not something imparted but is instead discovered through experience, intellectual and practical. At bottom, the greatest challenge posed by this shift comes down to the fact that community-based education and scholarship posit engagement and direct relevance as a counterweight to detached objectivity.

The context for this professional reorientation has often been a historical understanding of the evolution of higher education in the 20th century as well as the emergence of professionalism in American culture (Barber 1998; Bender 1993; Mathews 1998; Sullivan 1995). We have been trained within and teach within institutions of higher education whose structure, organization, and scientific culture were created in large part in the post–World War II period in response to a national crisis defined by the Cold War. Yet the ethos of professionalism and expertise that defined higher education's response to that particular crisis now contributes to public disillusionment with institutions that represent and legitimize a system that no longer addresses our most pressing national needs (Damon 1998). For the national crisis at the end of the 20th century is a crisis in our civic life (Bellah et al. 1985; National Commission on Civic Renewal 1998).

The issue for many students is, increasingly, how their education relates to this deeply felt crisis. In their educational experience, knowledge has been disconnected from their historical identity. For many faculty members, the question is how to transform education from detachment to engagement, connecting it to citizenship, incubating a renewal of civil society. The answer to questions such as these begins with providing opportunities for students to connect theory with practice, allowing them avenues for action, recognizing, as Emerson did, that "the final value of action, like that of books, and better than books, is that of a resource" (30). Engaged pedagogy trains historians to become the kind of scholar Emerson admired, discovering that "the world

— this shadow of the soul, or *other me* — lies wide around. Its attractions are the keys which unlock my thoughts and make me acquainted with myself" (29).

Approaching History Reflectively

When I read that we had to do 20 hours of community service, I was shocked and could not figure out why we had to do community service for the class . . . then I realized the importance of community "involvement" for a history class. . . . From our lectures and discussions we learned a plethora of information about democracy, individualism, and most of all community; however, without the firsthand experience, the words we read in the texts would have had little impact on our lives. . . . I had a personal attachment to the meaning of the words.

— Student, final paper

Throughout the course, Approaches to History: The Individual and Community in Democratic America, we interpreted texts — some of the key texts of American cultural history — and we engaged in community service experiences in the neighborhoods surrounding the university as a way of creating meaning from the past. Through discussions, journals, and written work we collectively searched for a broader understanding of our connection to history, community, and citizenship. The students approached their past by placing themselves in a larger historical narrative to become agents of history and participants in their democracy. Their mode of knowing was based upon relationships, connections created between them and their subject, connections that linked them physically, intellectually, and emotionally to the things they wanted to know. Incorporating community service into the curriculum brought together thought and action, knowledge and moral behavior, theories and personal identity, so that, as one student wrote in her journal, she "had a personal attachment to the meaning of the words" in the texts.

This course, offered as the senior seminar required for history majors (typically completed in junior or senior year), was designed specifically to incorporate community involvement with an understanding of the context and development of individualism, community, and democracy in American history. In addition to the assigned readings, students were required to engage in a minimum of two hours of community service per week. The class consisted of 14 students: 11 history majors, two political science majors, and one sociology major. There were six women and eight men, five seniors and nine juniors.

My original intent was to encourage all the students to become involved in service opportunities through the public school system so that we could share a common point of reference. However, by our second meeting the students had collectively developed the argument that by engaging in diverse service experiences they could learn more from one another and enrich our common reflection. Thus, one student worked as a tutor in an English-as-second-language program; one became involved with a youth program at the YMCA; one worked in the emergency room at a local hospital; one worked as a teacher aide in a local public elementary school. Two students paired up as teacher aides in a local private grammar school; one worked in an after-school program; and five offered their assistance to a voter information/political research organization. (I myself worked with an eighth-grade youth in a mentoring program.)

Students completed a Community Involvement Agreement by the end of the second week of the term. The agreement included a description of the nature of their involvement and the signature of their site supervisor. They themselves kept the original, and I kept a copy. At the end of the term, each student had to have his or her supervisor sign off on the agreement indicating that it had been fulfilled.

Students were graded on their written work and presentations. Seven elements made up their total grade, including their journals and their community involvement. The students collectively decided how much each component of the course was worth. During the second-to-last week of the course, one student suggested reassessing the point distribution. Consensus was easily reached that two parts of the course should count for more than had been originally agreed upon; namely, their community service and their key reflective writing — their journals.

Community Service-Learning

Participating in some type of service was essential to learning what was being taught — applying theory to reality. Service provided a greater depth and understanding of the readings. However, I must honestly admit that I was a bit resentful for being pulled from my narcissistic little world to work for the good of others. I got over it though.

The class could not function nearly as well without active participation of the students. Yeah, sometimes it was a real pain-in-the-neck to give up time for community service and traveling back and forth, but it was absolutely essential for beating some of these ideas into this thick head of mine.

By integrating action with learning, we can observe history from "inside" so to speak. As all historians are products of their times, this is almost a necessity to be a grounded historian who can comment on his times and conditions with the authority of experience.

Many of the ideas and terms we learned would not have come into focus or been believed had we not seen them in action for ourselves.

— Course evaluations

Over the last 25 years, service-learning has found justification in educational institutions as both an alternative pedagogy and as a movement aimed at transforming the culture of higher education (Barber 1992; Barber and Battistoni 1993; Kendall 1990; Stanton, Giles, and Cruz 1999). Ernest Boyer placed community-based education at the core of the creation of the "New American College," what he describes as "an institution that celebrates its capacity to connect thought and action, theory and practice" (1994: A48). Service-learning is a pedagogy of reflective inquiry linking students' involvement in community-based service with their intellectual and moral development. In its most fundamental sense, it is a way of connecting practical experience that meets a community need with academic study through structured reflection. The pillars supporting this approach incorporate a nontraditional pedagogy and epistemology (Palmer 1987). Connecting experience in the community to an academic curriculum requires adopting a reflective teaching methodology that integrates cognitive and affective development, or as bell hooks writes, "ways of knowing with habits of being" (1994: 43). The rich theoretical and pedagogical roots of service-learning can be found in the works of John Dewey, Paulo Freire, Robert Coles, Benjamin Barber, Henry Giroux, Parker Palmer, William Perry, Lawrence Kohlberg, Carol Gilligan, Cecilia Delve, Suzanne Mintz, Greig Stewart, and others (Delve, Mintz, and Stewart 1990; Saltmarsh 1996).

According to philosopher Jane Roland Martin, service-learning represents an educational paradigm that "integrates thought and action, reason and emotion, education and life" and "does not divorce persons from their social and natural contexts" — or their historical context (1984: 179-183). To achieve these results requires a change in pedagogy and epistemology; the relations of teaching and learning shift from procedural knowing to the collective construction of knowledge; the teacher is decentered in the classroom, facilitating via a problem-posing educational approach a dialogic search for knowledge. Students become self-directed and reflective learners; and teacher and students engage in a relationship of reciprocity where both are equally committed to creating a context for learning. Such an orientation on connected knowing legitimizes learning that takes place outside the classroom, recognizes multiple learning styles, and values learning based in experience.

Since this process of giving up old ways of knowing and learning in becoming a reflective historian can often be discomforting — as one student wrote in his course evaluation, "It was painful in the beginning, but the rewards were great" — a reflective teacher aims at educating the whole student and must be aware of not only what he or she knows but also the process of transformation toward becoming someone different from who he or she is. A reflective teacher ensures that the seminar is a place for growth and struggle as well as a place where knowledge is actively and collectively created. Finally, research on service-learning makes clear that its effectiveness as a pedagogy is directly related to both a close connection of community experience to the academic content of the course and the quality of the reflection that facilitates that connection (Eyler and Giles 1999; Eyler, Giles, and Schmiede 1996; Goldsmith 1995).

Reflective Journals

Jane Addams . . . began to address the question that is starting to arise at this point in our class — what does the individual do, what can they do, and what should they do.

I just had a heart attack. I thought I lost this journal. Usually I keep both of them together, but not this time. Yes, two journals. I found myself feeling certain private thoughts that had to be expressed, so I started another private journal.

(First Entry:)
I never had a journal before, and I don't really know what I should be doing. . . . I never really thought about what is history and how it relates to community.
(Last Entry:)
Today is the last day of class . . . and it is the last day of writing in this journal (I will continue to write in it now that I am hooked on it).

— Journal entries

Reflective journals were a key catalyst in encouraging students to search for the connections between their experiences in the community and their interpretations of the course texts. The learning dimension of service-learning emerges through reflective inquiry, and journals can serve as a powerful tool for reflection. Structured reflection is essential; as John Dewey once wrote, "mere activity does not constitute experience" (1979: 146). Time was spent early in the term discussing the purpose of journals and considering entries from Thoreau's *Journals* to explore the process of journal writing. There are a number of guiding principles I adhere to when using journals in a class:

• Journals are a tool of reflection where critical writing skills can be combined with critical thinking;

• Journal entries can take many forms — there is no formula for journal writing;

• Part of journal writing is discovering the *voice* to reflect in — discovering confident and empowered expression;

• Sharing journal writing is risky/revealing — it can foster group cohesiveness and provide challenge and support for further reflection (the process is enhanced if the teacher keeps a journal and shares entries with the students);

• Journal writing does not come naturally — it needs to be nurtured.

Students were required to do a considerable amount of writing for the course. Some assignments were very traditional analytical essays focused on the readings, whereas others were the weekly journal writings. The key to the latter was that the students' reflections broke down the pretense of objectivity and emphasized their "live encounter with subjects of study" (Palmer 1998: 37-38). That live encounter established the basis for the way in which they wrote in their journals and provided the catalyst for their developing an engaged style of thinking and writing that governed how they wrote about the texts they analyzed, and how they connected those texts and their experiences. In this way, their readings became real and their writing became a live encounter with living texts. Not only was the intellectual quality of their writing extraordinarily high, but their devotion to the analytical process became increasingly apparent as they engaged more authentically in their writing. Although the mantra of objectivity often includes an insistence on academic "rigor," the rigor of this course was not limited to an intellectual capacity to master the knowledge base of the discipline; it also included a rigorous capacity for critical thinking and writing that allowed the students to become better historians.

Every effort was made to have the intellectual and emotional struggle that takes place in reflection become safe and habitual. Students were initially asked to write low-intensity journal entries and to share their writing with the group. As this process became safer and more routine, the students moved to a higher level of trust and risked expressing more of their thoughts. At the end of each class, they provided the group with questions that served as the basis for journal entries as well as discussions — and as a means of weaving class meetings together. Their journals were "public" in the sense that they knew that they were expected to share their writing and that I would evaluate their entries as part of their grade. In some cases, this led students to keep a second, "private" journal, because the process of becoming reflective about their lives had become essential to who they were and what they did — and how they learned.

Journals, however, were only one tool of reflection. Classroom dialogue offered another venue for students to reflect upon their experiences in the community and the texts they read. As reflective learners, they developed an ability to approach the past and the present through a process of asking and answering: first, what happened; second, what does what happened mean; and third, what do I do with this information? In this way the past became connected to the present and the future, and their education to their capacity as active citizens.

Connected Knowing

I feel that this was one of the most difficult yet rewarding classes I have ever taken. . . . I feel that all students (not just history) would benefit from this class in a fundamental way. The issues confronted here are simply too unsettling to be tackled in a traditional academic format.

I have become more aware of my surroundings, have learned to look more deeply into the words of writers, and have learned to formulate my own opinions. Perhaps what I like best about this class is that it synthesized all of my years of book learning and applied it to why I was here in the first place. Lately I've been having difficulty justifying the cost of my education versus what I really learned about what is necessary in living. I was beginning to think my time was wasted; that history was a bunch of fluff that had no use in society anymore. . . . I don't think I ever really knew what it meant until I was trying to incorporate my experiences [in the community] with the many readings we worked with.

— Journal entries

By approaching history through experience and reflection, I was encouraging the students to become different kinds of scholars (just as I would have to be a different kind of teacher). By the time we read Emerson's "The American Scholar" as part of the course, they were quickly able to identify with the implicit warning Emerson sounded. By engaging the community, much as they would engage a written text, they embraced Emerson's imperative that "you must take the whole society to find the whole man" (25). Their experiences in a homeless shelter, an inner-city elementary classroom, an ESL program, or an after-school program left little doubt as to the meaning of Emerson's quips that "character is higher than intellect" (31) and "books are for the scholars' idle time" (28). They understood implicitly that in their prior educational experience, knowledge had been disconnected from their historical identity. This time, however, their experiences in the community allowed them to unpack each text they were reading in such a way that they had deeper insights into its meaning as well as deeper insights into their educational experience.

Each of the readings assigned in the course was employed to explore a particular cultural context and historical moment, as well as to illuminate the themes of individualism, community, and democracy (and their intersection). Similarly, the community-based experiences were the basis for exploring the meaning of those themes as the students encountered them in their lives. For the most part, the assigned readings were no different from what would be expected in a conventional upper-level cultural history course: John Winthrop's *Model of Christian Charity*, Tocqueville's *Democracy in America*, Jane Addams's *Twenty Years at Hull House*, essays by William James and John Dewey, the Lynds' *Middletown*, David Riesman's *The Lonely Crowd*, and Christopher Lasch's *The Culture of Narcissism* (see syllabus). Some readings were less conventional, chosen to generate discussion around topics such as community, activism, and the historian's professional identity — including Thomas Bender's *Community and Social Change in America*, Michael Ignatieff's *The Needs of Strangers*, Staughton Lynd's essay "The Historian as Participant," and "The Port Huron Statement."

As for the departures from traditional curricular design, one was the use of texts to focus on the meaning of concepts such as individualism, community, and democracy over the course of American history. Another was the utilization of community service experiences as a way of exploring the themes encountered in the written texts. However, the key difference was designing the curriculum in such a way as to connect the students' active participation in a community, their role as democratic citizens, and their personal and professional identity to the meaning of their education.

For that to happen, my role had to shift to facilitator and contributor to the construction of knowledge in the classroom. Clearly, I had a foundation and breadth of specialized knowledge as well as substantial experience to bring to our discussions. At the same time, each of the students also had a realm of knowledge and experience to contribute, both of which grew over the course of the term. What we collectively created was a transformative learning environment that changed the students, their approach to the discipline, and their relationship to the larger society. A full year after participating in the course, one student reported that "this course changed the way I perceive history. It helped me see how history is tied to current events."

"History," claimed another student a year later, "can be so amorphous, ethereal, but this course places history in a construct [and] turned us into *grounded* historians." These students had overcome the deadening disengagement and intellectual restrictions of objectivity; as a result, the past ceased to be an object and became, instead, a vital, interactive part of their lives.

Notes

1. A version of this essay was published as "Becoming a Reflective Historian Through Community Service-Learning" in the *Organization of American Historians Council of Chairs Newsletter,* Spring 1996, pp. 2-6.

2. All citations to Emerson's "The American Scholar" (1837) reference *The Complete Writings of Ralph Waldo Emerson,* Vol. 1, pp. 79-115 (New York, NY: William Wise, 1929).

References

Alinsky, S. (1969, orig. 1946). *Reveille for Radicals.* New York, NY: Vintage.

Barber, B. (1992). *An Aristocracy of Everyone: The Politics of Education and the Future of America.* New York, NY: Oxford University Press.

———. (1998). *A Place for Us: How to Make Society Civil and Democracy Strong.* New York, NY: Hill and Wang.

———, and R. Battistoni. (June 1993). "A Season of Service: Introducing Service Learning Into the Liberal Arts Curriculum." PS: *Political Science and Politics* 16(2): 235-262.

Bellah, R., et al. (1985). *Habits of the Heart: Individualism and Commitment in American Life.* Berkeley, CA: University of California Press.

Bender, T. (1993). *Intellect and Public Life: Essays on the Social History of Academic Intellectuals in the United States.* Baltimore, MD: The Johns Hopkins University Press.

Boyer, E. (March 9, 1994). "Creating the New American College." *The Chronicle of Higher Education,* p. A48.

Boyte, H., and N. Kari. (1996). *Building America: The Democratic Promise of Public Work.* Philadelphia, PA: Temple University Press.

Cooper, D. (February 1999). "Academic Professionalism and the Betrayal of the Land-Grant Tradition." *American Behavioral Scientist* 42: 776-785.

Cronon, W. (Winter 1999). "'Only Connect': The Goals of Liberal Education." *The Key Reporter* 64(2): 2-4.

Damon, W. (Oct. 16, 1998). "The Path to a Civil Society Goes Through the University." *The Chronicle of Higher Education,* pp. B4-B5.

Delve, C., S. Mintz, and G. Stewart, eds. (Summer 1990) *Community Service as Values Education*. New Directions for Teaching and Learning, no. 50. San Francisco, CA: Jossey-Bass.

Dewey, J. (1979, orig. 1916). *Democracy and Education*. The Middle Works of John Dewey, vol. 9, edited by Jo Ann Boydston. Carbondale, IL: Southern Illinois University Press.

Eyler, J., and D. Giles, Jr. (1999). *Where's the Learning in Service-Learning?* San Francisco, CA: Jossey-Bass.

————, and A. Schmiede. (1996). *A Practitioners Guide to Reflection in Service Learning*. Washington, DC: Corporation for National Service.

Freire, P. (1970). *Pedagogy of the Oppressed*. New York, NY: Continuum.

Goldsmith, S. (1995). *Journal Reflection: A Resource Guide for Community Service Leaders and Educators Engaged in Service Learning*. Washington, DC: American Alliance for Rights and Responsibilities.

hooks, b. (1994). *Teaching to Transgress: Education as the Practice of Freedom*. New York, NY: Routledge.

Kendall, J., ed. (1990). *Combining Service and Learning: A Resource Book for Community and Public Service, Vols. I and II*. Raleigh, NC: National Society for Internships and Experiential Education.

Keylor, W. (Summer 1999). "Clio on Campus: The Historical Society at Boston University." *Bostonia* 16(2): 20-23.

Martin, J.R. (1984). *Changing the Educational Landscape: Philosophy, Women, and the Curriculum*. New York, NY: Routledge.

Mathews, D. (1998). "Creating More Public Space in Higher Education." Washington, DC: The Council on Public Policy Education.

National Commission on Civic Renewal. (1998). *A Nation of Spectators: How Civic Disengagement Weakens America and What We Can Do About It*. College Park, MD: University of Maryland.

Novick, P. (1988). *That Noble Dream: The "Objectivity Question" and the American Historical Profession*. Cambridge and New York, NY: Cambridge University Press.

Palmer, P. (Sep./Oct. 1987). "Community, Conflict, and Ways of Knowing: Ways to Deepen Our Educational Agenda." *Change* 19(5): 20-25.

————. (1998). *The Courage to Teach: Exploring the Inner Landscape of a Teacher's Life*. San Francisco, CA: Jossey-Bass.

Reyes, M. (1998). "A Pedagogy for Citizenship: Service Learning and Democratic Education." In *Academic Service Learning: A Pedagogy of Action and Reflection*, edited by R. Rhoads and J. Howard, pp. 31 38. New Directions for Teaching and Learning, no. 73. San Francisco, CA: Jossey-Bass.

Richardson, R. (1995). *Emerson: The Mind on Fire*. Berkeley, CA: University of California Press.

Rorty, R. (1998). *Achieving Our Country: Leftist Thought in the Twentieth-Century.* Cambridge, MA: Harvard University Press.

Saltmarsh, J. (Fall 1996). "Education for Critical Citizenship: John Dewey's Contribution to the Pedagogy of Community Service Learning." *Michigan Journal of Community Service Learning* 3: 13-21.

Stanton, T., D. Giles, Jr., and N. Cruz. (1999). *Service-Learning: A Movement's Pioneers Reflect on Its Origins, Practice, and Future.* San Francisco, CA: Jossey-Bass.

Sullivan, W. (1995). *Work and Integrity: The Crisis and Promise of Professionalism in America.* New York, NY: HarperCollins.

The Individual and Community
in Democratic America

Course Listing: *CHST 1805, Sec. 1, Seq. 9: Approaches to History*
Spring 1995: Tuesday, Friday: 10:30 AM; Wednesday: 4:05 PM.
Class meets in Room 411 EL

Instructor: John Saltmarsh

"I believe once more that history is of educative value in so far as it presents phases of social life and growth. It must be controlled by reference to social life. When taken simply as history it is thrown into the distant past and becomes dead and inert. Taken as the record of man's social life and progress it becomes full of meaning."
-John Dewey, "My Pedagogic Creed" (1897)

Course Description:

This course will explore the historical meanings of individualism and community in American culture, focusing on the relationship of the self to the larger community of others and institutions, examining the historical dimensions of the tensions between the individual and society in light of the consequences for a democratic political culture.

In analyzing various approaches to historical study, the course has three components:
    1) analysis of primary and secondary source material to explore the traditions that define the tensions between individual aspirations and community values and assess how these have changed over time and in different cultural settings;
    2) analysis of readings to focus discussion on questions of method, theory, and evidence and the interpretation/analysis/writing of history in the exploration of the theme of the course; and
    3) service activity and reflection that will focus our discussion on approaching the contemporary context of our historical understanding, making connections between ideas and experience to integrate others' observations and interpretations with our own, to bring a certain immediacy to the readings.

Teaching Methodology:

Seminar. Discussion/dialogue will
    1) focus on common readings to explore the traditions surrounding the theme of the course and to provide the social context for the students' community service activity, and
    2) consist of reflection on experience of involvement in the community and the relationship between their experience and the readings/ideas of the course.

Service Experience:
A requirement of this course is that students will engage in community service activity for at least two hours each week (20 hours over the course of the quarter). Service assignments can be arranged by the instructor in collaboration with (1) the Tobin School in the Mission Hill Neighborhood next to Northeastern University or (2) with the John Shelburne Community Center in Roxbury.

The Tobin School in situated in one of Boston's poorest neighborhoods and is part of the Boston Public School System. It is the only kindergarten through eighth grade school in the Boston Public School System and serves a predominantly Latino and African American student body. The Shelburne Community Center is the only community center in Roxbury and for twenty-five years has focused its services to the ethnic and economic diversity of the residents of the area neighborhoods who utilize the Shelburne as a safe haven for their children.

Required Readings:

Jane Addams, *Twenty Years at Hull House* (1910)

Robert Bellah, et al, *Habits of the Heart: Individualism and Commitment in American Life* (1985)

Thomas Bender, *Community and Social Change in America* (1978)

Christopher Lasch, *The Culture of Narcissism* (1978)

Robert and Helen Lynd, *Middletown: A Study of Contemporary American Culture* (1929)

David Reisman, *The Lonely Crowd* (1961)

Tocqueville, *Democracy in America* (1835/1840)

Also: Classpack at Gnomon Copy

Course Schedule:

Week 1: April 5, 7 and
Week 2: April 11, 12, 14

Traditions and Definitions Approaches to History: Method, Theory, and Evidence, Bellah and Bender

Week 3: April 18, 19, 21: Christianity and Republicanism, Bellah and Bender

Week 4: April 25, 26, 28: Democracy and America in the early 19th Century Tocqueville

Week 5: May 2, 3, 5: Industrial Capitalism: Challenges to Individualism and Democracy, Addams

Week 6: May 9, 10, 12: The Self and Community in a Consumer Culture, Lynds

Week 7: May 16, 17, 19: Post-War America: The Quest for Individuality in a Mass Society, Reisman

Week 8: May 23, 25, 26: The Personal and the Political: Community Lost and Found: Approaching the Past and   the Future, Lasch

Week 9: May 30, 31, June 2: Presentations of Final Papers
{last week for Seniors}

Week 10: June 6, 7, 9: Presentations of Final papers

Week 11: June 12-16: Exam Week

"Democracy must begin at home, and its home is the neighborly community." (1927)

"Regarded as an idea, democracy is not an alternative to other principles of associated life. It is the idea of community life itself." (1927)

"Individuality cannot be opposed to association. It is through association that man has acquired his individuality and it is through association that he exercises it. [Individuality means] performance of a special *service* without which the social whole is defective." (1891)

"Information is an undigested burden unless it is understood. It is *knowledge* only as its material is *comprehended*. And understanding, comprehension, means that the various parts of the information acquired are grasped in their relation to one another - a result that is attained only when acquisition is accompanied by constant reflection upon the meaning of what is studied." (1933)
                                                            - John Dewey

Classpack Table of Contents:

Robert Coles, *Community Service Work*

Robert Coles, *Putting Head and Heart on the Line*

C. Blake and C. Phelps, *History as Social Criticism: Conversations with Christopher Lasch*

John Dewey, *The Democratic Conception in Education*

John Dewey, *The Search for the Great Community*

Ralph Waldo Emerson, *The American Scholar*

bell hooks, *Keeping Close to Home: Class and Education*

bell hooks, *Representing the Poor*

Michael Ignatieff, *The Needs of Strangers*

William James, *The Moral Equivalent of War*

Martin Luther King, Jr., *Letter from Birmingham Jail*

Jonathan Kozol, *Savage Inequalities*

Staughton Lynd, *The Historian as Participant*

Students for a Democratic Society, *The Port Huron Statement*

Henry David Thoreau, *On the Duty of Civil Disobedience*

Henry David Thoreau, *Journal*

John Winthrop, *A Model of Christian Charity*

Ellen Goodman, "Mentoring Kids in Crisis"

Required Written Work and Presentations:

1) A reflective journal:
The journal will focus on the community service activity and reflections on the experience and the connections between that experience and the literature of the course. You will be asked to keep a journal during the quarter. The journals are a reflection tool that will be shared periodically. There is the minimum expectation of weekly entries. Journals will be turned in for review the last day of class (and will be returned).   Journal: (%)

2) A review of *Habits of the Heart:*
The review/analysis should focus on the approach the authors took to creating historical understanding. What methodology(ies) do they employ? What theory guides their interpretation? What evidence do they turn to? Who are the authors (provide a cultural profile of the authors)? Be sure to incorporate at least two published reviews of the book in your essay and cite them properly. 3-5 pages minimum, typed, double-spaced. Due May 2.   Review: (%)

3) A small group presentation and short paper of one of the assigned books in the class:
The small group will present together and may collaborate on the written work, but each student will turn in a paper. The presentation and the paper will focus on
- the way in which the author(s) addressed the issues of individualism, community, and democracy in the particular book
- the author(s) approach (methods, theory, evidence) to the subject.
3-5 pages, typed, double-spaced. Papers are due two weeks after presentation.   Presentation: (%)
                                                                                        Paper: (%)

4) Final paper:
The final paper due at the end of the course will consist of an analysis of the service experience in the community, placing that analysis in a larger context drawn from the readings from the course and seminar discussions, integrating the students' own interpretations with those from the literature of the course. Your paper should integrate your experience in the community with the readings from the class to answer the question, "what is the relationship between my approach to the present and my approach to the past." 8-12 pages, typed, double-spaced. Papers are due for presentation during the last two weeks of the course, to be turned in on the last day of class.   Presentation: (%)
                                                                                        Paper: (%)

5) Class participation: (%)

6) Class attendance: (%)

7) Community service: (%)

Service-Learning and History:
Training the Metaphorical Mind

by J. Matthew Gallman

The integration of service-learning into history courses is not as easy as it appears. And it does not appear to be very easy. This essay is based on my experiments with using service-learning in two courses in American history while I was in the History Department at Loyola College in Baltimore.[1] I had taught the first course, American Urban History, several times before adding a service-learning component in the spring of 1995. The following year I developed a new course on Poverty and Welfare in American History, with a required service-learning component. This essay builds on those experiences to suggest some broader observations about the logistical practice and pedagogical theory of service-learning, particularly as they pertain to the teaching of history.

I will consider those logistical and pedagogical challenges in two stages. The first stage includes concerns common to most service-learning courses. The second considers some challenges and approaches that seem to be a unique aspect of using service-learning in teaching history. The inherent distance between that which is studied and that which is observed and experienced requires that history students, perhaps more than their peers in other disciplines, must develop a metaphorical — rather than a literal — understanding of their experiences.

Why Service-Learning?

I imagine that in some quarters the burden of proof placed on the decision to employ service-learning is particularly — I would say unnecessarily — heavy. That is, skeptics are likely to demand that service-learning be clearly and demonstrably the most effective pedagogical tool to teach the specific topics defined by a particular course. I think that many history courses can meet that test, but I would question whether such a demand is fair.

I first came to service-learning several years ago after participating in a day-long service experience with a class of first-year students. That day my class stained a deck at a residence for men who suffer from mental or emotional illness. I was personally struck by the experience, and particularly by the men who watched from the windows of their rooms as we worked. In their subsequent classroom discussions and written reflections, my students demonstrated that they were also moved by the day's activities.

Whatever the specific disciplinary benefits, I am convinced that service-learning has tremendous value in challenging our students to think about — and learn about — social justice issues. On that particular day I was not wearing my historian's hat; the experience was designed as an introduction to community service for first-year students, not as a discipline-based service-learning experience. But that is not to say that there were not important lessons learned. Following a truncated version of the "preparation, action, reflection" model, we prepared by spending a class period discussing our stereotypical images of the men whom we would be meeting, and that afternoon and again the next week we discussed what we had learned and observed.

On the day of our service, our actions were preceded and followed by invaluable discussions with the center's director. The reflection essays that my students wrote revealed that the experience had touched them at both an emotional and an intellectual level. They had learned at least a small amount about the interlocking challenges of homelessness, mental illness, and substance abuse. Moreover, they had received a taste of the complex relations between private philanthropies and public legislation. Finally, and I see no reason to discount this, at the end of the day the center had a deck stained that needed staining and the residents had truly positive experiences talking with — or merely watching — our students. Moreover, by the time they graduated, a disproportionate number of those students were heavily involved in some form of community service.

I introduce this non–service-learning episode to underscore the point that there are important benefits for students and the community *above and beyond* specifically disciplinary gains. Thus, I would suggest that the burden of proof for using this pedagogical tool ought to, in fact, be lower than that placed on other teaching innovations. The natural tendency might be for the historian to discount benefits that do not pertain to the topics at hand. But such thinking is really out of line with normal teaching practice. After all, as I construct a syllabus or conduct a class, I have many agendas in mind that are not directly associated with the historical topic under consideration. For instance, I am interested in how students express themselves, both in writing and orally, and I routinely create assignments and provide evaluations intended to develop those skills. Or more broadly, I join my colleagues in claiming that I am teaching critical-thinking skills that transcend specific course content. And finally, in selecting readings and running class discussions I try to broaden my students' understanding of diversity while also modeling a belief in gender equality. As educators we all do this sort of thing — to differing degrees — as a matter of course. When service-learning courses introduce students to social justice issues, encourage them to bridge the chasms between classes, or help them develop service interests and skills that may remain with them for life, those ancillary benefits are really no different *in kind* from the other goals and benefits we routinely weave into our teaching.

Why *Not* Service-Learning?

Although service-learning can be a superb pedagogical tool, there are good reasons *not* to take it up. Or, to be more precise, it is in the nature of service-learning that a poor or half-hearted effort could end up doing more harm than good, either for the students or for the community. Many of my colleagues have addressed service-learning's logistical challenges, and I do not presume to have any particular insights on the matter. Nonetheless, let me suggest five areas of particular concern in considering this approach.

(i) **Centers, Peripheries, and Eyesores:** As soon as we begin speaking of adding a service-learning component to a course we walk onto very treacherous terrain. That means not that we should rush back to safety but that we should tread very carefully. "Adding" a service-learning component to an established course's architecture is liable to look like the unsightly spare bedroom stuck on the back of an otherwise attractive home. If we think of it that way, our students will know right away and all will be lost. Service-learning will not work if treated as an additional topic or unit or, worse, as something that students wrestle with on their own time. Yes, it is appropriate to have time set aside for discussing service experiences and specific written assignments devoted to formal reflection. Such pieces are necessary, but in my mind not sufficient. Somehow the service-learning component must be woven into the fabric of the course, so that it becomes central to the academic experience. Students should regard this experience as a "service-learning course" rather than as a course with a service-learning component. That centrality can be conveyed to students in various structural ways, including giving service-learning particular attention in the syllabus, in the introductory class, and in the opening minutes of at least periodic class meetings. Even more important are those small occasions when the topic for the day is not *about* service, but the instructor points out a link between that topic and some aspect of the students' service experiences.

(ii) **Crises of Coverage:** It is only natural, particularly in using service-learning in an established course, to worry that service-learning will entail some loss of coverage. When we construct any course, we do so within pretty rigid parameters, defined by the number and length of class meetings. We probably also have some sense of how much total work we can expect from our students. Class time devoted to service-learning reflections will effectively bump class discussions that would otherwise have been included, or at least reshape them. I also believe in making similar adjustments to the homework portion of a course: I see the 15 hours of service and the accompanying written work as essentially replacing some other assignments, rather than merely adding to existing expectations.

Some educational theorists would urge skeptics to completely jettison the idea of coverage as an outdated concept that stands in the way of true teaching. I will leave it to them to fight that uphill battle, while suggesting that at least in the humanities there is simply no such thing as *full* coverage in any course, and thus it is really only a matter of including service-learning in our list of priorities in shaping a course. True, historians — and I suppose philosophers, English professors, and so on — will commonly insist that there is some baseline of factual information in each course below which they simply cannot fall. But we do not have to reopen recent academic battles about "the canon" to recognize that it is rather silly to speak of *necessary* coverage in a college humanities course. After all, I annually find it a tight fit squeezing my entire course on the Civil War and Reconstruction into a mere 14 weeks. This amuses my medievalist colleague, who speaks of decades the way I speak of historically crucial afternoons. The truth is that we routinely shape dramatically different courses into the semester (or quarter) structure. When we want to add new topics or materials we could try just to talk faster, but soon enough some heretofore "necessary" component is omitted and life goes on. If service-learning is worth doing, then it is worth making room for it.

(iii) The Poor Are Different From You and Me: A more serious stumbling block concerns those things that our students might learn, or think they learn, while doing their service. In one of the 1984 presidential debates, a frustrated Walter Mondale declared that his problem with President Reagan was not so much what the President did not know, but what he knew "which just isn't so." Service provides many opportunities for the unreflective student to learn things that just aren't true. I am most concerned about the natural, but dangerous, tendency toward what one might call personal empiricism. Most of my Loyola students worked at sites in Baltimore, where most of the low-income people they met are African-American. They then returned to a campus where the food service, housekeeping, and maintenance staffs were also composed almost exclusively of African Americans while members of the faculty and administration were almost exclusively white. If they had not been given some countervailing information, some of them would certainly have concluded — at least at the subliminal level — that (1) nearly all people on welfare are black and (2) nearly all African Americans have low incomes.

I can think of many instances where students' observations have led them to conclusions that I found worthy of further discussion. For instance, students occasionally return from meal programs criticizing those guests who ask for some other option rather than simply accepting the food offered. Students who have worked with tutoring programs sometimes draw cynical conclusions about seemingly expensive shoes worn by supposedly underprivileged boys; others return from a few hours with a child declaring that her mother is incompetent or worse.

How do we avoid creating a coterie of uninformed "experts" returning to campus with a set of reinforced negative stereotypes? One response is that many students are *already* doing community service, so service-learning is not really the problem and is potentially the solution. A better answer is to think hard about what our students will be experiencing and shape their preparations and reflections accordingly. Amateur empiricism can be countered with national statistics and with concrete images — guest speakers, videos, etc. — of nonwhites who defy those stereotypes. Anecdotes can be placed into a broader context. When one student complained about meal program guests asking for different desserts, another student pointed out that the man in question might have had few other choices of any sort during that day.

(iv) Do What I Do, Not Just What I Say: Leading effective reflection requires that the instructor has a good feel for the sites where the students are working. In my most successful service-learning course my students worked at five different sites. I was the director at one of these sites — an after-school program — and I had worked extensively at the other four. During the semester I worked alongside most of my students. I feel that my work at these sites had an important effect on my success as an instructor for several reasons. First, I love what I do and my students know that. I hope that contributes to their developing a sense of joy — rather than obligation or sanctimony — in doing service. Second, the things I have learned help me teach. Often students would mention individuals I knew and had worked with. Third, I feel that my actions model the process of learning that I want students to be going through with me.

It would be unreasonable to demand that service-learning instructors should be veterans of hundreds of hours of community service. But I would say that some familiarity with each site is necessary, and I would urge anyone undertaking service-learning to commit to spending time — at least as much as the students — engaged in service alongside his or her students. Not only will that help create the benefits noted above, it will also avoid the charge of hypocrisy that I think is poison to service-learning. In short, if we truly believe it is a good idea for our students, then we should want some form of service to be part of our own lives.

(v) Trains Running on Time: The final potential stumbling block is organizational. I have found that students really love active service, but they also really hate plans that go awry. Loyola College is very fortunate to have a superb service-learning system coordinated out of its Center for Values and Service. But whatever the local institutional structure, it is crucial that students being introduced to service, particularly as a course requirement, have as smooth an experience as possible.

Service-Learning and History: Distance and Metaphors

These broad structural and pedagogical concerns are an important foundation in creating a service-learning component in history, but they do not touch on the specific disciplinary challenges. What exactly are we trying to teach in a service-learning course in history? It may well be true that some students have an experience in which they truly empathize with an individual who is poor, or at least they feel that they see the world through that person's eyes, if only for a moment. But I do not think that such special moments can be the stated goal. They demand too much of the limited experience and of all concerned. The very idea that one could anticipate such a level of understanding belittles the complexity of poverty and of the lives of the people our students meet and work with. Moreover, such a demand would be bad history. The student who really does come to an understanding of some small portion of another person's life (for instance, the symbolic importance of a simple choice of dessert options) has not necessarily enhanced his or her understanding of history — unless he or she perceives some continuities between that moment and past realities.

In many other disciplines, service experiences can truly be treated as the raw material of the course. That is, my colleagues in sociology, composition, philosophy, education, psychology, theology, and political science can all construct service-learning placements intended to illustrate or illuminate specific themes in a particular course. The problem of chronological distance places the historian in a separate camp. That is, unless the service-learning experience is designed simply to raise issues at the most modern end of a chronological course, at some point the class must dig more deeply into the relationship between what is being experienced and the past under study. One of my graduate professors used to declare that "history does not repeat itself, but it does rhyme." Our task is to listen for the right rhyme. Or, to put it another way, in order for the present to inform our understanding of the past, we must search for the *appropriate* metaphors while avoiding those more likely to distort than illuminate.

One of my favorite sites in Baltimore was an informal meal program called Care-A-Van, operated by Loyola College volunteers. Twice a week Care-A-Van's student-volunteers bring sandwiches and drinks to a park outside City Hall where anywhere from 30 to 80 people, mostly homeless men, gather. After distributing the food, the volunteers stay around for an hour or so. Some of the guests drift away but many others remain for informal conversations. Over the course of weeks and months friendships are formed. My students and I learned many things from these afternoons, some important portion of which has helped us understand the past and the connection between that past and the present.

At the end of my course on Poverty and Welfare in American History, one Care-A-Van student, Bob,[2] wrote:

> *From talking to one person in particular, known only as John, I came to see that education really is what is lacking for most of the needy people who participate in the Care-A-Van program. He is always talking about how he would love to go into biology, and figure out how everything in the world works. He seems as though he would really like to make a difference. Unfortunately, he doesn't appear to understand that achieving such a goal is next to impossible. I feel bad for him, and others who truly want to get themselves out of their impoverished situation. In many cases, their condition is not a fault of their own, but rather a consequence of some accident early in their lives. I guess life just isn't fair.*

During the semester I had had long conversations with Bob and watched him go through a tremendous personal transformation in his views on poverty and in his thoughts about his place in society. I also knew John from Care-A-Van, and he had spoken fondly of Bob (who continued to participate in the program during the following semester). Did this relationship help Bob understand the experience of poverty in American history? There are certainly links to be drawn between Bob's understanding of John's life and our class discussions of the roots of poverty. For instance, many of the 19th-century reformers we read in class stressed the importance of education as a route to upward mobility. And when Bob suggested the crucial role of "some accident early in their lives," he drew an important connection between an essay that Mathew Carey (1971) wrote in 1837, an article on the early 20th century by historian Michael Katz (1990), and an anecdote that John had shared about his life.[3] The essays by Carey and Katz — and several other readings — stress the specific role of unforeseen accidents in dramatically changing individuals' circumstances. Thus, Bob was using his understanding of the past to help explain John's present. Most of John's life, insofar as Bob and I might know it, has little in common with the world of an Irish immigrant in 1850 or of a widow at the turn of the century, but in Bob's implied metaphor he pulled out two threads — the importance of education and the role of individual misfortune — that observers have consistently turned to to explain the problem of poverty.

Public Policy and Personal Understanding

Bob's implied metaphors, drawing links between John and individuals from the past, make good sense to me, but I am uncomfortable about asking my students to place individuals they have met into historic worlds they have studied. Such an exercise is likely to undermine many of the other benefits of the experience, leading students to approach the conversation with a checklist of traits in mind. A complementary approach would be for students to shift the analytic lens, so that an individual's relationship with society moves into focus.

A central concern in the study of poverty and welfare is to understand how the problem of poverty has been explained at any historic moment. One thread that runs through my course on Poverty and Welfare in American History is that reformers, politicians, and scholars consistently have differed over the relative weight of personal failings and external factors in explaining poverty. The 19th-century understanding of this discussion shaped a commonly recognized distinction between the "worthy poor" and the "unworthy poor." The assumption here was that certain categories of people — children, the elderly, the disabled — had fallen upon hard times through no fault of their own and thus should receive assistance freely and fairly easily. Others — the unworthy poor — were seen as victims of their own indolence or vices and therefore should receive only assistance that would not encourage further misbehavior. Over the last two centuries, the categories and labels have changed, but one can certainly argue that the fundamental premise has not: Policymakers and private philanthropists have always drawn distinctions between people deemed more or less eligible for assistance. These distinctions reflect contemporary assumptions about the origins of poverty and about those who are poor, and these assumptions, in turn, shape the experience of poverty.[4]

Through their service experiences, students are able both to observe individual manifestations of these abstract policy distinctions and, in some cases, to come to their own judgment about the appropriateness of those distinctions. One Care-A-Van student wrote:

> Another reason as to why we get the image we do of a poor person is because for years, the middle-aged man has been termed as part of "unworthy poor." There are hundreds of programs established to help the young children and single mothers . . . but little is done to help middle-aged men. Widows and the elderly have always been seen as deserving because "they have suffered circumstances beyond their responsibility" (Katz 1993: 10).
> ". . . Sentiment, however, did not shift in favor of dependent men, unless they were white. . . . Increasingly, males [were] divided into two groups,

adults [temporarily] out of work, and young minority men, unskilled,
unwilling to work, and dangerous" (12).

The student went on to acknowledge that "throughout my service, I have seen a lot of homeless either drunk or smoking and I have even found needles while cleaning the streets. However, one has to put oneself in a homeless person's shoes." In the subsequent pages of her essay, the student moved through many of those characteristics that she felt had placed the man of her Care-A-Van experience among the unworthy poor — theft, addiction, violence — and argued that these traits were the result, not the cause, of their material poverty. I would argue that in the process she was really placing herself in the shoes of contemporary policymakers and finding the fit uncomfortable.

Another student worked at Beans and Bread, a meal program in downtown Baltimore, and also attended an overnight sleepout at Fell's Point in Baltimore. She, too, pointed out the historic tradition of drawing distinctions between the worthy and unworthy poor while noting that "the only requirement for a meal at Beans and Bread is that the recipient be sober." She added, "I am personally thankful that Beans and Bread has no such discriminating criteria [between worthy and unworthy guests], for I would not have had the opportunity to get to know one of the most amazing people I have ever met." She went on to describe a long conversation with a homeless man:

> *I would love to write a whole paper on him and the conversation we had that night into the wee hours of the morning, but I will summarize it by saying that I learned a lot more than the fact that he is a man who has a job, and a huge heart, but not a home. I saw God in Clarence that evening. But I might not have had the chance to spend that time with him, because Clarence is also an alcoholic. He knows that his drinking is the reason for his condition . . . but does that make him unworthy of a warm meal and human interaction? I know now that I am in agreement with Beans and Bread on this one. The reason for his poverty, whether due to vice or misfortune, is not important. Food and the basic necessities for survival are rights, not something reserved for the privileged.*

The student's paper moved from this highly personal reflection back to a discussion of historic patterns, finally concluding that

> *What I have learned about the past helps me to understand the condition of our society today and has provided a framework of understanding the future. I know now that there are no molds into which one can neatly categorize "the poor" and that term doesn't describe a culture of people or a way of life, but rather a condition that should be temporary and is a result*

of many complex factors involving society as a whole more than any individual action or behavior.

I see many processes going on in this essay. The student was certainly developing a powerful, and not necessarily historical, concern for the human experiences of poor people. But I would argue that she was also thinking metaphorically, seeing links between the present and the past by asking how different individuals, institutions, and policies have categorized the poor. Notice that in her essay she not only considered, and rejected, the traditional distinction between the unworthy and worthy poor, but she also criticized the more contemporary discussion of a distinctive "culture of poverty" dictating human experiences.

Students who worked with a Tuesday evening women's group had yet another opportunity to see connections between historic policies and contemporary circumstances. One student, citing an 1827 report on urban poor relief, noted that "throughout history . . . women have been frowned upon for having bastard children and not worthy of receiving help." She went on to note that "as the [1996] welfare reform bill shows, women are still frowned upon for having bastard children and not worthy of receiving money." Several students with the women's group pointed out that the distinctive material and emotional challenges faced by the women in the group, many of whom were single mothers, were consistent with these historic challenges and were poorly addressed by the recent welfare reform legislation.

In these, and many other reflections, students drew either explicit or implicit connections between the worlds they observed and the debates about public policy they had studied. I see this as a metaphorical, rather than a literal, form of analysis because they were drawing connections between how people are viewed today — by legislators, charities, and voters — and how quite different historical actors, who had been categorized in comparable ways, were viewed by comparable policymakers at different historic moments. There is much to be learned by comparing how the Philadelphia Board of Guardians viewed unmarried mothers in 1827 with contemporary opinions about the members of the women's group. Of course it is important that the students recognize that they are learning about the policymakers and the policies, but not necessarily about the women themselves.

Places and Symbols

The sites where students do their service, and the places they visit, are themselves an important source for metaphorical analysis. Students in my service-learning courses both on Poverty and Welfare in American History and on American Urban History were encouraged to find links between their service sites and institutions from the past. For instance, we might have considered parallels between various meal programs and the "outdoor relief" of the early 19th century. Students from both the after-school program and the women's group likened the supportive communities that emerged from those programs described by Jane Addams (1965a, 1965b) in her essays about the settlement houses. Relatedly, some students contrasted the methods and goals of Charles Loring Brace's Children's Aid Society (1971), which advocated removing children from damaging urban environments, with those of after-school programs that follow Joseph Tuckerman's (1971) teachings by bringing volunteers into the children's world. These sorts of comparisons with past institutions are not to suggest broad similarities between essentially dissimilar bodies. Rather, selective appeal to the past enables the student who is thinking metaphorically to recognize those aspects of those bodies that do transcend historic change.

Urban institutions and the use of urban space could also be studied for their symbolic messages, beyond any particular material functions. In his essay on 19th-century institutions for the poor, Eric Monkkonen (1993) made the point that urban social welfare institutions — orphanages, hospitals, almshouses, and the like — were originally created with a sense of optimism and pride, reflected in their imposingly dramatic exteriors. Other scholars have pointed out the symbolic importance of the design and use of urban spaces, particularly insofar as those public spaces have become "contested terrains" between different racial, class, and gender groups.[4] In each of my service-learning classes we have also considered how novelists, photographers, and essayists have contributed to public perceptions of the urban environment and to the contemporary understanding of the role of that environment in shaping experience and behavior.[5]

These discussions of the symbolic importance of physical place recurred throughout both courses and offered various models of analysis for the metaphorically minded service-learning student. For instance, Beans and Bread is organized and run much like a small restaurant, whereas the couple who run Viva House — another Baltimore meal program — approach their meals as if they were welcoming guests into their home (which, in fact, they are). In both courses I had interesting discussions of the symbolic importance of these settings, and of the implied relationships between volunteers and guests, and how those relationships differ from other forms of "outdoor relief" that we had studied. On several occasions I have worked with students in public parks and playgrounds, which introduced opportunities to consider the use of public space at different historic moments. One group noticed that homeless men and women customarily slept in a Fell's Point park, only to temporarily abandon their places each morning when local residents arrived to walk their dogs. This divided use of public space is quite different from earlier urban patterns, but students could apply the urban historian's analytic tools to contemporary circumstances.

Placing the Student Within the Metaphor

Thus far I have suggested several distinct ways in which service-learning students can metaphorically connect the lessons of the past to experiences and observations in the present. Students may occasionally learn of personal histories that truly resonate with the experiences of people in poverty from past generations; they can often find evidence that the public policy debates of the present have clear roots in past discourse; and they can certainly recognize historic continuities in the symbolic roles of institutions and urban spaces. Whereas these approaches contain exciting possibilities, they also tend to remove the students from their own analysis. Some of the most profound historic insights (and personal gains) come when the students place themselves *within* this world of symbol and metaphor.

If a distinction between the worthy and unworthy poor is a crucial thread that runs through the history of welfare, the history of *reform* includes a recurring concern for bridging class distinctions. My students have read a wide array of primary sources in which benevolent-minded reformers tackle the problem of how they can best work to help end poverty or at least ease the individual lives of people who are poor. They have read the sermons of Joseph Tuckerman, the founder of Boston's first Ministry to the Poor; the speeches of Jane Addams, of Chicago's Hull House; and the more recent writings of Jonathan Kozol. These diverse voices share a conviction that there are huge benefits to be gained when people from different economic and social worlds come together to learn from one another (see syllabus).

In class reflections I urge my students to consider their experiences in the light of these insights. What are they learning, and how might that be akin to the experiences of Tuckerman, or a settlement house worker, or a Vista volunteer. One Care-A-Van student described

> the three goals of Tuckerman's mission [as] religious education, material help to the poor, and communication between the middle and upper classes and the poor. This communication, according to Tuckerman, would give those who were better off an inspiration to help the poor and encourage them to be advocates of the poor in their own circles.

Several pages later, he concluded that

> What we try to do [at Care-A-Van], besides providing traditional material aid in the form of food and warm clothing, is to get to know about the lives

and conditions of the people we help. . . . This helps everyone involved. . . . We get an unparalleled opportunity to learn things about life and people that we never would have heard elsewhere and renewed inspiration to come back into our own communities to let the people know what is out there.

The student who spoke so eloquently of meeting Clarence one evening drew the same connections between her learning experience and the sort of enlightenment advocated by Tuckerman and Addams. A student in an after-school program declared that the program was in keeping with Tuckerman's teachings, both because it "takes place in the center of a poverty-stricken community" and because "although the children and volunteers are of different races and come from unlike socioeconomic backgrounds, everyone views each other as equals."

As I developed the service-learning component in this course, I became more and more convinced that this is the best avenue for future exploration. Yes, students should always be alert to whatever they can learn about the lives of the people with whom they are working, and of course, there are important insights to be gained by considering the concrete implications of public policy. But the most profound historic lessons may be learned by looking within themselves. As their fears about unfamiliar people and places slowly dissolve, students should be alert to their own transformations. They should ask how their experience with multitudes of "otherness" is in keeping with Tuckerman's preachings, Addams's teachings, or Kozol's introspective reflections. What is the nature of distance — physical, economic, racial, cultural — in our society and in the worlds in which these reformers wrote? What are the students learning and what are they going to do with this knowledge? To what extent are they, like Addams and her colleagues, sometimes guilty of conceiving of problems and solutions from a limited class perspective? And finally, how can they place themselves at the center of their historic metaphor, using their experiences to better understand the shifting relationship between the middle classes and people who are poor?

Notes

1. This essay was written while I was still a member of the faculty at Loyola College and then edited to reflect the fact that I no longer work in Baltimore. I have, in fact, taught a very similar version of my service-learning course entitled Poverty and Welfare in American History as part of my new position at Gettysburg College.

2. I have changed all the names in this essay.

3. My students are introduced to these themes in lectures and in various readings, including Michael Katz's "The 'Urban Underclass' as a Metaphor of Social Transformation" (in *The "Underclass" Debate: Views From History*, Princeton University

Press, 1993); and Walter I. Tattner's *From Poor Law to Welfare State: A History of Social Welfare in America*, 5th ed. (Free Press, 1994).

4. This is a central theme in my course on American urban history. Many course readings touch on this issue but it is most prominent in Mary P. Ryan's *Women in Public, Between Banners and Ballots, 1825-1880* (Johns Hopkins University Press, 1990) and Larry R. Ford's *Cities and Buildings: Skyscrapers, Skid Rows, and Suburbs* (Johns Hopkins University Press, 1994).

5. The authors and artists discussed include Stephen Crane *(Maggie: A Girl of the Streets)*, Jacob Riis *(How the Other Half Lives)*, Walker Evans, Dorothea Lange, and Margaret Morton.

References

Addams, Jane. (1965a, orig. 1892). "The Objective Value of Social Settlements." In *The Social Thought of Jane Addams,* edited by Christopher Lasch, pp. 44-61. Indianapolis, IN: Bobbs-Merrill.

――――. (1965b, orig. 1893). "The Subjective Necessity for Social Settlements." In *The Social Thought of Jane Addams,* edited by Christopher Lasch, pp. 28-43. Indianapolis, IN: Bobbs-Merrill.

Carey, Mathew. (1971, orig. 1837). "A Plea for the Poor, Particularly Females. . . ." In *The Jacksonians on the Poor: Collected Pamphlets,* edited by David J. Rothman, pp. 1-20. Reprint, New York, NY: Arno Press.

Children's Aid Society. (1971, orig. 1854-1963). *Children's Aid Society Annual Reports, 1-10.* Reprint, New York, NY: Arno Press.

Katz, Michael. (1990). "History of an Impudent Poor Woman in New York City From 1918 to 1923." In *The Uses of Charity: The Poor on Relief in the Nineteenth-Century Metropolis,* edited by Peter Mandler, pp. 227-246. Philadelphia, PA: University of Pennsylvania Press.

Monkkonen, Eric H. (1993). "Nineteenth-Century Institutions: Dealing With the Urban 'Underclass.'" In *The "Underclass" Debate: Views From History,* edited by Michael Katz, pp. 334-365. Princeton, NJ: Princeton University Press.

Philadelphia Board of Guardians. (1971, orig. 1827). "Report of the Committee Appointed by the Board of Guardians . . . to Visit the Cities of Baltimore, New York, Providence, Boston, and Salem." In *The Almshouse Experience: Collected Reports,* edited by David J. Rothman, pp. 1-38. Reprint, New York, NY: Arno Press.

Tuckerman, Joseph. (1971, orig. 1826-1833). *On the Elevation of the Poor: A Selection From His Reports as Minister at Large in Boston.* Reprint, New York, NY: Arno Press.

HS368

POVERTY AND WELFARE IN AMERICAN HISTORY

Matt Gallman
Department of History
Loyola College

Fall 1996
x 2893
JMG@LOYOLA.EDU

Course Summary

This course will trace the history of poverty, and responses to poverty, in American history. The class will be structured around three interrelated clusters of questions. First, who were the poor? Second, what have Americans thought about poverty? Who, or what, has been blamed? And third, what have been the public and private policy responses to poverty? The discussion of these questions in an historic context will build to an examination of the contemporary challenge of poverty and welfare. How might the past inform our present discourse? A central component of this course will be a required service-learning experience. Teams of students will make several visits to service-learning sites and reflect on the relationship between historic patterns and contemporary circumstances.

Service-learning Experience

HS368 has a required service-learning component, which is integral to the course. In the first week of the semester you will be told about a series of available service-learning sites. Students will work - mostly in teams - at several sites, each of which will reflect a different aspect of the experience of poverty. You will spend roughly 15-20 hours at your site. At the end of the semester you will write a short essay reflecting on your experience and connecting what you have learned at your site with what you have read and learned during this course. If this makes you a bit nervous, do not worry. You will be well prepared before you visit your site and the Center for Values and Service will provide ample assistance. If you are already involved in community service, please see me.

Class Attendance and Participation

Attendance is mandatory. More than two unexcused absences will adversely affect your grade. Portions of most classes will be arranged around some form of discussion, either in small groups or as a class. You should come to class prepared to answer and raise questions concerning the assigned readings or in response to xeroxed handouts. Please try to arrive on time for the beginning of class.

Readings and Quizzes

This course has several different sorts of assigned readings. Trattner's From Poor Law to Welfare State is a good brief survey of the topic (be sure that you have the 5th edition). The "Underclass" Debate, edited by Michael Katz, is a collection of historical essays addressing various aspects of poverty and poor relief. Confronting Southern Poverty in the Great Depression is a collection of primary documents. Rachel and Her Children, by Jonathan Kozol, uses material from interviews to describe the experience of homelessness. And Poverty: Opposing Viewpoints includes recent articles and editorials on various aspects of the debate over poverty. In addition to these books, which should all be available in the bookstore, you will be reading quite a few articles and primary sources which will be distributed in class.

Some of these xeroxed titles are listed below, others will be announced and distributed as the semester progresses.

The success of this course depends on your consistent and careful preparation for class discussions. You should always come to class with notes on the assigned readings. To encourage strong participation, you will have occasional open note quizzes on the readings.

Written Assignments and Presentations

You will write five very short essays and one slightly longer essay:

- The short essays will be brief (roughly 2 pages) responses to the assigned readings. The dates are listed below. Specific assignments will be explained as the date approaches.

- The longer essay (3-5 pages) will combine a reflection on your service-learning experience with a broader historical discussion of the issues raised in your particular site. This assignment will be discussed more fully in class. Although you will be working with teams, each student must write her/his own essay.

All papers must be typed and proofread. Since the short essays are intended to provide a basis for class discussion, it is crucial that they be written before class. Therefore, there will be a particularly heavy penalty for late papers.

In the second half of the semester each team will make a class **presentation** about the particular issues raised in your service-learning and your independent reading. These presentations should be the logical extension of your second essays.

Examinations

There will be a midterm and an hour long final. Both will combine short essays and identifications. The final will cover the entire course but will stress material covered since the midterm. There will also be a final take-home essay.

Grading

Midterm Examination			-	20%
Final Examination			-	30%
In class	-	20%		
Take home essay	-	10%		
Short Essays (5 @ 5% each)			-	25%
Community Service Essay			-	15%
Class Preparation and Participation			-	10%
Reading quizzes				
Participation				

{Extremely strong participation may raise your grade; excessive absences will lower your grade.}

Academic Integrity

I assume that anything you do in this class is your own work unless I am told otherwise. You also may not rely on someone else's notes in taking the reading quizzes. Please review the section on Academic Integrity in the Student Handbook. You should include the signed Honor Pledge on every written assignment. In your papers all direct quotes should be identified with quotation marks and cited properly. The History Department has decided that any instance of intentional dishonesty on any assignment - no matter how small - will result in an automatic F for the entire course.

======
CLASS TOPICS

I. INTRODUCTION: UNDERSTANDING POVERTY

Tuesday, September 3rd   Introduction

Thursday, September 5th   Service-learning Intro
READING:
- Michael Katz, "The Urban 'Underclass' as a Metaphor of Social Transformation," in Katz, The "Underclass" Debate: Views from History (1993), 3-23.
- Eric H. Monkkonen, "Nineteenth-Century Institutions: Dealing with the Urban 'Underclass,'" in Katz, The "Underclass" Debate: Views from History (1993), 334-365.

Tuesday, September 10th   Varieties of Poverty
READING:
- Michael Katz, "History of an Impudent Poor Woman in New York City from 1918 to 1923" in Mandler. ed., The Uses of Charity, 227-246. {To be distributed.}

Thursday, September 12th Anglo-American Traditions
READING:
- Walter I. Trattner, From Poor Law to Welfare State (4th Edition), pp. 1-46.

II. 1800-1880s

Tuesday, September 17th   Indoor vs Outdoor Relief
READINGS:
- Philadelphia Board of Guardians, "Report of the Committee Appointed by the Board of Guardians ... to Visit the Cities of Baltimore, New York, Providence, Boston, and Salem" (1827).
- Mathew Carey, "A Plea for the Poor, Particularly Females..." (1837).
- Trattner, From Poor Law to Welfare State, pp. 49-75.
Essay #1 due in class.

Thursday, September 19th   Antebellum Innovations
    READINGS:
- Excerpt from Joseph Tuckerman, On the Elevation of the Poor: A Selection from His Reports as Minister at Large in Boston (1826-1833). {Note: If you run short on time, save the section on Children (pp. 111-39) for next week.}

Tuesday, September 24th   Scientific Charity
    READINGS:
- Excerpt from Josephine Shaw Lowell, Public Relief and Private Charity (1884).
- Trattner, From Poor Law to Welfare State, pp. 79-105.

Thursday, September 26th   Child Welfare
    READINGS:
- Excerpt from Children's Aid Society, Children's Aid Society Annual Reports, 1-10 (1854-1863).
- Tuckerman, On the Elevation..., pp. 111-39 (on children).
- Trattner, From Poor Law to Welfare State, pp. 110-135.

    Essay #2 due in class.

III. 1880s-1920s

Tuesday, October 1st   Historic Origins of the Modern "Urban Underclass"
    READINGS:
- Jacqueline Jones, "Southern Diaspora: Origins of the Northern 'Underclass'" in Katz, "Underclass" Debate, 27-54.
- Joe William Trotter, Jr., "Blacks in the Urban North: The 'Underclass Question; in Historical Perspective" in Katz, The "Underclass" Debate, 55-81.

Thursday, October 3rd   Muckraking & Progressive Reform
    READING:
- Trattner, From Poor Law to Welfare State, pp. 163-188, 215-270. (Read chapters 8 and 10, skim 11 and 12. Chapter 9 is interesting but too much to cover - read if you'd like.)

Tuesday, October 8th   Hull House: Urban Immersion
    READINGS:
- Jane Addams, "The Subjective Necessity for Social Settlements" (1892) and "The Objective Value of Social Settlements" (1892)
- Jacob Riis, "Pauperism in the Tenements" {All to be distributed before class}

    Essay #3 due in class

Thursday, October 10th   Service-learning Reflection

Tuesday, October 15th   MIDTERM EXAMINATION

IV. 1920s- 1960s

Thursday, October 17th   The Great Depression - 1
READING:
- Trattner, From Poor Law to Welfare State, pp. 274-300.

Tuesday, October 22nd   The Great Depression - 2
READING:
- Carlton and Coclanis, editors, Confronting Southern Poverty in the Great Depression. Specific assignment to be discussed in class.
Essay #4 due in class

Thursday, October 24th   The New Deal and Beyond

V. 1960-1990s

Tuesday, October 29th Building the Great Society
READING:
- Trattner, From Poor Law to Welfare State, pp. 305-332.
- Michael Harrington, The Other America, pp. 9-24, 155-170 (handed out in class).

Thursday, October 31st   Expanding the Great Society
READING:
- Trattner, From Poor Law to Welfare State, pp. 338-359.

Tuesday, November 5th   Collective Strategies
READINGS:
- Robin D. G. Kelley, "The Black Poor and the Politics of Opposition in a New South City, 1920-1970," in Katz, The 'Underclass' Debate, pp. 293-333.
- Thomas F. Jackson, "The State, the Movement, and the Urban Poor: The War on Poverty and Political Mobilization in the 1960s," in Katz, The 'Underclass' Debate, pp. 403-439.
Essay #5 due in class.

Thursday, November 7th   A War on Welfare?
READING:
- Trattner, From Poor Law to Welfare State, pp. 362-95.
- Short excerpts from Harrington, The New American Poverty and Charles Murray, Losing Ground.

VI. CONTEMPORARY CONCERNS IN AN HISTORIC CONTEXT

Tuesday, November 12th   Recent Debates
READING:
- Chapter 1, pp. 16-36 (#1-4); chapter 2, pp. 100-118 (#4-6); chapter 4, pp. 189, 203-220 (#3-5) [read introductions to the other essays in this chapter]

** This assignment consists of 10 short editorials/excerpts on different aspects of the recent poverty debate. Come to class with brief notes on each essay so that you can speak intelligently about what each author says (without having to flip through the book).

Thursday, November 14th   Rachel and Her Children
READING:
- Jonathan Kozol, Rachel and Her Children: Homeless Families in America (1988).

Tuesday, November 19th   Housing and Homelessness
READING:
- Poverty, chapter 1, pp. 54-71 [#7-8]; chapter 5, pp. 254-272 [#5-8]

Thursday, November 21st   Hunger and Meal Programs
READING:
- Poverty, ch 1, pp. 37-53 [#5-6]

Tuesday, November 26th   THANKSGIVING

Thursday, November 28th   THANKSGIVING

Tuesday, December 3rd   Children and Education
READING:
- Harvey Kantor and Barbara Brenzel, "Urban Education and the 'Truly Disadvantage'" The Historical Roots of the Contemporary Crisis, 1945-1990," in Katz, The 'Underclass' Debate, 366-402.

Thursday, December 5th   Race, Gender and Poverty
READING:
- Poverty, chapter 3, pp. 121-157.

Tuesday, December 10th   The Lessons of History?
READING:
- Michael Katz, "Reframing the 'Underclass' Debate" in Katz, The 'Underclass' Debate, pp. 440-477.
- Poverty, chapter 5, pp. 227-240.
Final Essay due in class.

Thursday, December 12th   HS368 FINAL EXAMINATION

Final Essay Assignment

Overview

Our discussions this semester have had three main components. Needless to say, our first concern has been with the history of poverty and poor relief. More recently we have been considering contemporary concerns and policy debates. And throughout the semester you have been engaged in a wide array of community service projects. For your final essay you will have the opportunity to reflect on these three components.

Assignment

Write a short (3-5 page) essay reflecting on your service experience in the light of the course's other components. What sorts of links can you draw between your experiences (and the site where you've worked) and the history of poverty and poor relief? How might your experiences (and your site) contribute to contemporary policy debates?

Specific Points

- You may select any form you choose, including a formal essay, a highly personal reflection, or any other form you'd like (a letter to Bill Clinton, an imagined dialogue with Joseph Tuckerman, a sonnet...).
- You may elect to write about other service experiences that you have had in addition to those for this course. You might even wish to incorporate the insights from your classmates' service experiences.
- You may choose to focus on a particular aspect of poverty (housing, children etc.) which connects most fully to your service experiences, or you may choose to organize your thoughts in a very different way. (For instance, a Beans and Bread volunteer might choose to focus on the role of institutions, the perceived importance of contacts between different classes, the particular problems of the mentally ill, or some clever combination of all these issues.)
- Be sure that your references to both the past and to contemporary discussions include explicit references to specific events, issues or authors. These references should be documented with footnotes or endnotes. I don't expect this essay to be absolutely comprehensive, but I do expect it to be grounded in the material that we have studied. Your challenge is to find a balance between personal reflections and factual materials.
- All essays are due in class on Tuesday December 10th.

** On your cover page please list your service experiences for the semester. This list should include: where you have been working, the number of times that you went, and a rough estimate of the total hours.

The Turnerian Frontier: A New Approach to the Study of the American Character

by Michael Zuckerman

It was Christmas vacation, not a time to talk about school. My caller knew it and introduced himself apologetically. He was, he said, Ralph Rosen, a colleague in the University of Pennsylvania's Classics Department. He had hesitated to call. He just didn't know anyone else to turn to. He'd agreed to teach a course in the spring, a freshman seminar in which his students would work at the John P. Turner Middle School in West Philadelphia. He'd heard that I had just finished a similar experiment that fall.

At first I thought that all he wanted was a few pointers, or perhaps commiseration for having yielded to the blandishments of another colleague, Lee Benson. Soon enough, however, I was intrigued with his course — a tantalizing comparison of ancient Athens and contemporary West Philadelphia — and caught up in exultant recollections of my own. It took me a while to catch his trepidation. I'm slow that way.

Ralph hadn't called to talk about tactics, or to seek my sympathy. He was willing enough to tell me about his course and to indulge my exhilaration at my own. But all he actually wanted, I began to realize, was to be reassured that he was not making a catastrophic mistake in sending his students into the community. As his unease got through to me, memories of anxieties of my own came flooding back. I had spent a fair part of my summer as Ralph now seemed to be spending his Christmas, worrying.

The course I'd just finished was one of my favorites. I'd begun offering it four years before, and it had clicked from the first. It pleased me immensely, and it seemed to matter to my students. I am a little at a loss to say why I agreed to jeopardize it — to toss away its culminating segment and substitute another that would oblige my students to spend a part of a day a week teaching at the Turner school — but I do know that I was appalled at the peril in which I'd placed myself, my students, and my course.

I spent a fair part of the summer thinking about my students and their treks to 59th and Baltimore. What if one of them were mugged, or raped? How would I live with my responsibility for it? What was my responsibility? What, indeed, was my liability? I spent time talking with a friend who runs the community service programs at a local private secondary school, reading the legal materials he sent me, and pestering people at Penn about the insurance coverage the legal materials said I had to have.

I thought about my students in other ways as well. I had 25 of them preregistered. I'd altered the rules of the game after preregistration; they could not have known what they were letting themselves in for. What if, when they learned of the changes at the first meeting of the class, they couldn't fit the teaching time into their schedules, or resented such coerced community service, or were simply scared? What if they all dropped the course?

The truth is that, even now, I have no compelling idea why I agreed to ask my students to help out at Turner and conduct a kind of research there. I did not and do not harbor any illusions about saving society thereby. I just did not and do not see any good reason not to try. I did not and do not have any confidence that obliging privileged and talented people to confront the problems of poor children in the cities will work. I just do not have any better alternatives. As Walter Annenberg put it when he pledged half a billion dollars to the public schools, "If anyone can think of a better way, we may have to try that, but the way I see this tragedy, education is the most wholesome and effective approach" (Mezzacappa and Sterling 1993: A1). I don't have half a billion dollars at my disposal. I do have a number of lively and adventuresome minds. It seemed a crime not to try.

Indeed, I am not sure that it is my turn to Turner that begs explanation. In many ways, the decision to connect my course with the West Philadelphia Improvement Corps (WEPIC) and to oblige my students to connect themselves with West Philadelphia seems the obvious one, self-evident and inescapable. I had never done it before because I had never had the wit to do it on my own and because no one had ever had the wit to ask me. Maybe that makes Lee Benson decisive after all. In his inimitable way, he asked.

I do not say this lightly. I suspect that there are a lot of us teaching in urban colleges and universities who grant our connectedness to our communities and grasp the urgency of our intertwined fate. We do not have to be convinced that our cities are going down. We read the papers, see the news, walk the streets. We know, or sense, the need. We know, or feel, that it is irresponsible, even unconscionable, to remain aloof. We cringe at the self-congratulatory insularity of the academy. But we do not know, or see, how to move beyond it.

History 443 is a course on American national character, a course with no transparent application to West Philadelphia or to the world of middle-school children in a rugged African-American neighborhood. But the longer I listened to Lee's invitation and importunity, the less that seemed to matter. I would have ample opportunity to figure out an application, however strained. I could not let slip the chance to take my students out of our cozy cloister.

Soon enough it dawned on me that I could reconfigure my course and accommodate a component on West Philadelphia easily, perhaps even excitingly. In the course as I'd organized it in the past, there were three segments: a first, theoretical part that afforded the students an array of competing conceptions of the American character; a second, substantive part that entailed an extended examination of voices often asserted to be quintessentially American (the puritans, Thomas Jefferson, Benjamin Franklin, Walt Whitman); and a third, hodgepodge part that mixed a disparate assortment of provocative readings on contemporary America. The second part provided a test of the theories in the first. The third part provided a test of the generalizations that survived the first two.

The third part was the key that would, I now decided, allow me my entry into West Philadelphia. I had never set the readings of that final segment before the students as a simple "test" of the constructions that still seemed tenable after we had worked our way through the first two units. Instead, I had always suggested that those texts be read in contexts of continuity and change. What of the American character and its trajectory through, say, 1960 still seemed evident in the 1980s and 1990s? What was gone, or going? What had come, or was coming, in its stead?

In the new format I now contemplated, I could still assign striking new works on contemporary America, but I could make them explicitly pertinent to West Philadelphia. I could still ask the students to compare contemporary America with that of the three and a half centuries preceding, and I could still require them to confront problems of persistence and transformation. But I could enrich those issues by keeping them steadily at the center of our enterprise and by explicitly introducing others of race, class, and ecological niche.

West Philadelphia in the age of Ronald Reagan and crack cocaine inevitably presented questions that the books I'd assigned in earlier incarnations of the course did not. In the past I'd asked students to think about how far our prior predications of character still prevailed in the present. Now I would also be asking them tacitly to consider how far such predications had ever prevailed outside certain privileged precincts of the land.

The readings that I finally chose — Jonathan Kozol's *Savage Inequalities,* Elijah Anderson's *Streetwise,* and John Edgar Wideman's *Philadelphia Fire* — proved to be complex as well as sharply critical works. (I had not read Kozol or Anderson when I chose them, and I'd only read Wideman when I'd chosen him, equally blindly, the last time I taught the course.) But I was not trying to radicalize the class or raise student consciousness in a militant manner. As I made clear at the outset, again when we launched into the West Philadelphia segment, and yet again when I sketched the final paper assignment, the discontinuities between the outlook of, say, Thomas Jefferson and the perspective of a West Philly gang member would be all too palpable. The more interesting task would be to tease out consistencies and convergences. Characterizations that could cover the essentially rural, white, relatively affluent world of Tocqueville's time and the essentially urban, black, relatively impoverished world of our inner cities would be very powerful characterizations indeed. I would be mightily impressed by such characterizations if students could develop and defend them.

But the insistent inner-city focus of the readings was not the crux of the reconfiguration of the course. Whatever the shift in subject matter, readings were still readings. The crux of the culminating segment was the confrontation of abstractions with experience. How did the glittering generalities of the books and of our classroom conversations hold up on the mean streets and in the crowded classrooms? How did "expressive individualism" or any of our other elegant concepts stand up at Turner where five-sixths of the students qualify as low-income recipients of meal subsidies and where only one-sixth of sixth graders score at the national average in reading comprehension and math computation?[1]

I wanted my students to get past the aura of artifice that hangs over even the most vivid passages of the most vivid books. I wanted them to have to integrate other people's observations and interpretations with their own. I wanted them to have something more immediate and undeniable than they'd ever had from books. Or something that would energize the immediacies they'd had from books. Or something that would reveal the power of books after all, something that would by its very thinness heighten the density and richness of the texts they read. I didn't really care whether they ended up affected more by their reading or by their immersion in the community. I simply wanted to complicate their intellectual consideration of the American character and intensify their experience in my course.

When I met the class the first day, I explained all this. There were about 40 students present, the 25 preregistered and the rest checking it out. The usual mix of buyers and window-shoppers.

Despite my best efforts at a brave front, I found myself plagued with nightmare anticipations. I'd already begun wondering how I would explain to my department chair the mass exodus I dreaded. But as the questions came from the class about my unconventional arrangements, I sensed — or thought I sensed — a positive response along with the inevitable resistance. There were a fair number of heads nodding eagerly as well as some tough questions about arrogant do-gooding and sharp aspersions on the presumptions of privilege. There was excitement among the students milling around me after I had dismissed the class as well as the usual uncommunicative, almost-sullen isolation as students drifted or bustled out of the room. It was hard to tell whether the ones who didn't hang around had to hurry to get to their next classes or whether they couldn't wait to get the hell out.

At the following class meeting, the group was visibly smaller. But as I called the roll, I realized that the attrition was a good deal greater even than appeared on a swift visual sweep of the room. All told, at least a third of those present the first day were gone; six or eight new students had turned up. Some of the goings and comings were reflective of the shuffling that always occurs.

The numbers were not much different than I encounter in courses that have no community component at all. But some of the shifting was quite clearly connected to specific logistical difficulties and vague social dreads. Students were sorting themselves out. Those who couldn't rearrange their schedules or their anxieties were leaving. Others, drawn by word of mouth, were arriving. When the dance was done, there were about 30 students in the class, and despite their residual uneasiness, they were a good deal readier for Turner than Turner was for them.

When I myself went to public school in Philadelphia in the 1940s and 1950s, there was no wasted motion. We settled into the regimen and routines that would prevail for the rest of the year within the first day or two. When my children went to school in the 1970s, 1980s, and 1990s, in the same privileged public schools of the city's nicer neighborhoods, there was still not much slack. Even now, in my daughter Elizabeth's first grade at Greenfield as much as in her sister Maria's 12th grade at Central, rosters and classes and teachers are set at the start of the term and remain essentially set for the rest of the school year.

But this regularity that I have always taken for granted is, as I learned that fall, one of the prerogatives of affluence. The mechanics of getting under way — e.g., the settlement of student and teacher assignments, the confirmation of classes, the arrangement of rooms — that take six or eight hours in the first day or two in my children's schools take six or eight weeks through the first month or two at Turner and in much of the city's system. It was, therefore, pointless to try to establish my students in a school assignment during the first half of the fall term.

Deferring the actual commencement of student duties to the end of October made the first visit from the WEPIC troupe — on the second day of class, shortly after Labor Day — almost as abstract an enterprise as any of the recondite conceptualizations of national character we were soon discussing. It also made the second visit, six weeks later, when program coordinator Cory Bowman came without the rest of the retinue, a fairly frenetic one.

Cory did not philosophize eloquently, as Ira Harkavy, director of Penn's Center for Community Partnerships, had done at the first WEPIC presentation. He did not sketch the situation at the school, as had Marie Bogle, a teacher at Turner, nor recount the challenges and gratifications of community service, as had Kim Van Naarden, a summer volunteer with WEPIC. His task was neither to inspire nor to reassure. He was in my class to explain actual options in actual time slots and to make actual assignments of actual students to actual teachers and courses.

But Cory is, in his way, as much a genius as Ira Harkavy. In our bare hour and 20 minutes, he outlined half a dozen programs to which my students could attach themselves, answered half a million questions, and recalled half a dozen additional programs and possibilities as he did so. It would have been a virtuoso performance if he'd merely gotten every last one of my 30 students into one or another of those dozen programs. It was a performance beyond virtuosity because my students showed almost no interest in the programs he first set before them.

Cory and I had spoken at length about potential placements. We had concurred that we would put our primary emphasis on a program in which Turner seventh and eighth graders studied community health issues and then in turn taught what they'd studied to students in the elementary schools in the area. The program was intricately and ingeniously conceived, and it promised to provide my students both an authentic prospect of doing good and an exceptional opportunity to do well in my course. The middle schoolers would be both tutors and tutees, and the reversals and reciprocities would afford my students a vantage point for their final papers far more expansive than any they could attain by, say, helping out in a generic classroom.

With my encouragement, Cory pitched the health tutoring program hard. To my astonishment, and for reasons I still do not really fathom, not a single one of my students opted for it. Cory never missed a beat, never registered the slightest surprise, never betrayed the mildest dismay. On the fly, he improvised an array of alternatives that reflected the keenness of both his knowledge of Turner's needs and his sensitivity to my students' aptitudes.

• One of my students was a Mexican American who was fluent in Spanish. Cory concocted a tutorial for him to do with a few middle schoolers recently arrived from Latin America.

• Three of my students were editors of the university newspaper. Cory arranged for them to become mentors to a small cohort of talented young writers, with whom they created a workshop in journalism.

• One of my students was the captain of the women's soccer team. Cory set her and another woman in the class with no special soccer expertise at all to teaching soccer at a nearby elementary school.

Other students worked with small groups of Turner youngsters on reading and creative writing. Still others taught alternative "ABC's" — aerobics, basketball, cooking — in the community school on Saturdays. One student taught math to adults preparing for their G.E.D. Another taught the history of West Philadelphia, and another the history of Africa. A couple simply continued the tutoring in neighborhood schools that they had been doing, on their own initiative, since their arrival at Penn two or three years earlier.

In retrospect, it is embarrassingly obvious to me that I didn't honor or even respect sufficiently the intensity of my students' engagement with their students. I didn't honor Ira Harkavy's vision — a vision he espoused when he came among my students, a vision I myself urged upon the class — one of community work as its own extraordinary kind of research. For when I brought in the traveling WEPICs on the second day of class, I inevitably cast them, contradictorily, as exhorters and comforters rather than as participants in the intellectual endeavor of the course. When I brought Cory back six weeks later, I invited him as an administrator rather than as a bearer of analytic or interpretive insight.

Furthermore, I simply never integrated my students' West Philadelphia experiences into our ongoing class conversations. I wish I could offer a thoughtful rationalization for that failure. I wish I could say honestly that I deliberately reserved such integration for the final papers that I asked of the class and that I didn't want to intrude on their primal reactions before they wrote those papers. But the truth is that I never thought of any of this. I proceeded passively, not purposefully. Even as I transformed the trajectory of the course, I remained wedded to the way I had always taught it from day to day. There were too many books I wanted to cover and too few weeks in which to cover them.

Fortunately, my students were not as attached to the luminous architectonic of the readings as I was. They were dealing with the problematic that I had put before them, even if I wasn't. They were essaying tentative connections between our readings and their experience in the community. They were seeking, all along, the integration that I had inadvertently declined to discuss.

I discovered my misfeasance by accident. Approaching the end of the course, I decided, veritably as an afterthought, to turn the last day of class over to the students to talk about their experiences in the community.

From the first time I taught History 443, I had taken the last day of class for my concluding summation of the sweep of the readings, though I had fallen into that format by accident too. An unanticipated cancellation and some subsequent juggling had left me, that first time, with a last day free after the completion of the assigned sequence of readings. That last day happened to fall on Earth Day. I thought I saw some intriguing connections between environmental issues and the burden of our readings and discussions over the preceding months, so I took Earth Day as a pretext to try to pull together in an oblique way the themes of the course.

In succeeding years the last day of the course had never fallen on Earth Day, so I had never tried to revisit that first extemporization of a synthesis. But every time I had taught the course since then, I had enshrined that original accident and reserved the last day for an alternative version of that initial conclusion. I had come to conceive such a slantwise synthesis as both a pedagogic imperative and an ethical obligation. I had come to agonize over its annual concoction.

I had almost settled on a gambit for my new finale when it finally occurred to me that it or any other such ploy would leave the course's WEPIC work utterly unacknowledged within the classroom. The students would, to be sure, wrestle with its import in their final papers, but that struggle would be an even lonelier and more isolating one than the teaching they had done. Suddenly it occurred to me that if I were to demand of them that they make connections between ideas and experiences in their essays, my demand would only be credible and resonant if we recognized such connections and modeled them in our classroom activity.

So I proposed to the class, at our penultimate meeting, that we spend our final session sharing experiences and discussing the meanings we made of them. The students were acquiescing, without either demurral or evident enthusiasm, when at one point I let slip an apology for the failure of closure that would attend this alteration of my original design. Suddenly, one of the graduate students declared that she preferred my first plan and asked me to revert to it. A second student, an undergraduate, insisted that he too would sooner hear the synthesis I had put together. And all at once the class came alive. To my delight as much as to my embarrassment, the rest of the students, one after another after another, graduates and undergraduates alike, resisted those calls and affirmed their eagerness to hear of their classmates' encounters at Turner.

The final session started slowly. As I look back on it, I think the reason was that none of the students wanted to seem unduly proud of his or her achievements. But as the stories slowly tumbled out, the pride became unmistakable. Almost everyone who spoke — and almost everyone spoke, sooner or later, more or less volubly — had accomplished something. A breakthrough with a student, an insight, a bond of trust. In some cases, authentic wonders.

The two young women who had set themselves to teaching soccer to a motley group of elementary schoolers on a muddy lot littered with broken glass had managed in a matter of weeks to create a program for 32 children, fusing them into a team and making them the marvel of the neighborhood. Indeed, their only failure was their very success: There was not, alas, another elementary school soccer team in the city for the kids to play.

The three young men who had taught journalism had managed in the same brief span to instill a sufficient competence in the technics of interviewing and investigation that their charges could conceive and carry off an issue of a Turner school newspaper. The youngsters developed a theme, did the digging, wrote up their findings, mocked up an entire paper, and ran it off on the *Daily Pennsylvanian* computers.

But as these three students — Josh, Kenny, and Chris — variously told the tale of their tyros' triumph, they all came back to the one youngster who had not shared in it. He was a brilliant writer. Indeed, he was, by common consent, a brilliant young man. He had thrown himself passionately into the workshop, and he had flourished there. He was seeing the point and the possibility of school, perhaps for the first time in his life. He was also doing badly — D's and F's — in all his regular classes for all the regular reasons. Then one day he was absent from the workshop. Inquiry revealed that he had been removed for disciplinary reasons. Someone in the school thought that he would work harder in his conventional classes if threatened with losing the one class that challenged him, a class that he cared about.

Two weeks later, my editors were still enraged. And as their rage swept the room, it set off a subtle sea change in the stories that other students told. The next wave of anecdotes centered on realizations that middle schoolers branded as backward in their reading ability could read relatively well if they were allowed to read sports or rap music magazines instead of the desiccated texts that their regular teachers insisted on. Several students spoke of their astonishment at the regular recurrence of violence, death, and tragedy in the lives of these children.

It may be worth warning readers, before I get much further into my recollection of that class, that they may recoil from — or even resent — a certain naiveté or harshness in some of my students' reactions. Those reactions assuredly represent the responses of extravagantly privileged youth to the shock of their brief immersion in the everyday life of a ghetto school. I can only plead on my students' behalf that the sometime simplicity and stridency of their responses suggest just how profoundly those students were touched by the glimpses they got of an America all too remote from the one most of them inhabit. In any case, when one member of the group asked the others what more they thought WEPIC might have done to help them in their unfamiliar assignments, there was no shortage of answers. For a brief period, the conversation turned from the pride with which it had commenced to a certain self-pity. Then it turned once more, this time to a new level of analysis.

One woman wanted to go back to the earlier discussion of violence. She had been appalled by the pervasiveness of harm and hostility in the drawings that she had asked her sixth graders to do. Another woman echoed her observations. She had been disheartened by the relentless emphasis on hurting and dying in the stories students wrote in her creative writing class. Soon the whole class was wondering why there had been so little discussion of violence in a course on the American character. Soon there was also intense debate on the place of aggression in American life and on the attitude that my students should have taken toward the aggression that seemed to them so rampant at Turner. Should they have ignored it, as they generally did, or should they have confronted it? Or was it perhaps an opening, an opportunity, to be worked with as Debbie and Audrey had worked with it to forge their soccer team?

Talk about the soccer team led to talk about teams, and then about peer groups, and then about the wondrous way in which the players policed themselves in Stefan's basketball class on Saturdays. A couple of students caught the connections between the peer groups prevalent at Turner and the peer-group structures that Anderson analyzed in *Streetwise* (1990). Virtually everyone noticed a nexus between such experiences in West Philadelphia and Tocqueville's (1945) observation of American affinities for organization and for submergence of individual selves in groups.

And as they did, their conversation exploded in luxuriant incoherence. They had created a matrix deeper and denser than they could control, or than I could have controlled if I had been directing the discussion. Some wanted to explore the dramatic contradiction between these manifest persistences of mutuality and the failure of collective concern that conditioned Bellah et al.'s (1985) findings of an ascendant individualism in contemporary America. Others feared that the prevalence of these peer loyalties would impede the development of a premium on personal achievement that even a ghetto youngster would ultimately find essential if he or she were to make his or her way in this country and this economy. Still others insisted that there was nothing wrong with such attachments, that cooperation was as natural as competitive self-assertion and probably healthier too. The team structures of the neighborhood could, like aggression and violence, be put to use as readily as they could be resisted.

The conversation never did coalesce again. Its subject skittered with every successive speaker, as multivalent as it was multivocal. But successive speakers seemed to become successively more perceptive — about what they'd encountered at Turner, about our class readings, and about the American character. If they never came to any consensus, they did warm to a richer, more intricate summation than I would ever have managed on my own. Indeed, the only point on which they reached any real agreement was that they hadn't had enough time at Turner. They resented the weeks they'd lost in the disorganization at the beginning of the school year, the brevity of their impact, and the discontinuity that it occasioned in the lives of their students. They were unanimous in urging me to teach the course in the spring the next time I taught it.

At the end of class, I went over to the department office and rearranged my teaching schedule for next year.

Our discussion had been deeply earnest. I had encouraged the class to speak spontaneously, even to shoot some from the hip. Instead, my students had spoken more deliberately — and more thoughtfully — than they had all semester. They had wanted to get things right. They were describing their own experience, and they were determined to be true to it.

On just that account, perhaps, they had spoken without any animating passion. But the passion that had been restrained in the presence of their peers poured forth in the privacy of their final papers.

In defining the final paper, I had asked the students to make contemporary West Philadelphia the center of their endeavor, but I had also obliged them to set their interpretation of the neighborhood in the context of our readings through the first two-thirds of the course. Since the part of the paper analyzing West Philadelphia was to be based equally on the reading and on their teaching experiences, and since the part placing that analysis in a larger context was to be drawn solely from the texts and our treatment of them in class conversation, the unmistakable implication of the assignment was to establish a gentle skew toward the readings.

But only a handful of my students chose to catch that implication or to honor it. A distinct majority disdained my directions and ignored their own obvious interest in following them. Though they had spent barely a half-dozen or dozen hours at Turner and five or 10 times as much time on the readings, most of my students wrote more about their work in West Philadelphia. In defiance of entrenched habits of docility and at some genuine peril to their grades, they wrote about what they really wanted to write about. And what they really wanted to write about was the immediate community that had enveloped them, more than the abstract ideologies that had elevated them.

Some part of this extraordinary impact of their experience in the community was doubtless due to the success that so many of them enjoyed. Like Tim, a number of them reveled in the realization that their help was "needed and appreciated." Like Brighid, they'd begun tutoring to improve their resume and discovered in the process that their motives had drastically changed. Stephanie had improvised a mini-course on the history of West Philadelphia. It had evolved so splendidly that the teacher whom she worked with asked her to return to continue it in the spring, and Stephanie had decided that she would do it, not least for "the ego rush" she got from the way her pupils welcomed her each week. She explicated that ego rush:

> I love it when the kids shriek my name when I walk in on Saturday morning. I love that the girls fight over who will hold my hand when we go outside. I love it when the children, my children, remember the structure of a limerick I taught them two weeks before. I love it when they remember to do their homework. I love it that they are all taking cooking class next year because I'll be the new instructor.

But some who had succeeded were disheartened as much as drawn on. Debbie exulted that her 32 fifth graders showed up to practice "twice a week . . . without fail" and that those "Warriors" — "a soccer team with no uniforms, no goal posts, and no other teams to play" — had achieved "a sense of unity and connectedness." Audrey, her co-coach, agreed that "the program was going well," yet still felt "shadowed by an overwhelming sadness." The used crack vials in the parking lot, the mothers who asked her whether she could spare any money, the littered lot that "shouldn't even be considered a playing field" — all reminded her relentlessly of "the hard realities faced by these children." "It would be nice," she wrote, if the school "could maybe clean up some of the dog shit all over. The kids are covered in it by the end of practice."

Jo-Anne discovered a bitter poignancy in touching her tutees' lives. She "began to understand Wideman's description of teaching in West Philadelphia. I'd go home with a sad feeling, a guilty feeling, knowing I should have done so much more. And that's what kept me coming back. It's also what finally drove me away." Jo-Anne never could quite come to terms with letters like the one she got from Chris: "Today . . . is our last Friday with Jo-Anne. I am really going to miss her very much. I spent many Fridays with her. Every time I meet someone they seem to go away, and I get depressed. I never thought she would go away so quick. . . . I guess this is good-bye."

But even such equivocal conquests as Jo-Anne's must have been comforts of sorts to students who often undertook their forays into the neighborhood beyond their ivied bastions with trepidation. As Brighid said, the African Americans with whom Penn students interacted were "either fellow students" or the people she had "been told to avoid during orientation week." Indeed, Jill confessed that finding herself one of the few "white faces [in] the whole school" was unnerving; to speak of her state of mind as "shock would be a complete understatement." Kenny feared that, "no matter what [he] did with these children, we would never be able to relate to each other." Jay "couldn't help but be slightly afraid" as he entered Turner for the first time, not because he was "scared of the kids" — who were, after all, mere middle schoolers — but because he was "afraid of being part of the 'them' for once." Debbie never did overcome her "dread" of driving alone to 60th and Cedar every Monday. Tony summed up a widespread sentiment when he pronounced West Philadelphia "a different country."

Despite the doubts and fears with which many of the students began — and in which some of them persisted — almost all of them expected to succeed. They are bright young men and women, and they are accustomed to meeting challenges. That is why they are at Penn. Their successes, therefore, delighted but did not seriously surprise them. Their failures astonished and absorbed them. The many who ultimately had rewarding experiences dwelt expansively on their accomplishments. The few who failed were, to judge by their final papers, affected more powerfully still.

Taken all together, much of their analysis proved inconclusive. Kenny confirmed Kozol's (1991) claims that inner-city schoolchildren are painfully aware of the education they are not getting. But Jill and Jo-Anne disputed

Kozol's insistence on the essential innocence of those youngsters, noting the precocity of their sexual knowledge and the intimacy of their familiarity with violence and death. Jacqueline thought the school imparted a "strong message" that "for most of these students" there could be "little expectation of success," and Stefan considered the expectations he encountered unrealistic. But Debbie denied that her Warriors were "doomed for failure." Where Kozol found that fourth graders had already given up the "degree of faith and optimism" with which they first came to school (1991: 57), she was convinced that her fifth graders had "kept the faith and retained their optimism." Rachel asked her pupils what they wanted to be when they got older and found two girls who hoped to be hairdressers, one who wanted to be a hairdresser and a lawyer, a boy who aspired to be Michael Jordan, and another who planned to be a veterinarian. None of them seemed to feel "worthless and devoid of hope." Audrey discovered that her charges could defer gratification, and Jo-Anne thought her eighth graders "motivated [by] a strong desire to achieve." Unlike the teenagers whom Anderson saw with little to lose by having a child out of wedlock because they had no "future to derail" (1990: 113), Jo-Anne's girls were determined not to become pregnant because they did "have plans for the future."

Jay found that the five boys with whom he was closest were all keen to stay in school and were, indeed, curious about college. But he also found that their aspirations to achieve were subordinate to their solidarity with one another. They skateboarded together, played basketball together, rented movies together. Their "posse," as they called it, provided them far more companionship and caring than did their families and more of a sense of themselves than any of them had separately. Stefan's students also took their sense of themselves from those they hung out with. They generally dressed as their friends did, and they always played together. It was their chosen "peers more than [any] individualism" that defined them.

Such observations confirmed and made vivid Tocqueville's perception of an American propensity to "draw apart with . . . friends, [each] in a little circle of his own," and leave "society at large to itself" (1945: 104). More than that, they made plain that the Frenchman's predications were in crucial ways incompatible with more modern formulations, notably Bellah et al.'s (1985) assertion of the ascendancy of expressive individualism in contemporary America.

Other observations lent themselves less neatly to one side or another of the contrary conceptualizations that we had developed during class discussions. The peer groups themselves were predicated on exclusion. They mocked Tocqueville's postulation of an American affinity for "self-interest rightly understood" (1945: 129). They amplified Bellah et al.'s emphasis on an elite American proclivity for "life-style enclaves" (1985: 71-75). But they did not asperse Tocqueville's analysis of invidious comparison and the uses of negative reference groups in America's "egalitarian" society.

Even among the disprivileged, there were, as my students saw, degrees of deprivation. Even among those who had little, there was disdain for those who had less. Stefan himself slowly came to the conclusion that certain clothes and other material possessions were not only tokens of peer-group identity but also talismans of status. They conferred "respect" on those who could come by them and made "outcasts" of those who could not. Kenny and Josh too grew convinced that the students in the WEPIC program considered themselves "an elite" at Turner. Kenny came to feel that "to define themselves" the ones in WEPIC needed the regular students at the school. Josh thought that the WEPIC youngsters deliberately distanced themselves from their fellow students. When he heard them blame their own schoolmates rather than barebones budgets and an antiquated plant for the filth of their school facilities — "People don't care . . . there are some nasty people at Turner" — he realized that "they did not consider themselves part of the community they incriminated."

Such realizations were fresh and sobering. Some others were stark and startling. They carried my students past any of the conceptualizations we had canvassed in the course into ideas all their own. Tony, for one, took Octavio Paz's premise that national character is not to be understood as a descriptive generalization of the predispositions and predilections of a whole people so much as a prescriptive idealization promulgated by an elite in the name of the nation; and he pushed that premise to its logical extremity and beyond. Against Kozol's impassioned appeals for justice to our own children, Tony wondered whether they are indeed our own, since they do not "fit" the prescriptive ideal that defines our character. Against Kozol's urgent insistence that "these are Americans," Tony finally "could not repress [a] shocking thought": "No, they are not."

Brighid's tutoring brought her to a different but equally disturbing apprehension. A few years earlier, a family sabbatical had occasioned her temporary enrollment in a London secondary school. There she had drawn "hexagons on graph paper for three months" in geometry and learned little more than "to fix water heaters" in science. Her school friends had been "violent, underprivileged, functionally illiterate students whom the British educational system had betrayed." Even when she learned that her school was the one school in the system obliged to accept the delinquents refused by all the other schools, she had still exulted that her own country did not deny educational opportunities to any child. In West Philadelphia, she found to her horror that her "naive" exultation was unwarranted. Even at Turner, a relatively good school by city standards, children were "written off by their society." Even at Turner, expectations were as abysmal as in the worst school in London. Equality of educational opportunity was not a discernible "element of American national character."

Jeremy was as appalled by his experience as Brighid by hers, but his dismay derived precisely from the parities between places. "All over" — in his home town of West Los Angeles as much as in West Philadelphia — he felt the same abounding "fear and mistrust." West Los Angeles might have "more ostentatious wealth — and just plain loose, flashy money — [than] any other town" he knew. West Philadelphia might have "less wealth . . . than . . . most places in the country." Still, in the one as in the other, benevolence "went out the window [when] nobody trust[ed] anybody." In the one as in the other, "no goodwill" appeared among people fearful that "their fellows [were] out to get them."

I do not hide my own impatience with America from my students. Though I usually make an effort to muffle it, they are not deceived. I have a certain reputation among them as a relic of the 1960s. But I do make clear that they do not have to mirror my ideas in their papers. I do demand that they think for themselves, and I do assure them that my courses are safe environments for doing so.

More than that, they believe me. In the other course that I taught that semester, I thought that I had perhaps intimated an unduly dispiriting assessment of the present prospect of historical study; my students, almost without exception, argued in their concluding essays that the conditions I thought constituted a crisis were in fact an unparalleled opportunity. In previous years, on the other occasions when I taught the course on the American character, I lodged largely the same criticisms of the culture that I did in this version with its community service component; my students, for the most part, countered in their final papers with chauvinistic pride in their culture and a sublime if chastened protectiveness of it.

Indeed, in this version, as long as the students in History 443 were still reading what their predecessors had read and discussing what their predecessors had discussed, their performances seemed to me essentially indistinguishable from those of their predecessors. On the last assignment, however, when they had to assimilate their experience at Turner as none before them had had to do, their writing took on a tone that I had never seen before. The very titles of their papers testified to the change that their Turner experience occasioned. "Sweatin' for the Man," "Inner City Blues," "Equality of Despair," "A Land of Exclusion," and the like blazoned from the beginning the preoccupation with racism, inequality, and injustice that pervaded the essays. I had never encountered a disenchantment so rampant in any previous set of papers in the course, or for that matter, in any other course I'd ever taught.

In short, something profoundly educative and even transformative occurred among my students in the schools of West Philadelphia. One after another, they bore witness to the ways in which a few hours at Turner "exploded" the "myths" they had maintained for years.

Audrey found it "hard to think about asking children under [such] circumstances to be thankful for the freedoms we [profess] in America," and equally hard to resist the conclusion that "the American dream has failed, though we can't face it." Jay wrote that "our nation . . . was built on a principle of inequality," and Jo-Anne judged the practice of inequality in the city's schools a "crime." Jen declared inequality, racism, homelessness, and violence the core of "what it truly means to be an American." Jay dismissed equality of opportunity as "nothing but a dream." Chris denounced "our top-heavy distribution of wealth" and the imminence of its "crushing us to death." T took "our entire social structure" to be "doomed." Jon, Andrew, and Amy all, uncannily, resorted to the metaphor of meltdown to describe an American people moving amid "guilt" and "despair" toward what Orin called "moral chaos."

Josh summed up the sentiments of a large part of the class when he enumerated the faiths that his fleeting experience in the inner city extinguished: "One society? No. We are white, black, rich, poor, each turning away in muted ignorance and contempt from those below us. Tolerance? Never. . . . The American dream? Get real."

One may recoil from the severity of these strictures. One may discount these indictments as excessive and even obsessive, overheated and even apocalyptic. But one would do well to consider how unlikely the revulsion of my students was, and how powerfully affecting, therefore, the glimpses of ghetto life that they got must have been for them.

My students are, after all, young men and women ill-equipped and ill-disposed to appreciate the plight of the poor. Virtually all of them have been brought up in comfortable circumstances, and more than a few of them in the lap of luxury.[2] As they often admitted in their papers, their very privilege has protected them from any extensive experience of the underclass and has afforded them a rich repertoire of defenses against its claims on their sympathy or even their attention. As they might have added, their privilege will probably insulate them even more completely in the future. They will go forth into a society in which places are increasingly allocated according to credentials, and they will go forth with the very best of credentials. Their successes will confine them to circles in which there will be scant incentive or audience for searing social criticism such as they ventured in their final essays, or even for experiences out of which such social criticism might grow.

If, then, their work in West Philadelphia allowed them no more than a brush with realities beyond those of their own past and prospective affluence, the worth of that work would be sufficient. If their teaching assignments at Turner afforded them no more than an inkling, for a few hours of a few weeks of their youthful lives, of how the other half lives, the importance of those assignments would still be palpable. But the hours at 59th and Baltimore did even more than open out to those students an ampler understanding of their country. Those scant sessions inspired in them thoughts that were actually their own rather than those of their milieu. And it is not beyond the pale of possibility that those thoughts may model for them a more independent way of meeting the world that could be considered educative rather than conventionally inculcative. We say that we seek such things for our students.

We say, too, that we seek to stir hope for the future in our youth, whose favorite movies and music are so often bleak and holocaustic. We say that we seek to instill compassion in those young people, whose ways are so often self-centered and mean. In the final papers that my students submitted, I sometimes saw a tempered optimism that promised to outlast the Panglossian patina I'd encountered in the papers of previous years. I sometimes saw a tenderness that made me melt.

Postscript

Frontier people in America were always a restless, westering lot. I and my History 443 course have also moved on since the "Turnerian Frontier" experiment described above, though we have not moved far or west. Where our pioneering predecessors vaulted across vast river valleys and mountain ranges, we merely went a couple of miles east. Where they ventured into the unknown, we came closer to home. Where they conquered a continent, my students and I conquered nothing, except perhaps a bit — a very small bit — of our ignorance and fear.

After my extraordinary experience at the Turner Middle School, I moved my course to the University City High School with immense trepidation. Still, the incentives to move were obvious. Turner was 20 blocks away by trolley. My students spent 15 minutes getting there even if they lived right by the trolley stop and the trolley came right away. Half an hour or more if they didn't and it didn't. And then the same coming back. But they could walk the three blocks to University City in five minutes.

But the difference in distance was more than just logistic. Turner was, in its own way, a very special school. Ira Harkavy, Cory Bowman, and the rest of the WEPIC group whose guidance was indispensable to our endeavor worked with Turner because Marie Bogle and a number of her fellow teachers, to say nothing of her principal, were indispensable to Ira and Cory. Ira spent 20 years sifting and false-starting to find the faculty nucleus he had at Turner. Those men and women made the school a place where WEPIC could walk the walk while others just talked the talk. They allowed Ira to be what he truly wanted to be, a provider of resources in support of grass-roots plans and purposes, because they truly took the initiative and set the school's direction. If they did not make Turner the jewel of the Philadelphia school system, they certainly made it a semiprecious stone in a diadem that had few enough even of those.

University City High School (UCHS) had, as I would soon discover, a number of committed and highly competent teachers. It also had, as I'd already heard, a dynamic new principal who seemed capable of transforming the school if anyone could. But there was a lot to transform. Appalling rates of absenteeism, parental poverty, and violence. Academic achievement scores far below the national average and very near the bottom even among city high schools. A dreadful reputation in the media and in the neighborhood. If my students were to confront the reality of the inner city, UCHS was a lot closer to it than Turner. If they were to take up the challenge of making a mite of difference in their own backyard, UCHS was transparently the place to start.

Nonetheless, I trembled to send them there. I worried for their sheer physical safety more than I ever had at Turner, where the students were simply smaller than mine. And I feared for their psychic safety far more than I ever had at Turner, where the students were still young enough for certain innocences and a poignant hopefulness that the high schoolers would not sustain. In short, I dreaded that my students would encounter a bitterness and despondency so profound that it would dispirit them.

I underestimated my students. In the years since I switched to University City, they have been disheartened by what they have seen and heard and felt. They have been appalled by things happening in the classroom and outside of it. They have even, on rare occasions, been threatened with physical harm or subjected to verbal abuse. But they have never asked out, never ceased doing their damnedest, never failed to keep their wits about them as they observed an America for which their privilege did not prepare them. They never quit, and they never quit learning. Indeed, as is the way of these things, they probably got more out of the experience than the students they were supposed to help. The rich get richer.

I asked them, one day during the year we left Turner, if they would rather we were still there. I should never have asked. I regretted asking as soon as the words were out of my mouth. But the words had flown from my mouth because class discussion had taken a carping turn that caught and amplified the doubts about the switch that had been nagging at me all semester. I'm not sure what I would have done, or even said, if the students had told me that they did in fact wish they were working with sweeter, less hardened kids. I am only grateful that they told me nothing of the sort.

The very students who had been complaining most vehemently were suddenly the most abashed. It had never occurred to them that there were alternatives. In truth, it had never occurred to them that there might be alternatives. Their complaints had arisen within their commitment. And as they pondered the possibility of a rather different experience, they deepened their commitment. They insisted that if they were to encounter the America of racially segregated schools and experience the fruits of the nation's impenitent inequality, they should be exactly where they were.

I stood amazed, that morning, at their appetite for reality. And I came to stand still more amazed, some weeks later, when I read their final papers. The carping that had driven me to my indiscreet query had clearly masked — or maybe enabled them to deny for a time — the rage that poured forth in those papers. University City was not the America that the celebrations of our national character promised.

More than that, I came to see, on the evidence of the papers my students wrote, that the carping also masked — or at any rate proceeded from — a dawning realization that they could connect with those UCHS kids. More than my students ever had at Turner, my students at the high school expressed an almost startled sense of camaraderie with the young people they taught, tutored, or coached. The difference in age between junior high schoolers and high schoolers — the difference that I had worried would only intensify the pain and fury of young blacks coming ever more acutely to realize that they were programmed for failure and exclusion — was also a difference that closed the distance between my 20-year-olds and those 17- and 18-year-olds.

Even at Turner, my students could grasp, ethically, that there but for the grace of God went they. At University City, my students could feel, existentially, that there, grace of God or not, they *did* go. They could see themselves, a couple of years before, in their tutees: the same sense of play, the same adolescent yearning, the same trepidatious anticipation of adulthood. More than once, they confessed their envy at the easy wit and sociability and sensuality — the command — of those they were formally set in authority over. And just because they came to grasp a kinship they'd never experienced so vividly before, they came to resent the blighting of those young black lives so like their own but for the accident of birth. So like their own *despite* the accident of birth.

When I sent my students off to the Turnerian frontier, I was overwhelmed by the ways in which their experience enriched their understanding of America. When I sent them to a nearer frontier, I was, if anything, even more overwhelmed, and their understanding was, if anything, even more enriched. Their service-learning was, by their lights, immensely satisfying as community service. It was, by mine, even more rewarding as learning.

Notes

1. These figures are taken from school data profiles of the Turner Middle School for the academic years 1990-91 and 1991-92, produced by the School District of Philadelphia and cited, with much more material to the same effect, in the final paper of University of Pennsylvania student Anthony "J" Fuentez: "The Just Nation: A View of American National Character," Fall 1993, pp. 4-5.

2. According to the only extant survey of the subject, 23 percent of Penn undergraduates had parents with incomes between $100,000 and $200,000 a year, and 27 percent had parents with incomes over $200,000 a year. These percentages are significantly higher than those at the other Ivy League schools. Samuel Hughes, "What Students Are Thinking — and Doing," *Pennsylvania Gazette*, December 1993, p. 23.

References

Anderson, Elijah. (1990). *Streetwise: Race, Class, and Change in an Urban Community.* Chicago, IL: University of Chicago Press.

Bellah, Robert, et al. (1985). *Habits of the Heart: Individualism and Commitment in American Life.* Berkeley and Los Angeles, CA: University of California Press.

Kozol, Jonathan. (1991). *Savage Inequalities: Children in America's Schools.* New York, NY: Crown.

Tocqueville, Alexis de. (1945). *Democracy in America, Vol. II,* edited by Phillips Bradley. New York, NY: Alfred A. Knopf.

Mezzacappa, Dale, and TaNoah Sterling. (Dec. 18, 1993). "A Giant Boost for Reform in Education." *The Philadelphia Inquirer,* p. A1.

Wideman, John E. (1990). *Philadelphia Fire.* New York, NY: Henry Holt.

Reflections of a Historian on Teaching a Service-Learning Course About Poverty and Homelessness in America

by Albert Camarillo

More than a decade ago, when first introduced to the idea of service-learning, I had only a vague idea of what "service" meant for students in an undergraduate course. Encouraged by the staff at Stanford University's Haas Center for Public Service and the dean of undergraduate studies to experiment with this unfamiliar pedagogical practice, I immediately had to consider two questions. Regardless of enticements of financial assistance for curriculum development, how could a historian build a service component into a history course? After all, history is about the past and, for the most part, historians are more concerned about the dead than the living. The thought of students in my Twentieth Century America or Introduction to American Urban History course performing their service as docents at local historical museums or historical societies — though surely a useful service to the public — simply did not appeal to me. How could I ask students, as young citizens of the nation, to engage in a service-learning project for which I myself had little passion?

Thus my second question: If I were to develop a service component for one of my courses, responding in fact to the dean's request for course proposals, how could I involve my students in an activity I regarded as a significant and meaningful contribution to society, not merely some pleasant service task to take students off campus for an hour or two each week? To make a service component or project successful, I concluded, I could not expect any less of the students than what I expected of myself. To push forward with a service-learning course, the service experience ideally would have to challenge Stanford undergraduates, educate them about the "real world," inspire them to contribute to the public good, and provide an intellectually stimulating environment.

Facing this tall order, I nearly abandoned all further thought of moving forward in this new direction, especially after concluding that none of my existing courses was a likely candidate for a service component. I was, however, encouraged by colleagues at the Haas Center to offer a pilot course, to experiment with service-oriented curriculum. Ten years later, the experiment continues, and my experience with teaching one of the first intensive service-learning courses at Stanford University has provided many important perspectives about my discipline, undergraduate learning, and public service. This service-learning experiment has also provided me with some of the most gratifying experiences I have had as a teacher of undergraduates.

In this essay, I describe how developing and teaching a service-learning course both broadened my appreciation for historical analysis and, at the same time, revealed the limitations of history as a way of understanding a contemporary issue. In addition, I reflect on how service-learning, as practiced in my course, has affected students and how it has affected me as an educator. A description of why and how I teach a course on poverty and homelessness provides the necessary background for these reflections.

Poverty and Homelessness in America

The topic of the service-learning course I developed integrated two interests, one associated with my intellectual agenda and the other tied to a societal concern and a personal interest I had as a local citizen. As a historian whose research focuses on ethnic and racial minorities in American cities, my writing, and much of my teaching, revolves around the history of some of the poorest populations in urban society.[1] But my research seldom extends past the 1960s, and I surely do not consider myself a scholar who studies poverty or homelessness. The latter term is of recent origin, and though it relates to a societal problem of long standing — Americans too poor to afford shelter — "homelessness" is associated with a social problem identified in the 1980s.

On one level, it was a bit of an intellectual stretch for this historian to move forward in chronology to engage an issue of recent vintage, but, at another level, the budding literature about homelessness revealed that urban minorities suffered disproportionately from this extreme manifestation of poverty. The linkage between historical and contemporary poverty in America's cities provided the intellectual bridge for my introduction to the study of homelessness. A challenge remained, however, because most historical analyses of poverty usually end with discussions of the War of Poverty in the 1960s, while the topic of homelessness in the 1980s and 1990s is still largely the domain of social scientists.[2] Was an interdisciplinary approach essential to teach this course?

A second, corollary interest drew me to the issue of homelessness as the topic for a service-learning pilot course. Like many Americans during the 1980s, I too was concerned about the increasing number of citizens who, for one reason or another, found themselves on the streets, sleeping in cars and in parks, and filling the temporary shelters hastily created to respond to this growing social problem. The media surely helped shape the image of destitute urbanites, homeless men in the nation's cities hovering over subway steam grates and standing in soup kitchen lines.

On the other hand, social commentators, such as Jonathan Kozol (1988), contributed to a realization that homelessness affected more than single men by exposing the brutality of a suffocating poverty among families who occupied hotels for the homeless in New York City. But the reality of homelessness first hit home for me when, in the mid 1980s, the first homeless shelter was opened in Menlo Park, California, a largely affluent suburban community located next to Stanford University — the community where I had lived for more than a decade.

"Homeless families in Menlo Park! How could this be?" I asked. I soon discovered that urban homelessness had a suburban analog. More and more suburban families with few resources were desperately searching for temporary and transitional housing. I immediately became involved with the local shelter and, within a few years, I was actively involved on a regional basis with nonprofit agencies attempting to deal with this mounting problem. When asked to consider designing a service-learning course several years later, my personal interest in homelessness as a concerned local citizen naturally connected with my intellectual interests about the condition of poverty, especially as it affected Latinos and African Americans, two groups with the highest percentage of individuals most at risk of becoming homeless in local society.

Thus, the service component of my Poverty and Homelessness in America course was tied directly to the shelters with which I had familiarity and was premised on the commitment of students to engage in a six-month-long intensive service placement (eight to 10 hours per week). It was also predicated on a commitment of the shelter sites to involve the undergraduates in substantive and meaningful placements involving direct service to the shelter residents. I expected and trusted that Stanford students, if provided some initial training and supervision, could play instrumental roles as quasi-staff in agencies and organizations chronically understaffed and underfunded. Students in my small group course (on average about 15) were assigned, depending on their particular interests, to one of six or seven different sites. These sites included family shelters, drop-in centers, and outreach programs for homeless youth, large temporary winter shelters for homeless individuals (located at a nearby California National Guard facility), and a public school classroom organized specifically for children of homeless families (located at one of the large shelters).[3]

The course extended over two quarters, with the first quarter consisting of two weekly sessions. The first session was dedicated to discussion of the required readings and the second served as a "reflections" session devoted to student reports about their weekly service experiences.[4] To facilitate student analysis of what they learned in the required readings and what they experienced through their service placements, three writing assignments were required: (1) interim and final placement reports that described their work at the shelters and included a discussion of how specific required readings related to their experiences at the shelters; (2) a traditional literature-type review essay to ensure the students were grappling with the required readings; and (3) a weekly journal in which they recorded personal comments, insights, and experiences related to their fieldwork.[5] The first two assignments were graded as was participation in classroom discussion. The second quarter of the course involved three or four group meetings and continuation of the placement work.

The course is listed as a regular Department of History offering and, over time, has continued to attract students from many majors in the social sciences and humanities as well as pre-med science majors. As I prepared to teach the course for the first time, it was clear it could not be taught strictly as a history course. But, as a historian, I did not want this course to become primarily a contemporary issues class in which students sat around a table discussing their feelings and trendy topics about homelessness. An interdisciplinary course would be necessary, and my effort to mount such a course provided an interesting intellectual perspective that allowed me to view the value and limitations of historical analysis.

Balancing Historical Perspectives and Contemporary Analysis

As I made plans for structuring the content and organization of the course, I knew that the topic of poverty could be addressed historically very effectively using the available secondary literature, but the topic of contemporary homelessness posed a problem. Ten years ago the literature on homelessness was in a nascent stage and most of the early studies provided either social science-oriented or policy perspectives. The "social commentary" literature was also just beginning to be published at this time. The syllabus for the course, consequently, included a mixture of readings from history, sociology, anthropology, policy studies, and social commentary literature. This was the first course in 15 years of teaching in which I emphasized literature other than history, and I was doubtful about the prospect of teaching an interdisciplinary course that de-emphasized the disciplinary perspective I knew best.

Since then, I have offered this course many times, and I have learned — through trial and error — how to encourage students to analyze contemporary issues with a historical sensibility.[6] This is especially difficult in a course of this type because it tends to attract students who, first and foremost, want to delve immediately into the contemporary problem of homelessness, and often view history as a subject to get through quickly so they can get to the "important stuff." As a result, my role as historian has been to remind and even insist that students consider how current problems are rooted in historical contexts.

To examine poverty in the late 20th century requires an understanding of how change and continuity in ideologies and policies over time have allowed poverty to persist and to take many forms in contemporary American society. The powerful explanatory value of history is, I believe, acknowledged by students — even those who were drawn to the course exclusively because of the contemporary saliency of the topic — when they can make direct historical connections between ideas, societal attitudes, public discourse, and governmental policies from eras long past. Students appreciate historical analysis when they understand the continuities, for example, between the public outcry in the late 19th century over the increase of street "paupers" and "vagrants" in American cities and the increasing number of legal statutes in municipalities in the late 20th century aimed at curbing the activity of "panhandlers" and homeless "street youth." When students, moreover, are asked to make associations between definitions of the "deserving" and the "undeserving" poor — a centuries-old dichotomy — they realize that ideas about the poor can transcend time and space and that contemporary images of "welfare queens" and people described as living in a "culture of poverty" are based on ideas with historical antecedents (Katz 1989).

Yet, the application of historical analysis tends to end where the study of contemporary homelessness begins, in the early 1980s. To examine the issues surrounding the homeless in contemporary America, reliance on social science and social commentary literature takes precedence over historical studies. Teaching a course on poverty and homelessness primarily as a history course reveals the limitations of historical inquiry, because historians, unlike sociologists, tend not to examine larger structural processes at play and hesitate to push their analyses in areas where traditional historical sources are not yet available. And while most historians are not trained to deal with quantitative methodologies, most social scientists develop and use databases in search of statistical factors that can explain the causes and effects of poverty and homelessness today. At the other end of the social science spectrum, anthropologists and social commentary writers focus more on individual lives and, thus, complement statistical analyses with deeply human, personal perspectives on the lives of homeless people.[7]

Though it was more difficult when first teaching Poverty and Homelessness in America to balance historical and social science literature, I have found it easier in recent years as more and more social scientists pay greater attention to historical context.[8] Nonetheless, an interdisciplinary course, especially one that draws students who would rather discuss current events than historical causation, requires attention to disciplinary balance.

Undergraduate Education and Service-Learning Curricula

What has motivated me most to continue to offer Poverty and Homelessness in America as a regular part of my teaching load is not the interdisciplinary character of the course. Rather, it is the meaningful engagement and greater understanding of both historical and contemporary issues that I see, year in and year out, as students in the course dynamically combine public service outside the university with traditional classroom learning. This combination of experiences gained from public service together with an intellectual foundation that provides a critical analysis of poverty and homelessness results in a rich educational environment, one that for me stands out uniquely in a teaching career of nearly 25 years.[9]

The factor that supercharges student interest in this topic is the dialectical relationship between the service and the learning. Exposure to homelessness through the service placement inspires students to wrestle intellectually with the required readings and motivates them to participate in discussions in which I often serve merely as moderator rather than discussion leader. At the same time, the service experience challenges students to examine personal and societal values, to pose a variety of questions about American institutions and policies, to think critically, and to understand better the crises faced by fellow citizens who find themselves in temporary shelters as they try to cope with the devastating effects of poverty. The service makes the students better learners and makes me a better teacher.

Students are, moreover, encouraged to assess the relevancy of the historical and social science required readings as they interact with and come to understand how and why families and individuals have fallen into the abyss of homelessness. In some cases, the literature provides satisfactory perspectives that substantiate what students learn from the children, the families, or the single adults they interact with in the shelters. The following excerpt from a student's interim service report in 1991 aptly describes his experience working with homeless individuals at a shelter in San Jose in relation to what he had read in Michael Harrington's *The New American Poverty:*

> *Even after taking a course on homelessness and poverty and working at the shelter for three months, I grapple with what it means to be homeless. In Michael Harrington's chapter on the "Uprooted," he writes that having a home is more than having a roof over one's head. He writes, "It is the center of a web of human relationships. When the web is shredded . . . a person is homeless even if he or she has an anonymous room somewhere." I*

agree that the guests at the shelter are still homeless; they are the uproot-
ed that society has ignored. Yes, they are not living on the streets, but it is
not enough to squeeze them into minuscule apartments with two or three
other people whom they have never met. If the shelter was a real home, the
guests would have privacy and more independence. At least they would be
treated like adults. At the shelter, I have seen the precariousness of which
Harrington writes. We have let homelessness in America slip away from
being only a problem of shelter into a more difficult and chilling problem of
isolation and ignorance. Harrington shows how many different kinds of
people are affected — the working poor, the young, and those who have
been laid off. Also, the mentally ill and those forced to turn to drugs and
alcohol still suffer from being homeless. I have encountered every category
at the shelter, and now I know how real it all is. The residents are REAL
people with nowhere else to go.

In other cases, the scholarly analysis simply does not sufficiently capture the human dimension of the problem or, worse yet, does not provide
adequate explanation for a complex social condition. "So often my experience seems so much different than those that are expressed in our academic books," a student noted in his journal. He continued:

Clearly, people are going to cast a picture [about homelessness] different
than mere numbers can explain but our books focus too heavily on the fem-
inization of poverty and the increasing number of homeless families. But at
Humanitarian House, we deal with individuals. Granted, there are women
there but it seems that people at the shelter are so often those deemed
undeserving and are overlooked.[10]

Through these public service placements, not only do students tend to turn
into more proactive and engaged young scholars, but they become more
involved citizens who contribute to the public good. They also develop
greater critical-thinking skills and offer penetrating critiques of society after
experiencing the lives of people who reside at the shelters.

Katz [in The Undeserving Poor] takes a stance on homelessness that I
am beginning to believe is for the best. I used to think that volunteerism
and charity organizations could make the difference. Now, I am convinced
that without making major economic and political-social changes in this
country, the poor and the homeless will always exist. Katz writes that most
Americans think of the poor as "them" rather than [as] "us." I see and feel
that every time I go to the shelter.

For most of the students, the service placements provide their first direct
exposure to people caught in the grasp of poverty. In addition, the course

often provides students their first exposure to literature that examines the conditions of homelessness. Together, these new factors can change the way they view the world, especially when they see glaring disparities all around them. Something as routine as a drive through a nearby shopping center can spark a critical perspective or introspection, as a student candidly remarked in her personal journal:

> The sign, as I exited the Stanford Shopping Center, glared in the sunlight: "Please Discourage Panhandling by Donating to Organizations Which Provide Assistance to Those in Need." Eight yards away, a man in ragged clothes and a baseball cap held up a sign saying, "Homeless Vet. Please spare some change." And there I was, passing these two emblems of our society on my way to Safeway before my Poverty and Homelessness class. The ironies in the situation were truly disturbing to me. More and more, I find it difficult to figure out what the appropriate reaction to poverty and homelessness really is and what my role as a community service provider means to this reaction. There was a homeless veteran asking for a handout outside of a posh shopping mall, symbolic of all the individuals I had read about in my class. There was the suggestion that donations to organizations which provide assistance to those in need is more appropriate than putting the money straight into the hands of the panhandler. There I was, empathizing with the individual symbol of oppression which has recurred in many of my studies and personal experiences while interning at the Rescue Center Shelter, and focusing my major on the very organizations which were being supported in the sign in an effort to discourage the actions of the individual . . . and in the end, I kept on driving.

Though students understand that providing public service can be a gratifying if difficult experience, they know that providing assistance for homeless people is the primary aim of their placement and that any academic and personal gain is secondary.[11] Importantly, most students leave the course and service experience with a greater understanding of the human condition. As one member of the class of 1996 put it:

> I realize that I am one of "them," those who are compelled to contribute time, energy, possibly a career, toward contributing, elevating, bettering. . . . I felt the need to be a worthy, active member of society. And with this society's constructs, there are very specific things that define what "contributing" is. So, going into this class, although I by no means was/am deluded into thinking I was going to do any great thing by interning, or that I was going to "save" anyone, it is difficult not to assume the role of a service provider, for it is a role that is very much projected onto us by social reality. I am feeling significantly uncomfortable with this projection, this reality, for it compartmentalizes us into categories of those in struggle vs.

those not in struggle/those offering service vs. those receiving service. . . .
Really, all I want to do is participate in a way that humanizes all partici-
pants. To not only humanize the homeless, but also to humanize myself, not
as a pillar of intelligence, stability, and potential, but as a human, perhaps
with very different experiences and circumstances, but as a human, and
thus an inextricable part of the human experience, of which we are a part.

Obviously, the impact of the service-learning curriculum on individual students varies depending on many factors, including their initial motivation and commitment, the nature of the service setting, personality, maturity, and previous public service experiences. In recent years, scholars interested in the pedagogy and structures of higher education curricula have turned increasing attention to service-learning. Some of these colleagues have offered useful ways to understand how students perform different types of public service in various service-learning courses. The identification of three distinctive motivations for service — charity, project, and social change — are particularly relevant for understanding why students become involved in public service and how to measure the potential outcome of the service they perform (Morton 1995: 21-23). These three types of service provide a framework for me to reflect on the dozens of students who have enrolled in my Poverty and Homelessness course over the years and to ask myself what motivated them to invest time and energy in the service placements and how the experience affected them.

Public service as "charity" suggests a relatively low level of commitment and short-term or one-time service. A recent survey administered to college undergraduates revealed that the vast majority of those who participate in public service do so "to help other people" (Astin and Sax 1998: 255). Though charity is a valuable civic contribution and can be inspired by wanting to help other people, it also suggests that those performing the service do not spend time understanding the subject of their charity. That is, people who perform charity are not necessarily interested in learning more about the issue or object of their charitable act. For example, the person who drops off food at a food bank for the needy and who performs this task one hour per week is engaging in an act of charity. If this person has no interest in discussing the reasons why people are dependent on the food bank, he or she is not likely to move beyond charity as a form of service.

"Project," as opposed to charity, requires a substantial commitment of time and energy to service, typically on a more regular basis, either short run or longer term. More important, service-learning as project includes a plan or objective for a desired outcome and requires serious consideration and understanding of the issue, problem, or topic. Though students might not actually experience the final outcome or realize the goal of the public service, the critical point is that the service is directed toward some specific aim and requires a level of understanding beyond the superficial.

The difference between public service as project and as "social change" is that the latter is service seeking to address or resolve root causes of a problem or condition. It requires an even more serious effort, a more long-term commitment — oftentimes involving an entire career — and it requires an even more intensive study and understanding of an issue or problem that can be resolved only through institutional change.

Charity, project, and social change as approaches to service-learning can run along a continuum, one building on the other. But these approaches can also be mutually exclusive. For the great majority of the approximately 120 students who have enrolled in my Poverty and Homelessness course thus far, "project" best describes their involvement in the service experience. The nature of the course requires more than charity; but it is the decision of students as they pursue careers after graduating from Stanford that determines whether they move into the social change domain, or whether they continue some form of project, or charity. Service-learning courses are transitory in the lives of young students. However, in my experience with undergraduates who have been involved in service-learning as project, I feel they are most likely to continue to include this approach to service in their lifestyles as adults. By contrast, there are a handful of students from my course who have been inspired so much by their service-learning experience that they have pursued careers placing them in positions where they could contribute to social change.

Service-Learning and the Education of the Educator

University faculty are generally not very well prepared or trained to handle the intense personal and extremely difficult ethical situations that students are likely to encounter when they serve as interns at a homeless shelter over a six-month period. The first time I taught Poverty and Homelessness in America, I was surely unprepared to provide expert counseling when particularly traumatic situations developed. Beyond serving as a source of support and suggesting that all perspectives should be considered, I really wasn't sure what to say to students who experienced such situations. For example, one student who had been tutoring at a family shelter watched in amazement as Child Protective Services (CPS) personnel converged on the facility one evening to take the child she had been tutoring and the child's siblings into protective custody while the police arrested their mother for alleged physical abuse. When my student asked CPS what would happen to the children (the father was absent and next of kin lived elsewhere) and was told the children would likely be split up in the foster care system, yet another dilemma associated with public service was brought into the classroom for discussion.

Though traumatic experiences such as this one have been rare, other troubling issues related to service-learning have arisen and been the topic of numerous reflection sessions. Though many years of teaching experience had equipped me to run seminars effectively when students discussed required readings, those students knew I was here treading on unknown territory. Together, we frequently used the reflection sessions to surface difficult and perplexing issues. Such a classroom environment, in which the students realized I was learning along with them, produced an open and supportive atmosphere in which they were willing to share thoughts and concerns. This environment spilled over into the discussion of required readings and, consequently, what students read in the literature often became related to their experiences in the public service placements. The result was a classroom full of young citizens eager to learn, inspired to grapple with the literature and test the limits of what academics and others said about problems, problems they themselves had encountered through their work at local shelters.

As educators, we look for ways to increase the effectiveness of our classrooms and to motivate students to learn. In general, Stanford students are motivated and very intelligent, but the environment created as a result of combining service with learning has not been duplicated in other traditional small group courses I teach. This was an important lesson for me to learn. At one level, I would like in every course I teach to infuse students with the enthusiasm and commitment to intellectual exchange and public service exhibited by students who enrolled in my course on Poverty and Homelessness. But, at another level, I am aware that service-learning curricula require more time and preparation than other courses. There is the extra time spent securing and placing the students at service sites, though a course assistant can certainly help in this area. There is the extra seat-time involved in adding sessions for students to reflect on and process the service experience on a weekly basis, time that should not be taken from sessions devoted to discussion of the required readings. There is the time involved in dealing with problems when placements go awry. And, as faculty supervisor for the student interns, one must accept additional responsibility by ensuring that the students' public service meets agency expectations.

Despite these additional allocations of time and responsibility, my experience with service-learning over the years always brings me back to teaching Poverty and Homelessness because of the gratification I receive each time a new group of students engages in public service and builds a foundation of knowledge about a topic new to most of them. How can an educator not want to return to a classroom setting, regardless of the extra effort required, where students are inspired and motivated to learn, and where one continues to learn oneself through their experiences? And, when students leave campus each week for their placements at local shelters, it is rewarding to know that one has created an opportunity for a group of active young citizens to contribute to the public good. Each time I teach this course, my faith in participatory citizenship for the public good is revitalized, and the importance of my career as an educator is reaffirmed as I work with students motivated intellectually as a result of the service-learning process. The experimental course I initiated a decade ago — one of the first service-learning courses developed at Stanford — is now part of the foundation of a steadily growing curriculum that provides students with opportunities to link their academic studies with public service.

Notes

1. Most of my early publications center on the historical experiences of Mexican Americans in California (*Chicanos in a Changing Society: From Mexican Pueblos to American Barrios, 1850-1930* [Harvard University Press, 1979]; *Chicanos in California: A History of Mexican Americans* [Boyd and Fraser Publishers, 1984]). My most recent book, *Not White, Not Black: Mexicans and Ethnic/Racial Borderlands in American Cities* (to be published by Oxford University Press), is a comparative history of Mexican Americans, African Americans, European immigrants, and Asian immigrants in American cities up to 1950.

2. The most recent bibliography on homelessness is included in Jim Baumohl, ed., *Homelessness in America* (Oryx Press, 1996).

3. Students at the family shelters either worked as assistant case managers, helping the staff case managers to provide resources and information for the residents, or they served as tutors working with grade school children in an evening tutorial project. Other interns performed a variety of functions, from developing new programs for shelter guests to serving as outreach workers providing services for homeless youth on the streets of San Jose.

4. The students are usually assigned to the service sites in pairs or teams. It was necessary for students to have a partner or group of peers with whom to share experiences derived from the public service placements.

5. The personal journals were an important part of processing the experiences of the students. They were required to keep their journal up to date. They were also required to submit the journal to me at the end of each quarter. These journals are quite remarkable documents, which capture the thoughts and feelings of undergraduates as they go through the public service experience.

6. I had team-taught a course in the 1980s with several colleagues from other departments in what was a multidisciplinary course, but my role was to provide the historical context and, consequently, as a lecturer I did not venture outside the cozy domain of history.

7. See, for example, Elliot Liebow, *Tell Them Who I Am: The Lives of Homeless Women* (Free Press, 1993).

8. See, for example, Peter H. Rossi, *Down and Out in America: The Origins of Homelessness* (University of Chicago Press, 1989); Christopher Jencks, *The Homeless* (Harvard University Press, 1994).

9. I have taught at Stanford — my first and only faculty appointment — since 1975; Poverty and Homelessness in America is the only service-learning course I offer. However, based on this experience, I have advocated for the expansion of the service-learning curriculum at the university and have been involved in helping other colleagues consider including service components in their courses.

10. The name of the shelter is fictitious. This student interned at an inner-city shelter in San Jose that catered to single adults, mostly men.

11. I stress the point that the service component of the course is a critically important part of their learning experience, but I also underscore that the service must take precedence over all else, including personal interests.

References

Astin, Alexander W., and Linda J. Sax. (May/June 1998). "How Undergraduates Are Affected by Service Participation." *Journal of College Student Development* 39(3): 251-263.

Harrington, Michael. (1984). *The New American Poverty*. New York, NY: Penguin Books.

Katz, Michael. (1989). *The Undeserving Poor: From the War on Poverty to the War on Welfare*. New York, NY: Pantheon Books.

Kozol, Jonathan. (1988). *Rachel and Her Children: Homeless Families in America*. New York, NY: Ballantine Books.

Morton, Keith. (Fall 1995). "The Irony of Service: Charity, Project, and Social Change in Service-Learning." *Michigan Journal of Community Service Learning* 2(1): 19-32.

History as Public Work

by Elisa von Joeden-Forgey and John Puckett

Academically based community service is a type of service-learning that integrates academic learning and civic engagement in powerful ways. This approach puts the hands-on investigation of societal problems at the core of the undergraduate academic program. It guides students to contribute meaningfully to societal problem solving in local venues, involving them in school and neighborhood improvement projects that provide unique opportunities for the production and use of new academic knowledge. It is serious "public work" — well worth the candle of the continuous planning and adjustments required to sustain it.

In an important book, *Building America: The Democratic Promise of Public Work*, Harry C. Boyte and Nancy N. Kari (1996) argue persuasively, on the strength of contemporary case studies in cities such as East Brooklyn, Seattle, and Baltimore, that the social and cultural divisions, civic disaffection, and fragmented communal life characteristic of *fin de siècle* America can be corrected through a resurgent civic activism that starts in the work-place. Boyte and Kari brilliantly propose the idea of public work as a general strategy for overcoming the dysfunctional central tendencies of postindustrial society. As their idea provides a useful way for conceptualizing academically based community service, we quote these authors at length:

> "Public work" is work by ordinary people that builds and sustains our basic public goods and resources — what used to be called "our commonwealth." It solves common problems and creates common things. It may be paid or voluntary. It may be done in communities. It may be done as part of one's regular job. In fact, adding public dimensions to work — recognizing the larger potential meaning and impact of what one does as a teacher or nurse, as a county extension agent or a computer programmer or a machinist or a college professor or anything else — often can turn an unsatisfying "job" into much more significant "work." The story of two bricklayers who were asked what they were doing conveys this sense. One said, "building a wall." The other said, "building a cathedral."
>
> In the fullest sense of the term, public work takes place not only with an eye to public consequences, it also is work "in public" — work that is visible, open to inspection, whose significance is widely recognized. And it is cooperative civic work of "a public": a mix of people whose interests, backgrounds, and resources may be quite different.
>
> Public work focuses attention on a point that we have largely lost in our age of high technology: We help to build the world through our common

effort. What we have built and created we can also recreate. Thus, public work suggests new possibilities for democracy. (Boyte and Kari 1996: 16)

Academically based community service is a powerful form of public work uniquely appropriate for American higher education. Indeed this strategy is thoroughly consistent with the historic mission of the American research university originally conceived and organized, in no small way, to help ameliorate the harmful social effects of industrialization and urbanization in America at the turn of the 20th century. To support our claim, we present the following grossly simplified historical sketch.

Prior to World War I, leading research universities linked their research and teaching agendas closely to the social problems of their urban environments (Harkavy 1996). At the University of Pennsylvania, for example, the early Wharton School focused teaching and research on social problems related to child labor in Philadelphia's textile factories and private control of the city's transportation networks and utilities (Harkavy and Puckett 1991a; Sass 1982: 55-89). In Chicago, at the turn of the 20th century, a close working relationship existed between the women of Hull House and the male sociologists at the newly founded University of Chicago, whose president, William Rainey Harper, emphasized the compatibility of research, teaching, and public service. Indeed, the early Chicago sociologists, who were scholars qua social activists, adopted the research interests and methodologies of the Hull House residents (Deegan 1988; Harkavy and Puckett 1994).

This reform orientation was undermined in the 1920s as conservative social forces and contexts favored tendencies within the American university toward the production of theoretical knowledge "for its own sake," the creation of ever more specialized academic departments, and the establishment of a narrow discipline-based reward structure. Between the wars and increasingly after World War II, these tendencies were given center stage and crystallized within the university as a set of permanent structures, operations, and behavioral expectations; as a consequence, the American university of the past 50 years has been an inwardly directed, discipline-centered institution, more and more isolated from society.

Today significant societal problems, in particular the devastation of our inner cities, have sparked a vigorous reconsideration in many quarters of the societal role and social responsibility of the American university (Bok 1990; Boyer 1994; Harkavy and Puckett 1994). Increased public scrutiny of the university's performance, scholarly critiques from *within* the American academy, and the impact of factors related to the university's own enlightened self-interest — for example, the intrusion of crime and threats to safety on urban campuses — have been key factors in this critical reformulation. The complex pragmatic problem raised by these criticisms is *how* the American university can once again become a mission-oriented institution; that is, *how* it can better serve society by developing humane applications of scientific knowledge to help those living in conditions of profound poverty and neglect. To restate the problem in Boyte and Kari's (1996) terms, it is how to reinsert public work at the core of the institution.

At the University of Pennsylvania, approximately 40 faculty members affiliated with the Center for Community Partnerships have adopted academically based community service (ABCS) as an effective way to accomplish Penn's historic missions of research and teaching, and to overcome the "false trichotomization" of research, teaching, and service (Harkavy and Puckett 1991b). Since 1991, approximately 95 ABCS seminars have been implemented campus-wide at Penn, with a spate of others being planned for the next several years under the auspices of a major grant from the Kellogg Foundation. Working in conjunction with the West Philadelphia Improvement Corps (WEPIC), an area-wide coalition that includes Penn faculty and graduate and undergraduate students, these seminars actively and directly contribute to school and neighborhood improvement projects in West Philadelphia. Our own work in undergraduate history has been conceived and organized within this broader framework of curricular activity at the University of Pennsylvania.

In this chapter, we argue that the intellectual and civic outcomes to be gained from academically based community service warrant serious consideration for the inclusion of this approach in the undergraduate history curriculum. To support this claim, we present examples and lessons learned from an ABCS course for undergraduate history majors that we introduced and taught jointly in the fall semester of 1995 at the University of Pennsylvania. (One of us, Forgey, taught the course separately for two consecutive semesters in 1996-97.)

HIS 204: Teaching American History: A West Philadelphia Workshop

In the winter of 1995, Michael Katz, chairperson of the University of Pennsylvania's history department, asked John Puckett, an associate professor in the Graduate School of Education (GSE), to consider organizing a service-learning course for Penn undergraduate history majors. For the previous eight years, Puckett had worked in several projects linking Penn's academic resources to the public schools of West Philadelphia, the university's proximate geographic community. Between 1989 and 1992 he had directed the West Philadelphia Student Research Apprenticeship Program, which included the development of an urban Foxfire-style community studies program and desktop publication facility at West Philadelphia High School. At a lunch meeting in the winter of 1995, Katz proposed that Puckett design a course on *doing* local history in West Philadelphia, an area that had been officially part of the city since 1854 and was home to a predominantly African-American (and increasingly poor) population since the late 1950s. Katz envisioned a group of Penn history majors working side by side with West Philadelphia High School students on local history projects, serving as mentors and teachers.

Puckett agreed to try to develop Katz's proposal, which would be offered in the fall semester 1995 as HIS 204, Teaching American History: A West Philadelphia Workshop. Katz made arrangements to have Elisa von Joeden-Forgey join Puckett to help plan and coteach the course. Forgey was a doctoral student and Ford Foundation intern in Penn's history department, with experience in collecting oral histories. During the spring semester we (Forgey and Puckett) met twice with Larry Devine, the Social Studies Department chairperson at West Philadelphia High School. Devine expressed a strong interest in the project and agreed to have two of his American history classes at the high school participate with the Penn undergraduates.

Over the summer, we outlined a course to encompass the following purposes:

1. HIS 204 would introduce Penn undergraduates to the history and social structure of West Philadelphia from 1854 to the present, with particular attention to the experience of African Americans in West Philadelphia. The course would be an integral part of the Center for Community Partnerships's West Philadelphia Bibliography and Information System. Papers authored by undergraduates in HIS 204 would be catalogued in this new program's repository and made available to the general public and to other researchers.

2. HIS 204 would introduce participants to the uses of local history; the methods, skills, and techniques for doing local history; and the sources and resources of local history, with particular attention to West Philadelphia. Students would learn about the richness and diversity of interesting, significant, researchable local history topics in West Philadelphia. They would acquaint themselves with city libraries and repositories for the study of West Philadelphia history, for example, the Free Library, Van Pelt Library, Temple Urban Archives, the Afro-American Museum, and the Pennsylvania Historical Society. Each student would develop an original paper on a local history topic. Weekly class meetings would be used, in part, for discussion of mutual interests, issues, and concerns raised by these research papers.

3. HIS 204 would engage Penn undergraduates as mentors to students at West Philadelphia High School. This component of the course would be conducted in conjunction with the West Philadelphia Improvement Corps (WEPIC) and the Center for Community Partnerships. The Penn students

would work with teams of high school students in two social studies classes to develop local history projects that would lead, on the high school side, to student and community publications; and contribute, on the university side, to the development of HIS 204 papers and the West Philadelphia Bibliography and Information System. To help orient them, participants would learn about the multiple contexts of academically based community service in West Philadelphia: the history of university-community relations, the origins and growth of WEPIC; the history, contexts, and social forces of West Philadelphia High School. Embodying itself a "neo-Deweyan" approach, the course would also introduce students to the general principles of John Dewey's pedagogy — a philosophy and progressive teaching strategy that underlies WEPIC project work.

The course consisted of two main parts: a weekly three-hour seminar at Penn (Mondays) and a weekly two-hour "recitation" at West Philadelphia High School (Wednesdays). During the recitation part, Penn students mentored high school students in two separate yet consecutive social studies courses taught by Larry Devine. The weekly seminar at Penn was intended to complement students' teaching experiences and to provide a forum for reflection and discussion among the undergraduates. At the beginning of the semester only the seminar met because the high school generally requires a month or so to get its courses in order. We used these early sessions to cover background material on teaching, oral interviewing techniques, the history of West Philadelphia, and the Philadelphia School District. Our 15 students, all history majors, began their actual teaching and project work in mid-October. Ten of them went to West Philadelphia High School (WPHS) on Wednesday mornings; due to scheduling conflicts, the other five went to Shaw Middle School on Thursday afternoons.

Local history project groups were formed in the following ways. At the high school, each undergraduate presented an idea to Larry Devine's third- and fourth-period classes; after these presentations, the high school students were asked to sign up for the project that interested them most. Interestingly, only one undergraduate was left without any students, and she was gracious enough to join another group. In the end, there were six separate groups pursuing the following topics: Islam in West Philadelphia, police-community relations (which developed into a history of MOVE), American Bandstand (which had originated in an arena three blocks from the high school), sports in the history of WPHS, local church history, and the West Philadelphia Free School.

At Shaw Middle School, Penn undergraduates worked with students selected by their teacher for this special history project, rather than with an entire class. Their topics included Clark Park, the impact of the Harlem Renaissance on West Philadelphia, and identity formation among African-

American girls in West Philadelphia. The Clark Park project was a continuation of a project the middle school students had already begun. One undergraduate visiting Shaw, Susan, showed an interest in doing an ethnographic study of History 204. Her duties were to participate in the Clark Park project while conducting interviews with the various participants at the two school sites and acting as the course archivist.

It is no exaggeration to say that nothing in their previous schooling had prepared our undergraduates for a course such as this — a course that would require them to enter a new, ill-structured, and perhaps daunting situation, construct an original research project, and figure out how to *lead* a team of high school students in carrying out that research. We observed in the early stages of the course that our students expected the events and relationships entailed in the high school component, somehow, some way, to be fixed in advanced. As Susan's final report clearly indicated to us, they were unprepared for, and more than a bit unnerved by, the degree of extemporaneous planning and jerry-rigging necessitated by a school-university collaboration.

This is not to say that we did not have a syllabus. We certainly did. Indeed, we did as much prior planning as possible to try to anticipate what our students would need as they entered West Philadelphia High School. For example, we scheduled two seminar meetings at the high school in the early fall. The purpose of the first meeting (September 25) was to meet Larry Devine and learn as much as possible about the high school; another teacher made an engaging informal presentation on the school's 85-year history, replete with slides from old yearbooks. The purpose of the second meeting (October 2) was to talk with a history teacher and students from another Philadelphia high school who had conducted local history projects of their own. For other seminar sessions in the early fall, we had our students examine substantive issues related to the course, for example, social forces and contexts that impinge on poor African-American children in West Philadelphia (Nightingale 1993); and methodological issues, such as oral history strategies (Yow 1994).

Other than a perfunctory orientation to Deweyan pedagogy (reading Tanner 1991), we took it largely on faith that our students would find their own way as mentors and teachers; we planned to use the seminar as a forum for working out the problems they would encounter. Happily, by the end of November, most had established effective teaching patterns and methods, and some had even been successful in inspiring their students to do extracurricular activities related to the local history projects. Because of this settling-in period, however, they did not have the time to pursue creative final projects with the high school and middle school students. Just as their work was getting off the ground, it was forced to come to a halt as the semester was ending.

The undergraduates were required to produce an article-length final paper based on their teaching experiences and on their research. Some of these papers were really exceptional, fusing teaching and research methodologies with substantive discussions of their primary topics in very sophisticated ways. The high school students were required to write a final five-page paper, outlining what they had learned and what questions they still had. We also conducted a Presentation Day at the high school, during which Devine's students presented their projects to the class. Unfortunately, it snowed heavily that day, so few people came. The performances of those who did attend, however, are on video.

The main strengths of the course fit loosely into two categories — academic and civic — and pertain predominantly to the undergraduates. The positive impact on the high school students is less evident. They were exposed to advanced college students and learned from them valuable information about the college application process and financial aid possibilities; they had an opportunity to receive intense personal attention, and in this way to improve their writing and thinking skills; and they visited research institutions and sections of the city that many of them had not seen before. Some high school students really took advantage of the resources offered by the Penn students and later praised the project. For example, Julie's student Frank at WPHS evaluated his experience with the project on the Free School as follows:

> I like the Free School because I never heard of it and I think it was a perfect idea. There was not one thing I didn't like about the West Philadelphia Free School and I also think that Ms. Novella Williams played a good part in it. I think that the project was the best thing that I did in Dr. Devine's class since I been there. Julie was the perfect partner to work on it with.

Julie reflected on Frank's written evaluation by noting that "Frank assured me that he was not just complimenting me so that I would give him a good grade on the project; he really enjoyed the work that we had done."

Academic Strengths

Many of our students, like Julie, were almost natural teachers, establishing honest, open, and respectful relationships with their students and inspiring their students to learn rather early on in the semester. She and others became interested in HIS 204 as a means of discovering whether they should pursue a teaching career. In her final paper, Julie explained that she had registered for the course because she was entertaining the idea of studying history in graduate school and pursuing a career in university teaching. Several others of our students have since pursued teaching-related jobs. Rachel is now teaching in private schools. Amy completed a master's degree in education. Susan participated in a government internship in Washington, D.C., which dealt in part with education.

The course also encouraged some students to devote more time to history study and research. Maria changed her major from biology to history. Two students, Fereschteh and Jeremy, have gone on to PhD programs at the University of London. Not only did students receive valuable teaching experience through HIS 204, but they also were able to test their interests and talents and buttress their self-esteem by performing well under intense, unfamiliar, and sometimes trying circumstances.

While much skepticism has surrounded this course and others like it, the final papers of our undergraduates testified to the fact that academically based community service can be academically sound. Because of the relatively small size of the course, we were able to provide students with a great deal of individual attention, something very necessary in a project of this nature. Students learned to utilize a wide array of sources and resources — archival documents, maps, oral interviews, ethnographic techniques, the built environment, videos, etc. — and to make this research knowledge active by translating it into their teaching. They took their students on several field trips to various libraries and institutes, including Van Pelt (Penn's main library), the Free Library, the University of Pennsylvania archives, Temple's Urban Archive collection, the Afro-American Museum, and the Historical Society of Pennsylvania. The rich texture of most of the final papers reflected this dynamic interplay among teaching, the use of many different sources, and the research process.

For example, Fereschteh commented that because she was herself Muslim, she "had a preconception that it would be relatively easy for [her] to access the community." It soon became clear to her that this was not the case.

This important understanding developed especially during our informal discussions with the high school students. I believe that this healthy dialogue presented me with issues which would arise in my exchanges with community members. For example, the students brought to life for me experiences that African-American Muslims must face in this urban environment. Specifically, the legitimate concern for security and protection within the community especially struck me. I was at first alarmed by how a local mosque . . . has informal security guards to protect the building and the community. . . . This lesson was valuable for me to understand because I learned to contextualize my observations rather than concentrate my energies on my alarmed reactions. Certainly this lesson did not prevent me from marveling at interesting innovations, like soul food halal restaurants!

In her case, the research and teaching processes could not easily be separated.

Because the history that students were reconstructing had an immediate relevance, they were exposed to the importance of the past to the present and to the demanding problematics of historical analysis. For example, Maria, who had become enamored by historical method, wrote the following about her research on the history of Clark Park:

> Research . . . has been my primary area of concern. While the amount of resources in Philadelphia was abundant, and the documents are well-kept, there were some difficulties. I was working almost exclusively with primary documents, some dating all the way back to the 1700s. This was fascinating and, more important, gave me the opportunity both to get information firsthand and also to get all the information, some of which may have been omitted in other sources. Still, there were inconsistencies among sources, illegible dates and handwriting, and also names and landmarks cited that are no longer existent. . . . When it has been relevant to the information I have presented in the paper, I have noted whether the fact is under contention, possibly wrong, or even just a guess.

She likened her research to a billiard ball: "By this I mean that my research flowed in a way similar to a billiard ball being hit in various directions. Once the ball rolls to a stop it is hit again, often in quite a different angle. . . . I moved according to where and how each set of resources or documents pushed me."

Her paper was a fine example of the pedagogical value of such an approach to history: She included a wide variety of sources, analyzed all critically at the level of her narrative, and was still able to tell a story. She was also prompted to think about the meaning of history and historical truth. This latter discovery was very much the product of the presentist context in which Maria, like all the other students, worked. She had collected oral narratives as well as local histories written by the neighborhood association, and had to weigh these against the documentary record.

Civic Strengths

Maria concluded her paper by discussing the interplay between teaching and research as she had experienced it.

> In regard to the kids, I learned many personal lessons through my interactions with them. At Penn, it is very easy to become accustomed to working with people in your same age group, at your same educational level, and often from the same socioeconomic background. However, these kids took

me out of that world quickly. I do not want this to sound like a charity case where I came from the almighty Penn and went to this school for the outcasts from Penn's exclusive world. This was not the case at all. In fact, it was a pleasure and quite enjoyable not because I felt good about myself for doing good deeds, but because I really enjoyed the company of the kids and learned a lot from them. As I have stated, they knew much more about the park than I did, than most people do, in the beginning. And their enthusiasm is something I have not seen in a long time.

This sentiment of community building was described more explicitly by Rachel, who worked at West Philadelphia High School:

I have lived in West Philadelphia for over three years now, but until recently, I never considered myself as a member of this community. Instead, for my first three years here I viewed myself as a privileged visitor to this area, and limited myself to the urban utopia confined within the boundaries of [Penn's] campus. Before taking this class, I had never ventured beyond 44th Street. More important, I never appreciated the area in which I now live the majority of the year, or the local people who are now my neighbors. Through working with the students, I learned a lot about my surroundings, but also about the people who live here. . . . Through working with the students at West Philadelphia High School, the students and I were able to learn about local history and American Bandstand while also learning about one another.

This undergraduate and her coteacher, Leslie, became involved in one of the most interesting teacher-student dynamics in the project. They had arrived at WPHS ready to discuss American Bandstand's unwritten policy of discrimination, and were surprised when the high school students responded with reticence, with one student announcing: "We're so sick of talking about racism. That's all people want to talk to us about. Can't we just talk about the dancing?" Eventually the two Penn undergraduates and the high school students were talking about racism as well as dance styles.

The breakthrough came, as both Rachel and Leslie have written, when they showed a video to the high school students in which two white Bandstand regulars admitted that they had learned their dances from black neighbors but were not permitted to say so on the show. After hearing this, the high school students began showing an interest in discussing discrimination, a change that Rachel attributed to the neutrality of the video in comparison with the power struggle that had arisen between the Penn teachers and the WPHS students. After the video, a wonderful trust developed between the Penn teachers and their students; one student even sang for them, and another told Rachel: "I had a really good time today. Bandstand is really cool." Rachel commented, "For the first time, I felt we were reaching the students on both the academic and the personal level."

All but one of the student papers reflected these sentiments. Undergraduates forged real bonds with their students, became deeply involved in the troubles, the prospects, and the fate of the public schools, and began to craft informed opinions about what they could do as individual adults, and what should be done on a larger societal level. Although we did not emphasize this in class, many of the students were more than willing to talk about what they had learned about themselves through their participation in HIS 204 and about how their impressions of the "inner city" had changed throughout the semester. When one high school student was shot (not fatally) in the West Philadelphia High School cafeteria in January 1996, several of our Penn students expressed concern and commented that after their positive experiences, such an occurrence was almost "unimaginable" to them. They spent one semester in a very troubled school in Philadelphia and came out not only feeling comfortable and secure there but also with real links to the community and with insights into the positive aspects of their students' lives.

Of course, they also gained personal knowledge of the struggles of the high school students they worked with. Amy discussed a few of these in her paper.

> I learned a lot from this experience at West Philadelphia High School. So many times it was hard to really grasp what the students were learning from me, but from their papers, which I made an extra effort to read, I had glimpses of the little things that I may have said or showed to them in class. . . . One of the students, Tamara, is a member of Hickman Temple and in her paper she shared what the church meant to her. Although she downplays the church's involvement in her life around the other students, I really could tell the church was special to her. She wrote about a particularly difficult time in her life in her paper. She had twin boys, and one of the boys became sick and later died. She wrote about how the church and the minister had always been there for her when her son was hospitalized and later when he died. I was really touched and surprised by this, too. I realized at that point just how much some of these students have been through and are currently going through, though most have smiles on their faces everyday and are always cheerful.

Commenting on what she would like to do in the future, Shawn presented her project, the Harlem Renaissance in West Philadelphia, and her experience with Shaw students as an organic whole. She suggested that knowledge about the past could serve to solve some of the problems of the present she had witnessed:

> While writing this paper, at the close of this program for the semester, I am

aware of what I would like to accomplish through continuing it. I would like to help combat these problems [and] seek a cultural rebirth as a solution. . . . I think that if I can revive the accomplishments of black Philadelphians in the minds of the city's youth . . . I can generate some interest in changing the patterns of the past. I can help them to recognize that understanding their history — in particular, the Harlem Renaissance and how it affected Philadelphians — gives them the potential to change whatever they want. A large-scale revival on my part is impossible, but a small one is not.

This concept, that local history can help young people think productively and creatively about their present and future, and about the present and future of their communities, brings to mind Frank's evaluation of the Free School. He saw in the Free School a potential solution to some of today's problems in urban education. With some nurturing, we believe, Frank's nascent interest could turn into a lifelong involvement in the improvement of Philadelphia's public school system.

These selections from Penn student papers demonstrate best the ways in which community service and academic pursuits can *amplify* each other, at both the high school and the college levels. Shawn, for example, came to appreciate the academic potential of academically based community service so much that she would have liked to require her middle schoolers to conduct community service work as part of their participation in the project.

Weaknesses

As many of our undergraduates pointed out, the great weakness of this course was structural. Since most problems could not have been anticipated, or could be solved only as they arose, this led to some confusion. We identified three major areas in the course that needed revising in its future iterations: time, logistics, and organization. In 1996-97, some of the changes we outlined were instituted, whereas other new problems were brought to the fore.

Time: In the one-semester format of the course many undergraduates did not feel they had enough time to research their local history topics adequately to teach the topics to high school students. They were researching and teaching in tandem, sometimes to the extent that they felt they were learning at the same pace as their students. They also expressed an interest in improving the high school students' writing skills, but felt they did not have the time to do this and simultaneously teach local history and historical research methods. Nor did they feel competent to teach writing skills to high school students. (Responding to this voiced concern, we engaged the

English Department's Writing Across the University program for a "one-shot" seminar on teaching writing — an expedient that was woefully inadequate given the literacy deficits of many of the high school students.)

Logistics: The five undergraduates teaching at Shaw noted that they often felt left out of the dynamic established among the majority of students, who taught at WPHS. In addition, they were critical of the fact that they were not allowed to work with an entire class, but only with students selected from a class by their teacher. All the Penn students, regardless of their school site or project, had difficulty with course logistics on various levels. For example, we lacked a central depository for such (limited) essentials as cameras, tape recorders, videotapes, film, cassettes, etc. — and we had to jerry-rig a supply service, often hand-delivering the requested item at the last minute to the Penn student or project site.

Other general issues included the undergraduates' occasional failure to inform us about planned or unplanned absences, including absences at the high school, and an unpredictable and utterly confusing high school schedule (four separate bell schedules, any one of which could be in operation on a given day depending on the school-wide events scheduled). Furthermore, we were unsuccessful in getting our students to use the course listserv to share ideas, questions, and difficulties. Indeed, we were not able to get them to self-reflect until their final projects. Toward the end of the semester, when the seminar met informally to discuss students' progress, attendance was spotty.

We suspect that these logistical problems were, in no casual way, linked to the time problem of the course. Quite simply, our students were being pressed in several different directions, not the least of which was the requirement that they complete a final (academic) paper for the course. In the end, that project became their overriding priority.

Organization: Undergraduates were frustrated that their projects were not part of the regular curriculum, either at the high school or the middle school. They also complained that because of this, they had no authority to assign homework and almost no means of tempting their students to complete assigned work. Put another way, they were dependent on their own personal resources to persuade their students to work on the projects outside of class. In most cases, their strategies failed to elicit this additional level of participation.

Year Two

In the course's second year, 1996-97, while Puckett was on a Fulbright fellowship in Germany, Forgey instituted some of the changes that had suggested themselves after its first run. Most important, HIS 204 became a year-long course, organized at a single school site. Participation over two semesters was not required, but strongly encouraged, and exactly half of the fall students re-enrolled in the spring. (Of the others, one left the university due to personal problems, and two had to take other courses to satisfy curricular requirements.) The Penn students spent the fall researching their local history projects, devising syllabi for the spring, and collecting teaching materials. On site at West Philadelphia High School, they worked on writing assignments and began to flesh out local history project proposals with their students. In the spring, the undergraduates read heavily in African-American and urban history, with a special emphasis on trends in Philadelphia.

Difficulty in accommodating one-semester students produced new problems. For those enrolled only in the fall seminar, the course, which emphasized preparation for the spring semester, lacked an end point; for those who joined in the spring semester, the course reproduced the time crunch of the first year: Students were researching, learning, and teaching all at once.

However, the benefits of a year-long course to the high school students were clear. They began to see the projects as part of their regular high school curriculum and the Penn students as an aspect of their schooling. (Time and again, West students voiced their resentments at the fly-by-night involvement of many well-intentioned volunteers whose inconsistent or short-lived projects led to feelings of abandonment.) Thus, by the spring semester when they realized that their team leaders were in the fray for the duration of the year, West students developed much deeper relationships with their mentors. There was, however, some difficulty for those teams whose Penn mentors had left after the fall semester. They complained about being short-shrifted. In an effort to mediate this admittedly unfair situation, Forgey and Devine gave them the option of joining other groups *or* starting an entirely new project with one of the new Penn students.

The year-long format also afforded more time to take West Philadelphia students on field trips. Class trips were organized to Temple's Urban Archives, the African American Cultural and Historical Museum, and the University of Pennsylvania. This gave Penn students an opportunity to emphasize aspects of their work that fell outside of their history projects but were intimately related to the objectives of the course itself: college preparation, mentoring, and nonacademic activities, such as meeting their West Philadelphia students for pizza. The latter appreciated this, and many cited the field trips as the best part of the project.

For those Penn students who could commit to a full year, the course offered a better opportunity to pursue creative projects that employed multimedia in presenting historical research. One group, which was studying the arts in African-American Philadelphia, did complete a student-designed mural in the high school building with the help of Philadelphia's Mural Arts

Program. Still, the undergraduates' ability to execute projects with their students was constrained in part by time and in part by a dearth of resources combined with logistical hurdles. West Philadelphia students expressed again and again their interest in video and drama, and were frustrated that these things were not possible within the course as it existed. Penn students often talked about the pedagogical potential of a multimedia project that would engage many different layers of their students' intellects and section their projects off from the daily life of school. They themselves were eager to explore creatively new ways of doing history. Multimedia projects would also lend themselves to the production of truly public history, and this public role would help both undergraduates and high school students see themselves as useful and talented contributors to their communities.[1]

Suggestions for Future History Courses

Our experience in HIS 204 teaches us that academically based community service courses in history are best conceived and organized as full-year courses — problems of continuity created by undergraduates leaving and entering the course notwithstanding. We also think that the most effective structure is to locate all the project work in a single high school and to have one overarching thematic focus, for example, the Underground Railroad and African-American labor history. This thematic focus must, however, be decided jointly and consensually by the undergraduates and the high school students. We further recommend using the fall part of the course to have the undergraduates (1) read in the chosen historical theme (with a parallel line of reading for the high school students), (2) get to know the high school, (3) plan the project work with the high school students, and (4) receive training in writing instruction. The spring semester would then be devoted to project implementation and further reading in the chosen theme.

Conclusion

In this chapter, we have argued that adding public dimensions to an undergraduate history course can strengthen the civic learning of students without sacrificing academic quality. Indeed, in light of the (in most cases) highly original academic papers developed by our students in HIS 204, we would argue — and we trust we have effectively illustrated this point — that our approach has strengthened the academic learning of Penn undergraduates.

We are very much concerned about the context in which academic learning takes place. Stated more precisely, we are concerned that at some point there be a nexus in each undergraduate's university education between the academic program and social activism. In his 1749 "Proposals Relating to the Education of Youth in Pennsylvania," Benjamin Franklin, founder of the University of Pennsylvania, wrote that the "great *Aim* and *End*" of education is to cultivate in youth an "an *Inclination* join'd with an *Ability* to serve mankind, one's Country, Friends and Family" (Smyth 1907: 396). Updated in our own "Neo-Franklinean" terms, the great aim and end is not only to cultivate knowledgeable, civic-minded citizens who have an ability to positively shape America's future but also to advance constructive social change in the here and now.

This agenda requires college and university professors to recognize the larger potential and meaning of their scholarly activity. Our own work over a span of several semesters has acted on this proposition in that we have tried to link the academic and civic learning of undergraduate history students to a larger agenda of academically based community service and support for a broadly based school and neighborhood improvement project in the university's proximate geographic community. Recalling Boyte and Kari (1996), we would argue, finally, that our approach helps transform undergraduate history, not only by treating students as *producers* rather than consumers of knowledge, but also by providing venues wherein knowledge production serves immediate public needs and purposes.

Note

1. Many other collaborations, specifically with arts-related organizations and agencies, are possible, and the course could serve as a strong catalyst for forging relationships between nonprofits, city agencies, and Philadelphia public school classrooms. Students could write and perform plays inspired by their historical research; they could make videos to be presented to the community; they could desktop-publish photo essays and display their photos at local galleries; and they could desktop anthologies of community lore and history. University resources would need to be devoted to developing these relationships and supporting students' projects, but the benefits gained, we imagine, would be substantial.

Theater Arts 250, an academically based community service course taught by William Yallowitz in spring 1998, illustrates the potential of such activity. In that course undergraduates have collaborated with University City High School (West Philadelphia) students and members of the Black Bottom Association to create the Black Bottom Performance Project. The Black Bottom was a poor but vital African-American neighborhood in the 1940s and 1950s — a neighborhood whose residents were displaced by institutional development, including Penn's, in the 1960s. The theater project engaged Penn students in several sets of activities: studying and applying the theory of community theater; conducting oral history research on the Black Bottom; helping to teach acting skills, oral history interviewing, and history through the performing arts to high school students; and writing the script for "Black Bottom Sketches," a musical play based on oral history interviews and performed by a cast of nearly 30 people, including University City High School students, Penn undergraduates, and community members of the Black Bottom Association.

References

Bok, Derek. (1990). *Universities and the Future of America.* Durham, NC: Duke University Press.

Boyer, Ernest L. (March 9, 1994). "Creating the New American College." *The Chronicle of Higher Education,* p. A48.

Boyte, Harry C., and Nancy N. Kari. (1996). *Building America: The Democratic Promise of Public Work.* Philadelphia, PA: Temple University Press.

Deegan, Mary Jo. (1988). *Jane Addams and the Men of the Chicago School, 1892-1918.* New Brunswick, NJ: Transaction Press.

Harkavy, Ira. (1991a). "The Role of Mediating Structures in University and Community Revitalization: The University of Pennsylvania and West Philadelphia as a Case Study." *Journal of Research and Development in Education* 25(1): 10-23.

———— . (1991b). "Toward Effective University-Public School Partnerships: An Analysis of a Contemporary Model." *Teachers College Record* 92(4): 556-581.

———— . (1996). "Back to the Future: From Service-Learning to Strategic Academically-Based Community Service." *Metropolitan Universities* 7(1): 57-70.

———— , and John L. Puckett. (1994). "Lessons From Hull House for the Contemporary Urban University." *Social Service Review* 68(3): 299-321.

Nightingale, Carl M. (1993). *On the Edge. A History of Poor African-American Children and Their American Dreams.* New York, NY: Basic Books.

Sass, Steven A. (1982). *The Pragmatic Imagination: A History of the Wharton School, 1881-1981.* Philadelphia, PA: University of Pennsylvania Press.

Smith, Albert H., ed. (1907). *The Writings of Benjamin Franklin, Vol. 2.* New York, NY: Macmillan.

Tanner, Laurel N. (1991). "The Meaning of Curriculum in Dewey's Laboratory School (1896-1904)." *Journal of Curriculum Studies* 23(2): 101-117.

Yow, Valerie R. (1994). *Recording Oral History: A Practical Guide for Social Scientists.* Thousand Oaks, CA: Sage.

History 204
"Teaching American History: A West Philadelphia Workshop"

305 Williams Hall
Monday 2-5
Fall Semester 1995

Professor
John Puckett
Associate Professor, Graduate School of Education, C-19, tel: 898-7389; e-mail: johnp@nwfs.gse.upenn.edu. Office hours: M, 12-2; T, 3-4:30; and by appointment

Graduate Assistant
Elisa Forgey, Department of History; Assistant Director, West Philadelphia Bibliography and Information System; e-mail: jvon@sas.upenn.edu

The purpose of this experimental course is threefold. First, it will introduce Penn undergraduates to the history and social structure of West Philadelphia from 1854 to the present, with particular attention to the experience of African Americans in West Philadelphia. This course is an integral part of the Center for Community Partnerships' Program in West Philadelphia Information Systems, Data, and Bibliography. Papers authored by undergraduates in HIS 204 will be catalogued in this new program's repository and made available to the general public as well as to other researchers.

Second, this course will introduce participants to the uses of local history; the methods, skills, and techniques for doing local history; and the sources and resources of local history, with particular attention to West Philadelphia. Students will learn about the richness and diversity of interesting, significant, researchable local history topics in West Philadelphia; they will acquaint themselves with city libraries and repositories for the study of West Philadelphia history, for example, the Free Library, Van Pelt Library, Temple Urban Archives, Afro-American Museum, and Pennsylvania Historical Society. Each student will develop an original paper on a local history topic. Weekly class meetings will be used, in part, for discussion of mutual interests, issues, and concerns raised by these research papers.

Third, this course will engage Penn undergraduates as mentors to students at West Philadelphia High School. This component of the course will be conducted in conjunction with the West Philadelphia Improvement Corps (WEPIC) and the Center for Community Partnerships. The Penn students will work with teams of high school students in two social studies classes to develop local history projects that will lead, on the high school side, to student and community publications; and contribute, on the university side, to the development of HIS 204 papers and the West Philadelphia Bibliography and Information System. As an orientation, participants will learn about the multiple contexts of academically based community service in West Philadelphia: history of university-community relations, origins and growth of the West Philadelphia Improvement Corps (WEPIC); history, contexts, and social forces of West Philadelphia High School. Itself a "neo-Deweyan" approach, the course will also introduce students to the general principles of Deweyan pedagogy—a philosophy and progressive teaching strategy that underlies WEPIC project work.

Part I: Orientation

September 11   Course Overview: Review of Syllabus, Course Readings, Project Work, etc. Presentation on West Philadelphia Improvement Corps (WEPIC) as Context for Course.

September 18   Introduction to Philadelphia and West Philadelphia, Part I: Social Forces and Contexts; History of University of Pennsylvania in West Philadelphia

Readings: Nightingale, *On the Edge*, pp. 1-75; *Bessin, "Modern Urban University"; *Tanner, "Meaning of Curriculum in Dewey's Laboratory School"

September 25   Introduction to Philadelphia and West Philadelphia, Part II: Social Forces and Contexts

Readings: Nightingale, *On the Edge*, pp. 79-165; *Halpern, "Children on the Edge: An Essay Review"; *Cohen, "The Last Boy Scout"; *Novek, "Buried Treasure"

Week of September 25: Meeting at West Philadelphia High School. Larry Devine, chair of the social studies department, will provide an orientation and tour of the high school; Kenny Johnson, the high school's roster chair, will review the history of West Philadelphia High School; Linda Hansell, director of the PARTNERS program, will discuss mentoring in West Philadelphia.

October 2   Introduction to Local History

Meeting at West Philadelphia High School with teachers and former students from LaSalle High School, site of local history projects—what works, what doesn't work, etc.

Readings: *Metcalf & Downey, *Using Local History in the Classroom*, pp. 1-126

Note:
Larry Devine, John Puckett, and Elisa Forgey will provide a separate orientation for students at West Philadelphia High School.

Part II:
Local History Projects in West Philadelphia:
Getting Started

October 9   Doing Oral History

Presentation by Elisa Forgey

Readings: Yow, *Recording Oral History*, chap. 1, pp. 1-31; chap. 2, pp. 32-54; chap. 3, pp. 55-83; chap. 6, pp. 143-166; chap. 9, pp. 220-244; *Portelli, "Death of Luigi Trastulli"; *Palmer et al., "'I Haven't Anything to Say': Reflections of Self and Community in Collecting Oral Histories"

Week of October 9: Meeting with social studies classes at West Philadelphia High School; Lee Cassanelli and Elisa Forgey conduct "demonstration" oral history (life history) interview with West Philadelphia High School students

October 16   Fall Break: No Class Meeting

                              Week of October 16: Each Penn student will conduct a peer interview with a
                              partner from HIS 204; read Yow, *Recording Oral History*, chap. 5, pp. 116-142;
                              and write a two-page response paper on how the context of the interview
                              influences the nature and tenor of the information received. Assisted by Elisa
                              Forgey, high school students will conduct their own life history interview with a
                              West Philadelphia community member. Penn students will meet with teams of
                              high school students to find common research interests and to define local history
                              project.

Part III:
Local History Projects in West Philadelphia:
Research and Writing

October 23   Final Topic Selection. Discussion of Peer Interviews and Response Papers.

                              Readings: Oral presentations on specialty books published by American
                              Association for State and Local History. You will choose one of the following
                              AASLH books for an individual or team presentation to the class:

                              Local Schools
                              Houses and Homes
                              Public Places
                              Places of Worship
                              Local Businesses
                              Transcribing and Editing Oral History
                              Artifacts and the American Past
                              Local Government Records

                              John Puckett will order selected books through the Pennsylvania Book Center. At
                              this class meeting, students will introduce their proposed project work to their
                              peers for comments and suggestions.

                              Week of October 23: Penn students will meet and make arrangements with their
                              research teams at the high school to begin collection of local history materials.

October 30-November 27   Informal Weekly Class Meetings (Proseminar): Discussion of Issues and
                              Concerns, Assistance with Research and Writing

                              Week of October 30 to Week of November 27: Penn students will meet at least
                              once weekly with their teams at West Philadelphia High School to collect local
                              history materials related to the various projects. Larry Devine, John Puckett, Elisa
                              Forgey, and Cory Bowman (WEPIC) will assist with logistical arrangements for
                              the projects as needs arise.

December 4   Class Meeting: Debriefing

December 11   Course Papers Due

Course Requirements

The major requirement is a 20-30 page paper (journal article length) on a topic of local history, to be conducted in conjunction with students at West Philadelphia High School. For notes and bibliography, use the format of the *Chicago Manual of Style* or Turabian's *Manual for Writers*—latest edition for both. This paper is to be printed or typed double-spaced. Include a title page, with your name, course number, and date on it; and paginate the paper after p. 1. Use regular typing or computer paper; do not use erasable bond or linen paper.

Course grades will be determined as follows: Course paper (60 percent); class participation, including discussion of readings (20 percent); high school participation and mentoring (20 percent).

Required Texts

(Books are available at the Pennsylvania Book Center, 3726 Walnut Street)

> Carl Nightingale, *On the Edge*

> Valerie Yow, *Recording Oral History*

> Book selection from list provided by American Association of State and Local History

> Bulk Pack Readings (Available at Campus Copy Center, 3907 Walnut Street)

Reclaiming the Historical Tradition of Service in the African-American Community

by Beverly W. Jones

As a 20-year service-learning practitioner, I have noticed limited engagement of African Americans in the discourse on community service and service-learning at conferences and in the research and publication arena. Is this limited interest due to the fact that there is a dissonance in understanding service-learning's relevance to rebuilding inner cities? Is a Moynihan-like belief in neglect (U.S. Dept. of Labor 1965) outweighing the assets of the African-American community as the preferred strategy for creating viable, sustainable, and nurturing environments? Or is the fact that the history of communalism and benevolence once a part of African-American life and history has not been utilized as a bridge to understanding the theory of service and creating healthy communities, a civil society? What does it take to create from neighborhood groups confident leaders who can come to the table ready to tackle the serious problems we face? The questions posed above lead back to a need to reclaim the historical connections of communalism brought by Africans to America as the framework of African-American involvement in the service movement.

History 4050: Seminar in African-American History

History 4050 is a service-learning course taught to North Carolina Central University (NCCU) upper-level juniors and seniors. The course has five goals:

1. Link the African-American historical tradition of communalism to social enterprise through service;

2. Document the role of NCCU in community rebuilding;

3. Define civil renewal and trace its development in Durham, North Carolina;

4. Provide students with an understanding of the life and culture of one African-American community before they engage in service experiences;

5. Provide students with an opportunity to practice civic arts as they search for civic values to support and strengthen community efforts.

Communalism: A Code Word for Service

The first part of the course provides students with the theory necessary to understanding service as a form of community building. Joseph's *Remaking America: How the Benevolent Traditions of Many Cultures Are*

Transforming Our National Life is the required reading for this section of the course. (See the syllabus at the end of the chapter for the course's reading list.) According to Joseph, African-American notions of community service are rooted in a traditional African legacy of connectiveness and intergenerational obligation. African metaphysics emphasized three basic aspects of humanity. The first was the idea that individuals and communities have the capacity to celebrate life, even in despairing situations. The second was that individuals in communities are visionaries who have the creative power to manifest their visions. The third idea was that the individual's identity is communal. The individual operates in a network that provides economic, religious, and political functions. African mutual aid societies, for example, traditionally stressed instruction and provided financial aid for the burial expenses of their members. Such connectiveness defines a civil society where the quality of life for one concerns all members of the community. The communalism of Africans created civilities of respect, trust, and mutual interest and support. Enslaved Africans brought this communal orientation with them to the Americas as they were dispersed in the diaspora, and the tendency to form voluntary, benevolent organizations not only survived the slavery experience, but was significantly shaped by it.

African Americans in the slave community viewed themselves as a familial group with a common life-style and interests. This group might include community leaders, conjurers, preachers, and peer group members. These individuals felt a responsibility to nurture, protect, and educate the younger members in the family. Younger slaves exhibited a respect for their elders and often cared for those members too old to care for themselves. In addition, slave communities protected and fed runaway slaves. Many slave narratives and interviews with former slaves exemplify this communal attitude.

A cooperative slave community allowed African Americans to survive the harsh conditions of slavery. Recognizing that their fates were connected, many slaves pooled their meager resources to benefit the entire community. Slaves built houses; sewed; wove baskets; and washed for one another. In some instances they shared food from their garden patch, if they were fortunate enough to have one. In addition, slave communities protected individual members from harsh conditions and abuse at the hands of the master.

Outside the slave community, benevolence expressed itself in the creation of mutual aid societies, fraternal organizations, and churches. These institutions often operated like the extended family network in the slave quarters. Black benevolence groups provided financial resources among free blacks and helped to ease the transition from slavery to freedom. The earliest, formed in 1787, aided in the development of the black church. Throughout the African-American experience, the church has been instrumental in the struggle for black liberation and citizenship. Early black churches served as stations along the underground railroad and provided food, clothing, and shelter for many of the runaways escaping the bonds of slavery.

Churches were also centers for education and recreation. The first historically black colleges and schools were associated with black churches that often provided them with financial and human resources. In 1865, the American Missionary Association (AMA) founded Atlanta University, and the American Baptist Home Mission Society helped establish Virginia Union University and Shaw University. The Methodist Episcopal Church founded what later became known as Morgan State University, and the AMA founded Fisk University in 1866. A year later, the AMA founded Emerson and Talladega colleges and the American Baptist Home Mission Society founded Morehouse.

In the late 1800s, institutions such as North Carolina Central University worked assiduously to rebuild civil communities, promoting self-help efforts at community reform, organizing nursery schools, calling attention to education disparities, and linking the community to the university. During the 1950s and 1960s, the legacy of such efforts was thousands of local grass-roots organizations that raised money, collected and distributed food, and recruited volunteers to participate in demonstrations and boycotts. At the same time, black churches often served as centers for mobilization. During this push for social justice, the black community looked within, as it had during slavery and its first years of freedom. However, as urban communities were plagued by seamless poverty, epidemic crime, and physical deterioration during the 1970s and 1980s, such concerted efforts at rebuilding were lacking. Hence the central importance of higher education institutions engaging in collaborative partnerships with local community groups to seek a regeneration of the spirit of communalism and the social enterprise ethics of the African and African-American traditions.

Reclaiming the Service Mission of North Carolina Central University

In this part of the course the required readings include W.E.B. DuBois's *The Souls of Black Folk*, which explains the importance of historically black institutions in the development of black leadership, and this author's own "Rediscovering Our Heritage: Community Service and the Historically Black University," an article that discusses the development of the Community Service Program at one historically black institution, North Carolina Central University.

Over the past decade, NCCU has repositioned itself to take a leading role in rebuilding African-American civil society. Like most historically black institutions, it was founded in order to "seek the regeneration of the Negro," as outlined by DuBois. In 1910, James E. Shepard founded NCCU to develop in "young men and women the character and sound academic training requisite for real service to the nation." Service, in this context, could be considered a code word for community-based work and community-civil regeneration.

NCCU is geographically surrounded by communities with deteriorating physical structures but viable social and culture institutions. The university has repositioned itself to partner with these communities to improve their quality of life and create means of capacity building. This dramatic repositioning began in 1993 with the appointment of Julius Chambers as chancellor. Chambers, who left the position of executive director of the NAACP Legal Defense Fund, brought to NCCU a vision of service and self-help. He revised the mission of the university to promote "the consciousness of social responsibility and dedication to the general welfare of the people of the State of North Carolina, the United States, and the world." The new mission further states that the university recognizes the mutually reinforcing impact of scholarship and service on effective teaching by expecting "faculty and students to engage in scholarly and creative as well as service activities that benefit the larger community." This mission reflects John Dewey's belief that educational institutions should focus on "developing the social intelligence of their students through service" (1898: 17).

From Theory to Practice: Key Component of Civil Society Development

The required readings for this section are Medoff and Sklar's *Streets of Hope: The Fall and Rise of an Urban Neighborhood;* Hoopes's *Oral History: An Introduction for Students;* and McKnight and Kretzmann's "The Problem: Devastated Communities." Medoff and Sklar's work creates an opportunity for students to examine Boston's Dudley Street Neighborhood Initiative and compare it with the North East Central Durham initiative. Hoopes's book provides the framework and tools for conducting oral histories, the final essential element of the course. Students conduct 20 interviews of residents, local and county government officials, community agencies, businesses, and NCCU faculty, all of whom have played an intimate role in the community-rebuilding efforts of North East Central Durham. From their interviews and their reading of McKnight and Kretzmann, they delineate the key components needed for community revitalization:

- creation of a beneficial partnership (university and the community);
- community assets mapping;
- responsiveness to needs articulated by the community;
- multiple agency support;
- a single-issue focus (e.g., lead poisoning);
- community capacity building (community ownership of project).

Community Rebuilding in North East Central Durham (NECD)

For the fourth and final class-based part of the course, students also read Morse's "Five Building Blocks for Successful Communities" and Roseland's "Mobilizing Citizens and Their Government." Both works prepare students to understand the NECD community.

In 1993, in response to the City of Durham's Partnership Against Crime efforts, NCCU joined city and county government, businesses, postsecondary institutions, and community residents for the purpose of revitalizing and reclaiming a community in the most drug-infested, deteriorating area of Durham — North East Central. A steering committee representative of this coalition developed five task forces focusing on: (1) family and child support, (2) economic development, (3) religion, (4) youth, and (5) health. Members of each task force included the same mix of university, community, and government representatives.

An assets and needs survey was then conducted by the Institute for the Study of Minority Issues at NCCU. The survey indicated strong economic interest on the part of operating businesses, economic investment potential among black churches, and three public schools with quality programs that could be leveraged for further development. A complementary needs survey identified four primary community concerns: (1) reducing crime, (2) creating jobs, (3) developing health maintenance programs, and (4) encouraging children to stay in school.

Though North East Central Durham is located eight miles from the university, NCCU responded to the community's requests through research projects, student tutors and mentors, grant writing, and curricula restructuring. Each activity and funding proposal was approved by the steering committee. To date, the most promising results of this effort have come from the task force on family and child support and the heath maintenance task force. Though numerous meetings were necessary to solidify trust between partners, faculty from the Human Sciences Department have now successfully fostered the concept of "community rebuilding" by assisting the community in the development of a Family Resource Center. At the same time, one elementary school in the community is receiving support from NCCU's School of Education to improve the curriculum and training techniques of teachers. Finally, the Health Education and Biology Department are partnering with NECD in a health maintenance initiative designed to address a major environmental injustice; namely, infant and early childhood lead poisoning — a problem found often in inner cities throughout America. Two courses in Health Education and Biology have incorporated service-learning components of lead poisoning in their curricula.

Other service-learning activities have also helped to transform North East Central Durham. In the Health Education 4200 class, Aging and the

Aged: Health Perspectives, students have produced taped interviews as part of their required home visits to the elderly. In addition, students make a minimum of five visits to nursing homes where they do whatever they can to assist the staff and patients. Many of the students have continued the relationships with the elderly beyond the end of the class.

Conclusion

Comments from student journals indicate their understanding that the service proclivities of African Americans are rooted in African culture. The communalism that characterized the African experience was reborn through African-American community renewal, resulting in viable, safe, and caring communities. Students also realize that understanding the history and culture of a community helps them to appreciate better the ethos of service. Only by understanding a people's history can one learn to build on its assets.

References

Dewey, John. (1898). *Developing the Social Intelligence of Their Students*. Carbondale, IL: Southern Illinois Press.

U.S. Department of Labor. (1965). "The Negro Family: The Case for National Action" (The Moynihan Report). Washington, DC: Greenwood Publishing Co.

History 4050
Seminar in African American History
Dr. Beverly W. Jones

SYLLABUS

This service-learning course will probe the historical meaning of service in the lives of African Americans- from the communalism of Africans to community renewal in the 1980s and 1990s. Our goal is to isolate those variables that enable communities to nurture, empower, and develop a society for the common good. It is hoped that students will be better prepared to work collaboratively with communities once they have understood their history and assets.

The history of North Carolina Central University provides a case study of the role of higher education in community building and civil society renewal. Students will utilize oral history as a way of interpreting community development and civil renewal.

Learning Objectives

Students will be able to

1. Connect the service proclivity of African Americans to their African traditions.
2. Understand the role of HBCUs (Historically Black Institutions in community and civil society renewal.
3. Connecting the service mission of North Carolina Central University to their involvement in service
4. Explore two community development initiatives as examples of civil renewal.
5. Understanding the history and culture of the Durham community as an essential framework before
6. student service involvement

Required Readings

- W. E. B. DuBois, Souls of Black Folk (Illinois: University of Chicago Press, 1903).
- John Hope Franklin, From Slavery To Freedom (New York: Alfred A. Knopf, 1974).
- John Henton, John Melville, and Kimberly Walesh, Grassroot Leaders for a New Economy: How Civic Entrepreneurs Are Building Prosperous Communities (San Francisco: Jossey-Bass Publishers, 1997).
- James Hoopes, Oral History: An Introduction for Students (North Carolina: University of North Carolina, 1979).
- James A. Joseph, Remaking America: How the Benevolent Traditions of Many Cultures Are Transforming Our National Life (San Francisco: Jossey-Bass, 1995).
- Beverly W. Jones, "Rediscovering Our Heritage: Community Service and the Historically Black University," in Successful Service-Learning Programs: New Models of Excellence in Higher Education, Edward Zlotkowski, ed. (Bolton, MA: Anker Publishing Company, 1998).
- John L. McKnight and John P. Kretzmann, "The Problem: Devastated Communities," in Building Communities From the Inside Out: A Push Toward Finding and Mobilizing Communities Assets (Evanston, IL: Center for Urban Affairs and Policy Research, 1993), 1-11.

- Peter Medoff and Holly Sklar, <u>Streets of Hope: The Fall and Rise of an Urban Neighborhood</u> (South End Press, 1994).
- Suzanne Morse, "Five Building Blocks for Successful Communities," in <u>The Community of the Future,</u> edited by Frances Hesselbein, et. al. (San Francisco: Jossey-Bass Publishers, 1998), 229-236.
- Mark Roseland, "Mobilizing Citizens and Their Government, in <u>Toward Sustainable Communities:</u> <u>Resources for Citizens and Their Governments</u> (Gabriola Island, BC: New Society Publishers, 1998), 181-197.

Grading

Journal	10%
Two Short Papers	25%
Oral Histories (Oral Presentation)	15%
Oral History (Written)	15%
Final Examination	35%

Grades

A	100-90
B	89-80
C	79-70

Journal

The purpose of keeping a journal is to provide a means for critical reflection on your experiences in the class and in your visits to North East Central Durham as an interviewer. Entries should be once a week. They may record questions, perceptions, feelings, and reflections. They may be hand written (legibly, leaving space for comment) and kept in a bound journal or notebook; typewritten and kept loose leaf notebook

Class Schedule

First Week
I.   Introduction, explanation, and expectations

Second Week
II.   Roots of Service in the African American Experience
     A.   African Tradition to Reconstruction
     B.   Jim Crow to Twentieth Century

     Reading: James A. Joseph. <u>Remaking America</u>
                  John Hope Franklin, <u>From Slavery to Freedom</u>

Third Week
III.   Service Role of Historically Black Institutions
     A.   Service Mission
     B.   Case Study: North Carolina Central University

                 1.   North East Central Durham
                 2.   Knolls Community Development
                 3.   Eagle Village

Readings: W.E.B. DuBois, The Souls of Black Folk
                Beverly W. Jones, "Rediscovering Our Heritage"
                Peter Medoff and Holly Sklar, Streets of Hope
                Douglas Henton et al., Grassroot Leaders for a New Economy

Fourth Week
IV.   Durham: In Perspective
        A.   "Durham Marches On" (filmstrip)
        B.   Panel: Durham Residents- Life in Durham

Fifth Week
V.   The Practice of Public Work
        Readings: John McKnight, Building Communities From Within
                      Suzanne Morse, "Five Building Blocks for Successful Communities"
                      Mark Roseland, "Mobilizing Citizens and Their Government"

Sixth-Seventh Weeks
VI.   Oral History: Theory to Practice
        A.   Definition
        B.   Tools
        C.   Developing Interview Questions
        D.   Mock Interviews
        E.   Assignments of Interviewees

Eighth - Eleventh Weeks
VII.   Oral Interviews
        Oral Presentation of One Interview

Twelfth Week
VIII.   Paper Presentations

Thirteenth Week - Final Examination

Service-Learning as a Tool of Engagement:
From Thomas Aquinas to Che Guevara

by Bill M. Donovan

As the essays in this volume indicate, historians who use service-learning do so with several goals in mind. Much of the attention given to service-learning has been directed at its wider implications, primarily in its potential to promote civic and community consciousness among a generation of young people who, investigators of social trends pronounce, are retreating from traditional forms of social engagement. In this essay I step back from that broader discussion to focus on service-learning in the classroom, specifically its value to enhance student understanding of historical issues and processes. In addition, I wish to address some of the pragmatic considerations involved for historians considering using service-learning in their own classrooms.

The following discussion is based on six years of experience in using service-learning in undergraduate courses ranging from freshman surveys to upper-division classes directed toward history majors. Service-learning is not a one-shoe-fits-all teaching strategy. Each course has presented specific opportunities and obstacles. Effective service-learning necessitates employing service exercises appropriate to a course's goals, assessment procedures, and the types of students being taught — freshman or upper-division, traditional or nontraditional.

Addressing Academic Reservations

Before describing specific courses, I want to address very briefly some misconceptions about service-learning, and then explain the motivations that led me to apply service-learning in my teaching. At first glance, service-learning might appear to provide few benefits for undergraduate history courses. Most historians already struggle to include the quantity of information that we consider necessary for our students to understand course material. Hence, the suggestion that we consider implementing another exercise in a time-constrained semester or quarter seems impractical at best. Furthermore, unlike our colleagues in political science or sociology, we mostly discuss individuals and members of groups who are dead, and often have been so for centuries. The social, political, intellectual, and physical environment in which they lived no longer exists in an obvious sense. How, consequently, is sending students to work in soup kitchens, hospices, or tutorial programs applicable to any courses other than perhaps contemporary history? To this question must be added other, more academically generic reservations. Does not service-learning compromise academic rigor by lowering intellectual content? Is service-learning essentially another fad, made additionally questionable by a coterie of political and social agendas?[1]

Let me begin with the simple fact that sending students to work outside classroom and university walls is neither new nor revolutionary. Experiential education in the form of student internships, for example, has long been a respected aspect of undergraduate education. The rise of public history and museum studies has accelerated the prevalence of internships in a wide variety of venues. Many history departments, including my own, have institutionalized such learning by creating separate classes solely set aside for internships.

As for academic rigor and intellectual content, these concerns, while legitimate, too often serve as a smoke screen intended to prevent discussing pedagogical methods and objectives about undergraduate teaching and broader issues of historical objectivity. To the charge of political and social agendas, Matt Gallman's essay in this volume directly responds in a most convincing manner. Student evaluations habitually give high marks for difficulty and intellectual challenge to academic courses that use service-learning. I have never found it necessary to compromise on reading lists or written assignments in terms of length or difficulty. But, as I will explain, I have changed texts and some lectures to ensure that students view the service requirement as central to the course.

Next, I want to argue briefly a point of difference between faculty as historians and most of the students who enter our classrooms. This point centers on the concept of connection. Many historians appropriately lament intellectual disconnection, how specialization in the profession together with their own specific scholarly interests make it difficult to share their work, even with colleagues in their own departments. But in truth, we have available to us strong and meaningful intellectual (and often social) bonds to others via regional and national organizations in our field of study. Furthermore, electronic discussion groups tied to the Humanities-Net have enormously broadened the accessibility of intellectual exchange.

But, most important, we feel connected to the past; we appreciate its importance and find contemporary relevance in its study. For most of us, history is both vocation and avocation. We realize that individuals never operate in a vacuum. We understand, and take comfort in, the belief that we are part of the tide — ancient and geographically disparate in origin — of individuals, ideas, and events that have preceded us; we are recipients of and contributors to an intellectual heritage, one that will continue beyond our lives. We believe our contributions to this intellectual inheritance, and our place in this greater tide of civilization, no matter how small, have intrinsic value.

Consequently, we believe our research and teaching can make a difference, even if the outcomes of such activities are not immediately apparent.

But surveys and anecdotal evidence indicate that few traditional-age college students share such perceptions. For them, the past is dead and thus irrelevant; individuals are powerless in the face of huge corporate, financial, and political institutions that more often than not are fundamentally corrupt. Traditional-age students have grown up with television talk shows such as Ricki Lake, Oprah, Geraldo, and Jerry Springer, programs that emphasize emotion over reason, a mistrust of authority, and skepticism about expertise. Television journalism reinforces this scenario with the inevitable and often inappropriate "How do you feel?" question, as well as frequently shoddy investigative reporting.

Nationally, parental divorce rates among entering college freshmen are nearing 50 percent, and a far greater percentage of students have undergone psychological counseling before entering college than even in the recent past. Consequently, young men and women are arriving on our campuses with different emotional baggage and social expectations than did the generations teaching in the classroom (Levine and Cureton 1998).[2] Many students arrive with little to no experience in the workplace, or without substantial personal interaction outside their own social and economic stratum.

Service-Learning in the First-Year History Survey

It was this absence of workplace and social experience that first motivated me to consider service-learning in my freshman History 101 Modern Civilization survey. HS 101 is one of the two core history classes that all Loyola College of Maryland students must take. Almost all students take HS 101 during their freshman year. The faculty at the college have a great deal of autonomy in deciding the texts and exercises in their sections, most of which reflect the strengths and interests of individual instructors.[3] One of my course's themes is exploring different assumptions about the lives and behavior of people in the past, whereas a second theme concerns the rise of the urban working class.

Several year ago, I had shown slides of the Great Depression and began discussing the interaction of politics and economics. Early in the discussion a couple of students said they could not relate to the depictions in the photographs: The scenes were simply too foreign.[4] Their disclosure began a much broader discussion about poverty, individual responsibility, and society's responses to economic and natural crises. Several of the more vocal students presented a neo-Malthusian argument about problems of contemporary unemployment, underemployment, and poverty, whereas others essentially repeated the assumptions of the liberal economic thinkers we had read earlier in the semester. One student, for example, asked whether it was really worthwhile for the First World to aid populations in distress such as the hurricane and earthquake victims in Bangladesh. Another half-seriously suggested that the food served in Baltimore's soup kitchens was likely better than that provided by the college's food service. Let me emphasize that these students were not making an overtly prejudiced argument. But many believed that a great deal of poverty was a matter of choice, and, given the services available to the poor, was neither wretched nor difficult to change.

Eventually, some questions on my part together with the observations of other students gently demonstrated the fallacy of such assumptions. Yet afterward in my office I wondered how many students had been actually convinced that their initial arguments contained problematic assumptions about history, economics, and human behavior. Moreover, with so great an unfamiliarity about contemporary poverty and low wage earners, how much could such students actually comprehend of historical poverty and working-class politics? In Alfred North Whitehead's words, how could I as a teacher bring to my students' notice, "some fundamental assumptions which . . . appear so obvious that people do not know what they are assuming because no other way of putting things have ever occurred to them" (1952: 26).

The key assumption to test was the students' concept of choice. My students largely come from middle- to upper-middle-class families. They grow up in environments in which choice is taken for granted in virtually every aspect of their lives, in decisions ranging from buying toothpaste and cars to selecting colleges and careers. Indeed, a frequent complaint among students is that they often have too many choices. My initial idea was to have students go and eat at a soup kitchen to experience a lack of choice in the food they ate, the tables they sat at, and the time at which they had to eat.

In the fall of 1992 I approached Erin Sweezey, then one of the service coordinators at Loyola's Center for Values and Service, with this idea because I knew that faculty members in other disciplines had used the center as a resource to create service-learning projects.[5] While Erin liked the idea, she thought the experience too intense for our freshmen and suggested I try another exercise. From those conversations sprang the HS 101 Urban History Project.

In putting together the Urban History Project, Erin and I discussed several issues central to its success or failure. Naturally, the first issue focused on the type of service most appropriate for the course. In addition to its intellectual fit, we looked for a project that would be meaningful to the students and to the agency at which they worked. Service site selection also had to take into account the time constraints of student schedules, together with the needs of community partners. We discussed questions of transportation, staffing problems at various agencies — who would direct the students, what kind of orientation they would have before beginning, what the agencies would expect of them — assessment, liability, student apprehensions, a mandatory or optional service requirement, and how not to reinforce cultural stereotypes.

Creating the Freshman Urban History Project

The Project has evolved considerably since I introduced it in the fall of 1992. These changes reflect my own learning process as to how best to use a service component in teaching. They also reflect student suggestions and criticisms from the Center for Values and Service's questionnaire that students answer along with the college's teaching evaluation form. After the term is over, instructors review their course questionnaire in order to consider the strengths and weaknesses of their service component. They can then make suggested changes before the next term.

In my Modern Civilization classes, the effect of historical events — wars, technological changes, economic depressions, and so forth — on ordinary individuals and families has become a fundamental (albeit by no means exclusive) point of departure in lectures and readings. I also want students to explore different concepts of individual and societal notions of responsibility. In the list of required readings my students study the questions Las Casas posed to Charles V in A Brief Account of the Devastation of the Indies. Robert Darton's "Great Cat Massacre" opens up the issue of the effect of changing technology on artisans, social mobility, and notions of violence. Novels such as Zola's Germinal and L'Assommoir, and the film Matewan lead to discussions of working-class communities and family life.

Students have four service options.[6] Beans and Bread is a small (250 people maximum) meal and outreach program located in the inner city very close to a neighborhood dominated by student bars and expensive restaurants. Our Daily Bread, located in the center city, is a much larger meals-only program that serves more than 800 people a day. Students work as greeters, servers, cooks; bus tables; and clean up after all the patrons have left. Let me add that faculty, staff, and administrators commonly offer to work alongside students at the same tasks. Care-A-Van is a program in which five to seven students take a college van downtown to offer food (usually sandwiches they have just made), beverages, and conversation to homeless people.[7] U.N.I.T.E. (Urban Needs Introduced Through Experience) is a weekend immersion program in which students stay at a college-sponsored inner-city shelter for direct service, discussion, and reflection. On Saturday, they must go outside the shelter to eat, having only two dollars for all their meals. Students find this a powerful and sobering experience.

Mandatory or Optional?

In this course, I decided to make the service mandatory as opposed to optional (or what is sometimes called a "fourth-credit option"[8]). Because the Urban History Project is bound to the central themes of the course, I treat it as I would an additional text. Students who for whatever reason are opposed to the service assignment write a short paper on some historical subject related to the lives of ordinary people. In the main, only one or two students per section ask to write papers.

Much discussion among Loyola's faculty and the college's Advising Department has centered on the question of whether courses with a service-learning component should be so listed in semester course schedules. The rationale for indicating a service-learning component is that students who are either unable or strongly opposed to service-based work have the option of taking another section. However, most service-learning faculty choose not to list their courses as such. They maintain that the college has several courses with mandatory projects for which students have to go off campus; for example, astronomy. Yet these courses have no special listing. While I agree with this argument, I myself now post my classes that have service-learning components. I should add that no student has ever dropped one of my courses because of its service-learning component.

Time and Monitoring

How many hours should a service project take, and how often should students work at their sites? My freshman project is smaller in scale than those of my upper-division courses. Freshmen already have a lot to handle in making the transition to college life; in light of that often difficult transition, I primarily seek to introduce service-learning and allow the students to see how useful it is in understanding course issues. Along with the course syllabus, I give my freshmen a page of questions they should consider in order to give some structure to their experience.

Early in the semester a service-learning coordinator and two or three students briefly speak to my classes explaining the service-learning opportunities open to them and the mechanics of signing up and going to the sites. Small information packets are passed out containing a booklet about the Center for Values and Service and the assistance it provides; a service contract, which the site provider signs to indicate that my students have shown up and the type of work they have performed; and a liability release form.

The coordinator explains transportation arrangements and emphasizes the importance of showing up on time and showing respect to the population the students will be working with. The students accompanying the coordinator are usually sophomores who undertook a service project in their freshman year. I ask the upperclassmen to speak largely to reassure the freshmen — recounting their experiences, answering questions, and giving suggestions from a student's point of view. The class then has a week to sign up at the center, which posts a list of dates and times reserved for my students. The center sends me a copy of the sign-up sheets so I can remind students of their service date. Before the date of the last class, the center sends me the names of any students who have not fulfilled their service requirement.

When the Urban History Project first began, freshmen went to a site once, but student evaluations advised that future classes should go more often. Many students wrote that they had arrived at the site too nervous to pay much attention to their surroundings. By the point when they became comfortable, it was often time to leave. At present, students go at least twice to the sites, spending between four and six hours there on each visit.

Student Reflection – Discussions, Papers, and Grading

It has become commonplace to say that student reflection gives service-learning its distinctive value as a teaching tool, separating it from traditional community service. When done well, reflection synthesizes the experience outside the classroom with the intellectual activity inside it. Structuring good reflection, however, is far from uncomplicated. In perhaps the most helpful book on reflection in service-learning, Harry Silcox points out that "the vagueness of any single definition of reflection . . . [and] the lack of any concise description of reflection by most who use the word . . . indicates the confusion that exists about reflection and its use as a learning tool" (1995: 3).[9]

Most faculty members employing service-learning use a combination of class discussion and written reflection. I find that a series of class discussions seems most effective in my freshman classes. The first reflections are deliberately brief and seek to discover the extent to which students are thinking about their service in relation to lectures and readings. For the early modern period, pointing out the differences between past and present social and economic conditions is as valuable as finding the linkages. For example, the question to what extent the "good poor" still exist generates student discussion about who defines social attitudes and how such perceptions reflect change and durability in the social order. These first discussions also serve to reassure students who have not yet done their service, and they help the class discern whether the service, in fact, is reinforcing stereotypes. Discussions become longer and more sophisticated as class lectures and readings reach the era of the Great Depression.

Toward the semester's end, students write a two-page reflection paper in which they discuss their service in light of the course's lectures and readings. Students are instructed that their papers are to be neither self-congratulatory essays nor saccharine laments about poverty. I make it clear that papers are graded on the content of their analysis, with points deducted for sloppy thinking and writing. On occasion, I have also asked students service-related questions in their final examination essays. These questions vary depending on that semester's readings, but I generally ask about changing social conditions and attitudes vis-à-vis specific historical circumstances in a manner that does not simply repeat the focus of their reflection paper.

Service in Other History Courses

While the Urban History Project operates well in my first-year survey course, it is not necessarily suitable for the other courses in which I employ service-learning. Students in my upper-division History of Latin America: The National Period course and my Military and Society in Latin America course do not work in soup kitchens. Instead, they work with various agencies such as the Mayor's Office on Hispanic Affairs, the Hispanic Apostolate, several area churches, and other nonprofit organizations in the Baltimore-Washington, area that deal with Latin America. Service projects range from adult literacy tutoring and initiating a public relations campaign on behalf of a Protestant church's undertaking to buy school books and supplies for a group of Nicaraguan children, to putting together a video on the Chiapas insurrection and showing it in area high schools. Such projects reveal Baltimore's growing Hispanic population to students.

One student wrote that the lectures and readings on the killings and destruction in Central America had not really made an impact on her because the statistics were so overwhelming. But after speaking to a young man from Guatemala, who had to flee for his life, she now genuinely understood the tragedy of events there. For her, as for many other students, the human connection of the service project opened her intellectual understanding.

For an honors course focusing on the West between late antiquity and the Renaissance, a completely different approach proved necessary. Students read John Boswell's *The Kindness of Strangers: The Abandonment of Children in Western Europe From Late Antiquity to the Renaissance* as one of their required texts. I had originally chosen Boswell for several reasons that had no connection to service. But I decided to see whether doing service was possible in such a course. As it turned out, students worked with children and adolescents at risk. Some worked with children in residential facilities, while others worked in an after-school program at an elementary school.[10] Their service led to some extended and spirited discussions on the meaning of love and abandonment in contemporary and medieval society.

Last spring, I was assigned to teach our department's mandatory course for majors on historical methods. As one of their final projects, I asked students to design a semester-long upper-division course of their choosing. They had to provide a syllabus, a readings list, a short analysis of each lecture topic, and the types of test and writing assignments to be required. I asked them to include, if possible, a service requirement appropriate to their course. They had to describe the service component in detail and explain why it related to the course.

I must admit my surprise at the variety of courses they created. For example, one student constructed a history of modern Russia in which students worked with the area's sizable Soviet immigrant population. Others created courses on American women, the history of violence, and the history of Baltimore. An ROTC student created a course on modern American military history in which the students had to work at VA Hospitals and Care Centers, or with the Vietnam Veterans of America. Students had to keep journals on what they did, saw, and heard. These journals provided the basis for class discussions and the students' research papers.

Despite all this creativity, I wish to conclude by reiterating my belief that service-learning is not appropriate for every course. Nonetheless, it is a highly flexible learning tool. Faculty members should have reasonable expectations as to what they seek to accomplish. Careful planning is essential for a successful service-learning course. Not every student will find the service project as exciting or as necessary as the instructor. But many will find their service and the class in general one of their best undergraduate experiences.

Notes

1. In this regard it is no coincidence that so many references are made to John Dewey. Those opposing service-learning on the grounds of maintaining historical objectivity or rejecting so-called "political correctness" should consider consulting Peter Novik's *That Noble Dream: The "Objectivity Question" and the American Historical Profession* (Cambridge University Press, 1988). Moreover, I wonder how the texts and lectures of those who object to service-learning would fare under similar scrutiny.

2. The long-running Harvard Study on incoming freshmen also supports these points. Grade inflation and inadequate preparation for college further complicate the learning environment, to no small extent by creating unrealistic expectations among incoming students.

3. The department guidelines for HS 101 suggest an average reading load of 200 pages per week, that students generally read complete texts as opposed to excerpts, and minimum writing assignments of 15 to 20 pages (mine have been as many as 40 pages) per semester, and that all exams be bluebook essays. The department does not allow multiple-choice or true-false exams in any Loyola history course.

4. This is a common experience. Dr. Ilona M. McGuiness has written, "Here at Loyola, many of our student come from relatively privileged and sheltered backgrounds. Their responses to sensitive sociocultural and political questions are sometimes limited by the parameters defined by their own experience and by the received opinions they bring into the classroom. Their unfamiliarity with people who live in circumstances far different from their own is often reflected in the rhetoric of their oral and written discourse . . . class discussions tended to be delicate while students learned to distance themselves . . . [and] to concentrate on how their ideas could be presented effectively to an audience which included but was not limited to people sharing their own points of view" (1995: 4-5).

5. Since then, Loyola's Center for Values and Service has established both teaching workshops and one-day retreats in which faculty who use service-learning discuss their experiences with other faculty considering adopting it. In the fall of 1999, the college further strengthened its commitment to service-learning by offering two tuition-free scholarships to outstanding students committed to service during their undergraduate years and funds for students and faculty to travel to national conferences on service-learning.

6. In the fall semester of 1999 I changed several of the course sites owing to the impending move of Our Daily Bread and the great popularity of Beans and Bread, which made it impossible to obtain sufficient placements for my classes.

7. Care-A-Van is a student-founded and student-run program. Students must have at least one prior service experience before going on Care-A-Van.

8. Faculty members may choose to offer the fourth-credit option. This gives students another credit counting toward their grade-point average though not for graduation. Students who take this option usually do at least 30 hours of service during the semester. It also involves more reflection than do many service-learning classes.

9. The best recent work on using reflection is Dwight Giles and Janet Eyler's, A Practitioner's Guide to Reflection in Service-Learning (Vanderbilt University Press, 1996).

10. The class worked with students of low-income single-parent households, in residential and day treatment centers with adolescents with behavioral problems related to family breakdown, trauma, and deprivation.

References

Levine, Arthur, and Jeanette S. Cureton. (1998). *When Hope and Fear Collide: A Portrait of Today's College Student.* San Francisco, CA: Jossey-Bass.

McGuiness, Ilona M. (1995). "Educating for Participation and Democracy: Service Learning in the Writing Classroom." *The Scholarship of Teaching* 1(2): 4-5.

Silcox, Harry C. (1995). *A How-To Guide to Reflection: Adding Cognitive Learning to Community Service Programs.* Philadelphia, PA: Brighton Press.

Whitehead, Alfred North. (1952, orig. 1925). *Science and the Modern World.* Mentor ed. New York, NY: New American Library.

Serving and Learning in the Chilean Desert

by Marshall C. Eakin

For the past few years I have worked with a group of colleagues at Vanderbilt University to promote service-learning on our campus. My interest in service-learning arose out of more than a decade of advising and working with our student-created and student-run Alternative Spring Break program.[1] Since 1998 I have cochaired an ad hoc committee on service-learning that has met with our provost and has been looking at how we might consolidate and promote the disparate service-learning activities on campus. At times, I have found myself in an odd position. I am not an expert on service-learning. In fact, most of what I know about service-learning has come as a result of this collaboration with colleagues and through personal investigation. Furthermore, I found myself promoting efforts to support a type of course that I had never even taught. I watched enviously as colleagues in sociology or education created and taught courses that established ties with the Nashville community. Working with these committed and creative colleagues pushed me to create my own service-learning course. As a historian of 19th- and 20th century Latin America, however, teaching a service-learning course that draws on my professional expertise takes a bit more effort and planning than would a course on homelessness in our community or the local juvenile justice system.

The principal catalyst behind the creation of my course was a student. As a freshman, Rachel McDonald participated in Alternative Spring Break in Lima, Peru, in March 1996. Energized by the experience, she began on her return to look for a faculty member who might teach a summer course in Lima that involved working with the urban poor. On the advice of one of my colleagues in the history department, she appeared in my office in the spring of 1996 and made an impassioned plea for me to help her find someone to create this course. Impressed by her commitment, I resolved to work with her and seize on this opportunity to create my own service-learning class. I had two simple objectives: to introduce students to Latin America and to get them involved in community service.

A variety of problems (including the Peruvian hostage crisis in Lima in late 1996 and early 1997) gradually turned us away from Peru and toward Chile. A former advisee and Latin American studies major, Will Clark, had worked in Santiago for several years after graduation, eventually setting up Outreach International, an organization that sends groups to do service work in Chile.[2] By the fall of 1996, Rachel had been awarded a prestigious Ingram Scholarship, an award given to a highly select group of Vanderbilt students who show an exceptional commitment to service.[3] During the summer of 1997, Rachel went on Will Clark's program to Pachica, a small town of some 200 inhabitants in the Atacama Desert in the far north of Chile. Her group worked at Kuyasapu, an agricultural high school run by the Methodist Church. When Rachel returned in the fall, we resolved to push ahead with my service-learning course, to base it in Pachica, and to hold it in May 1998. Thus was born Latin American Studies 294: Contemporary Chilean Social Problems in Historical Perspective.

The Course

Once I had arranged for an appropriate site, I began to construct a course that would draw on my training as a historian of Latin America and that would provide students with a historical perspective on the social issues they would be confronting in their work in Chile. I also wanted to strike a balance between academic and service work. One of the primary obstacles to the promotion of service-learning at Vanderbilt (as well as at other schools) has been the unfounded suspicion of faculty in the College of Arts and Science that service-learning is simply academic credit for personal experience.[4] Consequently, I wanted a course that would be academically rigorous as well as committed to service; one that balanced reading, writing, and service work. The course had to provide students with both experience (in the field, so to speak) and context (reading and reflection).

After consulting with Will Clark, his contacts in Pachica, and my colleagues, I came up with the following plan. Our group would work part of the day, have the late afternoons to read and write, and then hold discussions in the evenings. I put together a package of readings that provided students with a general overview of Chilean history, with an emphasis on the Aymara culture of the Andean region, and a look at issues in the mining region of Chile's Norte Grande ("Greater North"). (See *opposite* for the contents of the classpak.) My plan was to have the students read the materials, just as they would for a class at Vanderbilt. Then they would discuss them each day in a sort of round-the-clock, on-site seminar. After roughly a week in Pachica they would write an essay, with another essay to follow about a week or so later. Finally, they would keep daily journals reflecting on their experiences and the readings. I planned to read and comment on the journals on a weekly basis. The journals, I hoped, would help me gauge the ability of the students to keep up with the assignments and process their experience. They would also help me guide the discussions.

After such a long process of development and planning, my service-learning course nearly failed to get off the ground. In January and February 1998, the Vanderbilt Office of Overseas Study duly advertised the proposed

Readings from Chile
Classpak

Bringle, Robert G., and Julie A. Hatcher, "Implementing Service Learning in Higher Education," *Journal of Higher Education,* 67:2 (March/April 1996), 221-39.

Epstein, Jack, "An Indian is Half of La Paz's Odd Couple," *Christian Science Monitor* (16 February 1995).

Klubock, Thomas Miller, "Working-Class Masculinity, Middle-Class Morality, and Labor Politics in the Chilean Copper Mines, " *Journal of Social History,* 30:2 (Winter 1996), 435-63.

Long, William R., "Amid the Concrete of Modern Bolivia, Ancient Aymara Culture Blooms," *Los Angeles Times.*

O'Obrien, Thomas F. "Rich Beyond the Dreams of Avarice: The Guggenheims in Chile," *Business History Review,* 63 (Spring 1989), 122-59.

Rivera, Mario A., "The Prehistory of Northern Chile: A Synthesis," *Journal of World Prehistory,* 5:1 (1991), 1-47.

Textbooks

Collier, Simon and William F. Sater. *A History of Chile, 1808-1994* (Cambridge: Cambridge University Press, 1996).

Kolata, Alan L. *Valley of the Spirits: A Journey Into the Lost Realm of the Aymara* (New York: John Wiley and Sons, 1996).

new course (along with two others) for our Maymester session.[5] A proposed course in Israel failed to attracted enough students, and a fully subscribed course on Guatemalan archaeology had to be canceled due to safety concerns.[6] The associate dean, who had worked out all the arrangements for my course, had set 15 students as the threshold for making the course feasible. He had also agreed to let Rachel McDonald go along as my paid teaching assistant, since she knew the site so well and had worked with the contact organization. The cost of the program to students would be $3,100 (a $985 program fee and $2,115 in tuition for three credit-hours), plus airfare to and from Chile (approximately $1,200).[7] Our early March deadline passed with just seven students signed up. A late rush of applicants pushed us up to 12 students by late March, and we got approval to go with a smaller-than-planned group.

Of the 12 students who signed on, one was a sophomore, two were seniors, and the rest juniors. None of the students had any extended experience in Latin America. Three of them had been in Mexico for periods of one to two weeks. Nine of them had never been out of the United States. Seven had some ability to converse in Spanish, although the most fluent had had no more than five semesters of Spanish. The other five spoke no Spanish at all. Three of the students were majoring in Latin American studies and two in Spanish. Although I had managed to tap into the pool of students interested in a Latin American experience, my great disappointment was that no more than one or two of the students seem to have been drawn to the course because of a background in service.

Most of the group met with me for a briefing session in mid-April, and we met again on Saturday, May 3, for a two-hour orientation session with Will Clark and the codirector of Outreach International, Lloyd Stratton. Both Clark and Stratton had several years experience working in Chile, and both had worked in Pachica with our contact agency, EMANA (Extensión Metodista al Niño Andino, or "Methodist Extension Programs for Andean Youth"). They gave us a slide presentation about the site and an orientation to both Chile and Pachica. Most of the group met at the Nashville airport the following afternoon for our flight, and several others met up with us in Dallas for the overnight flight to Santiago. (One intrepid student went down a couple of days early, and a second would follow a day later.)

The Experience

Our time in Chile was split into three segments: (1) a brief introduction to the country with two days in the capital, Santiago, (2) two weeks working in Pachica, followed by (3) several days seeing more of the Atacama Desert, with two final days in Santiago. The idea was to combine an intense service experience in a small locale with a wider experience in the Norte Grande and a brief look at the nation's heartland. I was especially interested in having the students gain an appreciation for the country's incredible geographical diversity. Chile has some of the world's most unusual geography, stretching some 2,600 miles from the tropics (18 degrees South) to the Antarctic (55 degrees South), yet averaging only some 90 miles in width. The towering Andes form the eastern border with Argentina and Bolivia, while a narrow coastal shelf north of Santiago is almost entirely desert. The central valley has a Mediterranean climate, and with some six million inhabitants, metropolitan Santiago is home to one out of every two Chileans (as well as to some of the worst smog in the world!). The Norte Grande is another world entirely. The Atacama Desert is the driest region on the planet, and in some areas no rainfall has ever been recorded (Collier and Sater 1996: xvii-xix).

Pachica is at the northern end of the desert. Some two hours by car to the east of the thriving Pacific port of Iquique, Pachica is a small town of some 200 inhabitants located in one of the many valleys that cut across the high desert. Altitude (approximately 5,000 feet) mediates the tropical temperatures, and in May those temperatures range from high in the low 80s to around 60 at night. Pachica has some of the clearest air on the planet; the sun is direct and strong, and the stars are brilliant at night. (According to an old saying, the Atacama Desert is "geology by day and astronomy by night.") The region is dry and dusty, but irrigation canals bringing water down from the Bolivian Andes make possible limited agriculture. Although the North is known primarily for its mining economy (especially nitrates and copper), the local economy around Pachica revolves around the raising of alfalfa, corn, llamas, pigs, sheep, goats, and small animals such as chickens, rabbits, and guinea pigs.

In the late 1980s, EMANA canvassed the northern region looking for a site for an agricultural high school. Led by Stanley Moore, a Methodist missionary and agricultural expert with 30 years experience in southern Chile, EMANA picked Pachica for the school site after the community agreed to donate the land and to work with the school.[8] Inaugurated in 1992, Kuyasapu ("Good Harvest") now has about 150 students who come from all over northern Chile. They live in dormitories, eat in a common cafeteria, and attend classes in another set of buildings. In addition to a traditional high school academic curriculum, the school concentrates on teaching the students how to cultivate crops and raise animals. One of its primary missions is to promote Aymara culture and pride in the students' indigenous heritage. The Aymara, a people once comprising the southern half of the Incan empire, today number more than three million in Bolivia. In northern Chile, however, their population has declined to some 20,000-50,000. Furthermore, although their language and culture remain strong and vibrant in Bolivia, most Chileans of Aymaran descent have been losing their linguistic and cultural heritage in a society that has long denigrated Indians. Kuyasapu specifically seeks to inculcate in its students pride in their indigenous past through the study of Aymaran culture and language.[9]

In Pachica, our group lived in two of the guest residences at the school (the 11 women in one building, and the three men in another). Although the school has plumbing, most buildings have no running water. Water is brought in by truck from nearby irrigation canals and pumped into tanks on top of the buildings or into oil drums in front of the residences. The only running water is from the tanks on three of the buildings. Bottled drinking water is brought in from Iquique. The locals wash their clothes and bathe in the irrigation canals (practices we ourselves quickly adopted).

Our group generally ate breakfast in the cafeteria from 7:30 to 8:00 each morning, and on weekdays we then worked after breakfast until 12:30 pm. Lunch was served at 1:00 (followed by siesta, a custom the students very quickly came to appreciate and adopt as their own). We worked again from 3:00 to 5:00. Late afternoon was available for reading, writing, and occasional social activities, and dinner was served at 7:30. Most evenings we held group discussions from 9:00 to 10:00 pm. On several occasions, there were evening lectures about Aymaran culture, and one night we enjoyed a presentation of Andean music by the school band. Needless to say, our days were full — and usually exhausting.

On weekends the students had a freer schedule and greater flexibility. They could use their time to catch up on their reading and writing and to take excursions. One Saturday, we took a tour of the region around Pachica with stops to see thousand-year-old geoglyphs and petroglyphs, and to visit Humberstone, an old nitrate mining complex that is now an immense ghost town. We also squeezed in a couple of dances with the students in the cafeteria, soccer games, hikes in the surrounding mountains, and lots of personal interaction with the high school students. John Elmore, the resident director of the school (and a native of Alabama), had brought back gloves, bats, and balls from a recent trip home, and several of our group taught a large group of girls and boys to play softball. Perhaps the highlight of our local excursions was a trip to the nearby home of a local woman who provides most of the town's baked bread. The "bread lady" showed us how to make dough, and then gave us a demonstration of how to cook it in her clay oven. At 72, she works irrigated fields along with her 83-year-old husband and their son, and she regularly cooks and sells bread in Pachica. When the students asked the secret of her health and longevity, she replied, "Eat well, work hard, and when there is a party, party." Needless to say, this went over quite well with the students.

The bulk of our service work at Kuyasapu consisted of two main projects. The first, and least popular, was clearing a large field to prepare for planting alfalfa. Although farmers in surrounding fields grow alfalfa, the school has always purchased it and trucked it in to feed the school's livestock. (The Kuyasapu students regularly work in the fields producing corn, vegetables, and onions.) We set out to clear a weed- and rock-covered field on our first full day in Pachica. The hot (and very direct) tropical sun and the grueling work of weeding and then breaking the soil quickly convinced students that the life of the Andean peasant was not for them. We spent close to half of our work days (mainly at the beginning and end of the trip) clearing the field. The Kuyasapu students came with us on our first day to show the gringo city slickers how to use hoes and shovels. Discussions between our group and the Kuyasapu students were some of the most interesting and important during our entire stay.

Our second, and more important, project was completing an outdoor laundry for the school. When we arrived, a previous group and the school's shop crew (Pedro, Manuel, and José) had already built the bulk of the structure. Alongside the boys' dormitory, they had poured a rectangular concrete slab about 80-feet long and 10-feet wide. They had built a 10-foot-high cinder-block wall on three sides, leaving open the long side facing the dormitory. Along the length of the long wall they built about two dozen concrete sinks. Over the period of about a week, Pedro, José, and Manuel would put up a steel frame for the roof, put in copper tubing and faucets, and build a metal tower for the water tank. Our job was to paint the structure, put up the straw roof, build clotheslines, and help put up the water tank.

Setting up the clothesline turned out to be a lot less popular than painting. The rocky desert soil required the use of picks and shovels as we dug some 13 post holes, each two feet deep and two feet in diameter. We then had to make concrete and pour it using wheelbarrows and shovels. Making the concrete was long, backbreaking work. The school had purchased bags of cement that we then mixed on the concrete slab with local gravel and water. Pedro and Manuel directed the process while we used shovels to mix and wheelbarrows to cart the concrete to the post holes.

When we finished the laundry near the end of our second week in Pachica, the group was justly proud of its accomplishment. Kuyasapu students immediately flocked to the new facility, which saved them the trouble of lugging buckets and laundry down to the irrigation canals below the school. With so many students using the sinks, the laundry also quickly became an important social gathering point complete with loud music blasting from boom boxes. The Vanderbilt students found this project much more fulfilling than working in the fields, largely because they could see a permanent physical monument to their labor. (I have observed the same type of reaction by students on Vanderbilt's Alternative Spring Break. They would much rather build something than provide services. They need to see some visible and lasting result of their work.)

The academic dimension of the trip was just as grueling, albeit in different ways, as the service work. Students had a tough time balancing the physically exhausting, time-consuming service work, social interaction, and the academic load. Every night they wrote in their journals, and I collected and read their journals weekly. These journals constituted the most revealing and satisfying part of the class for me. Most students (after some initial prompting) quickly moved beyond description to reflection on the readings and their experience of Chile. At times, the connections were very direct. As they were reading an article on the efforts of the copper mining companies in the first half of the century to shape the behavior, sexuality, and morality of the miners, we spent a Saturday afternoon touring Humberstone, once one of the largest nitrate mines and company towns in the country. As students toured this ghost town they could see the physical embodiment of the efforts at social control described in the article.[10]

At other times, the students wrote about their efforts to understand their daily experiences in Pachica and Chile. A number of them reflected on how vastly different their lives and life choices were when compared with those of their young friends at Kuyasapu. They connected, at times, on how limited the options seemed to be for their new friends. Nearly all the students in our group wrote in their journals about and debated the impact of our visit on the Chilean students. They worried, in fact, that we might contribute to their seemingly unquenchable thirst for U.S. music, television, and movies — a trend our group found unsettling and ominous. In some journal entries, the students expressed a fear that Chilean culture, and especially Aymaran traditions, would be overwhelmed by U.S. popular culture.

Besides reading about 40 pages a day and writing journals, students wrote two essays of about 1,000 words each. This was a chore for a generation raised on computers. One student had brought a laptop computer and small printer, but the rest had to resort to pen, pencil, and looseleaf paper as they took notes, drafted essays, and revised. In the days leading up to the due dates for the two essays, the students became almost feverish in their efforts to read, digest, and write. Each time, due to the workload, excursions, and fatigue, I pushed back the due dates to give them enough time to finish their work. The results were excellent. Although not all students had the same ability to grasp the arguments and analyze the readings, all their essays showed a much deeper and more thorough grasp of the material than any comparable set of essays I have received in my regular classes at Vanderbilt. The discussions that followed delivery of the papers were also very good. Everyone had read the material very closely and could make contributions to the analysis of the readings and their significance.

Group discussions and individual conversations were often the most rewarding moments on the trip. Group discussions varied enormously in their quality and level of student participation largely depending on the physical labor, excursions, and activities of the day. By 9:00 on some nights several of the students were exhausted and had trouble focusing on the material at hand. At times, I would hold discussions before dinner to avoid the fatigue problem. On two occasions, we held our discussion while hoeing in the fields, thus truly combining academics and service. Group dynamics worked fairly well, although I faced the usual problems of trying to draw out the more reserved students, and working to rein in the more outspoken. Since I firmly believe that teaching is a conversation, one of the most rewarding features of this course was that discussions did not simply begin and end during a specific class time. The conversation was ongoing, sometimes one-on-one, at other times in small groups. These exchanges were often very intense, personal, and infinitely more effective than the standard classroom lecture.

Evaluation

One of my great frustrations with the standard teaching format is that contact with the students is so infrequent and episodic. In most classes, we see students fewer than three hours a week, spread out over two or three days. If we are to connect with our students, we must do so quickly and somehow entice them to come back for more, either for discussions outside the classroom, or for additional classes. This very intense, one-month, service-learning course represented a wonderful opportunity to connect with students in ways rarely possible on campus. Living and working with the students, teaching virtually round the clock, made this both a very demanding and a very rewarding experience. I feel that the students learned more about Chile than they ever would have back in Nashville in a regular class, and that several of them also made a deep personal connection with Latin America that would have been impossible without direct field experience.

One of the most important connections the group made was with the students at Kuyasapu. Although the non-Spanish-speaking students were frustrated by their inability to communicate as effectively as the Spanish speakers in the group, everyone established friendships with Kuyasapu students. Indeed, the more capable Spanish speakers became intermediaries for non-Spanish speakers, something that strengthened group bonds while improving the language skills of the Spanish speakers. Members of the group also learned to reach out even when they did not have the language skills. One of the strongest friendships formed was between an artist in our group, Bianca, who spoke no Spanish, and a young woman from the school who spoke no English but shared Bianca's love of art. Constant daily interaction with the Kuyasapu students added a dimension to our service work that was invaluable. It made our readings and work more vivid, personal, and real for the students in the group.

In short, students learned more and were more profoundly affected by this service-learning experience than would have been possible in a traditional class with the same readings, writing assignments, and requirements back on the Vanderbilt campus.[11] I also learned an enormous amount about the students, their plans and outlook on life, and what life is like (from the student perspective) on the Vanderbilt campus. Much like my experiences with Alternative Spring Break, this kind of intense contact with students gave me insights into them and campus life that I would never otherwise have had.

Despite the rewards of this type of teaching experience, the course was not without its problems. First, teaching this type of class, especially overseas, requires an enormous amount of preparation, and while in Chile enormous responsibilities that rarely come with on-campus classroom teaching. As with all service-learning courses, the instructor has to do a lot of preliminary work to arrange for a site and to work with the contact agency. Recruiting students, orienting them, making travel arrangements, and keeping track of predeparture preparations are activities far beyond the standard Vanderbilt course. (Although having a teaching assistant was an enormous help in this regard.) Second, the downside of the intense and rewarding contact with students on a 24-hour-a-day basis was having to deal with problems, not only of logistics but also of interpersonal relations. With some 14 people in our group, we inevitably faced a wide variety of personalities and some intragroup conflict. In addition to the usual responsibilities of teaching, I had to become something of a counselor, mediator, and father figure. In fact, the greatest challenge in the course was not logistical or intellectual, but helping to foster and nurture positive group dynamics. In the end, we all got along and the group was cohesive, but this required enormous emotional energy on my part.[12]

In the end, the course worked, and quite well. Its service and academic components converged successfully. The two components would have fit together even more precisely and effectively, however, had the service been more directly historical in nature. As a historian, I was able to provide students with the context of the people, cultures, and economy of Pachica, the Norte Grande, and Chile. The service work they did gave them direct experience helping and working with Chileans, and a good sense of contemporary connections with the Chilean past. But the bond between the context and the experience would have been more direct and vivid, I think, had the service work been more closely tied to recovering the past. Had we been working, for example, on the restoration of the ghost mining town of Humberstone, recovering and organizing archives in the region, or helping restore an archaeological site, the service work would have been more intrinsically historical in its nature, and thus more directly connected to Chilean history.

Returning to my original goals for the course, I feel that I was more successful in achieving the first than the second. These students were introduced to Latin America and immersed in Latin American society. They will never see Latin America with the same eyes again. Several, I am sure, will return to the region soon, and a few will pursue coursework in Latin American studies over the next two years at Vanderbilt. (One student went off to Cuba for a three-week course in June.) Two or three will probably go into careers that involve working in Latin America or with Latin Americans. For that handful of students who had already considered a future in Latin American studies, this experience, I am quite sure, reinforced their plans. I am less sure about my second objective — getting the students involved in community service. This objective is harder to gauge. My teaching assistant, Rachel McDonald, was already committed to service as a lifelong commitment. Of the other students, my sense is that their experience did reinforce (at least intellectually) the importance of service and service-learning. Perhaps two or three came back with a stronger commitment to service.[13]

As for the experience's impact on me, the course has deeply reinforced my commitment to service-learning. Having now taught a service-learning course of my own, I can speak from firsthand experience with my colleagues about the pedagogical value and personal rewards of teaching such a class. With those colleagues already receptive to service-learning, I am now able to share my experiences and what I have learned. To those colleagues who are skeptical, I can now speak with greater authority and precision about the academic rigor and importance of learning through service.

Finally, my experience convinced me of the need to work harder to push Vanderbilt to the next step in service-learning — the appointment of someone on campus as service-learning coordinator.[14] After years of working with other committed faculty and staff, the time has come for us to have a person who can channel the institution's various efforts toward more systematic program building. We need someone who can advise, coordinate, promote, and publicize service-learning on our campus. Only through such coordination will we succeed in moving on to establish service-learning as an important and integral part of our students' education. When this finally happens, courses like this one not only will be able to have an impact on students, faculty, and the communities they serve but also will be able to contribute to a larger effort to make more effective both service and learning.

Notes

1. A small group of students began Vanderbilt's Alternative Spring Break in 1986. The first year some 50 students worked in Nashville, on a Native American reservation in South Dakota, and in the Appalachian region of east Tennessee. In the spring of 1998 more than 300 students went to 23 sites in 16 states, Mexico, and Peru. For more information, contact the organization at asb@ctrvax.vanderbilt.edu.

2. Outreach International is located in Birmingham, Alabama. Its email address is inoutreach@aol.com.

3. E. Bronson Ingram, president of the Vanderbilt Board of Trust (1991-95), and his family created the scholarships in 1993 for students with excellent academic credentials and an exceptional commitment to service. Each year, Vanderbilt selects four or five new recipients who receive half-tuition fellowships, as well as summer funding for self-designed service projects. The full group of Ingram scholars meets monthly throughout the academic year in a special seminar.

4. To avoid the possibility of resistance from faculty who might object to this type of course, I gave the class a Selected Topics listing (LAS 294), which requires only department approval and does not require going through a series of committees at the college level. At Vanderbilt, a course may be taught three times under this miscellaneous rubric before it has to go through full-scale course approval.

5. Vanderbilt's spring semester normally ends around May 1, and its first summer session generally begins during the first week of June. May sessions are supposed to offer intense courses (three hours a day for four weeks) on topics that are not normally offered during the regular year. Faculty have been encouraged to create courses for overseas study during this month between the end of the academic year and the beginning of summer school.

6. Earlier that year a group of students from Maryland on a short study-abroad course in Guatemala was attacked, and several students were raped. This incident, a State Department advisory, and concern about growing civil violence in Guatemala eventually persuaded Vanderbilt faculty and administrators that the proposed summer course should be canceled.

7. Obviously, Vanderbilt tuition is quite steep at $705 per credit hour. Students, however, who stayed in Nashville and took a three-credit course would pay the same tuition. They would likely pay close to $985 for housing and food for a month, so the extra cost of the program was, in fact, the airfare to Chile and back.

8. Information on the school and its history comes from conversations with Stanley Moore in Pachica and Iquique from May 6 to 21, 1998.

9. For an excellent overview of the Aymara world, both pre-Columbian and contemporary, see Alan Kolata, *Valley of the Spirits: A Journey Into the Lost Realm of the Aymara* (John Wiley & Sons, 1996).

10. The article is Thomas Miller Klubock, "Working-Class Masculinity, Middle-Class Morality, and Labor Politics in the Chilean Copper Mines," *Journal of Social History* 30(Winter 1996): 435-463.

11. This is borne out by student evaluations of the course in both their written comments and the numerical ratings (which were as high as any course I have taught in my 15 years at Vanderbilt).

12. Another emotional drain was my concern for the safety and health of the students. We had just a few moments of anxiety on the trip. Our first afternoon in Pachica we all hiked through a narrow canyon up and down steep rock faces using ropes. Several times I had visions of students tumbling down rocky slopes. Fortunately, no one fell. On another occasion, one student nearly broke his arm. More seriously, four students came down with Hepatitis A nearly three weeks after the end of the class. Most likely, they contracted the virus while we were traveling during the final days of the trip.

12. One student stayed on in Chile and worked through June with an organization that helps street kids in Iquique.

14. For an excellent overview of ways to institutionalize service-learning on a college campus see Bringle and Hatcher (1996).

References

Bringle, Robert G., and Julie A. Hatcher. (Mar./Apr. 1996). "Implementing Service Learning in Higher Education." *Journal of Higher Education* 67(2): 221-239.

Collier, Simon, and William F. Sater. (1996). *A History of Chile, 1808-1994.* Cambridge: Cambridge University Press.

Classical Studies and the Search for Community[1]

by Ralph M. Rosen

It has always fascinated me how the academic discipline of classical studies is conceptualized in our society. A profession that was not very long ago held to provide a universal education for anyone aspiring to be a functional and informed citizen in Western society has gradually come to be seen as a haven for antiquarians and pedants, far removed from the concerns of the modern world. There are many reasons for this perception (and surely classicists themselves must bear some of the responsibility), but I am still astonished at the assumption that the study of Greco-Roman antiquity is a pursuit fundamentally "irrelevant" to today's concerns. I keep remembering what drew me into the profession in the first place: learning, for example, about the oral poetics that informed the great Homeric epics while I was discovering analogous poetics in jazz and blues; following the first presidential campaign in which I could vote while studying the democratic machinery of classical Athens; observing year by year the quickly shifting sexual politics of modern America while discovering that many classical texts had articulated similar concerns. In short, just about everything I encountered within classical studies was enthralling precisely because it was profoundly implicated in some way with the contemporary world and my own life within it.

It is true, however, that the classical curriculum that most institutions have inherited does not on the surface reflect the vibrancy and "relevance" of the field, nor does it often convey the passion and personal engagement of its practitioners. I have spent many years now trying to counteract the stereotypes about the classics, and have always found this a real rhetorical challenge. Time after time I have been asked by suspicious parents why their child was studying classical antiquity, or worse yet thinking of majoring in the field. Time after time I found myself reciting the usual line about the classics as the fountainhead of so many aspects of Western culture, whether it be law, science, literature, or philosophy. I would even venture to suggest that a person well-versed in Greco-Roman antiquity might be a more savvy and acute citizen, better equipped than others, perhaps, to confront a complex modern world.

Some parents were consoled by this argument, but others quite rightly wanted to know more specifically how classics could serve an accountable function in the education of their sons and daughters. I slowly realized that no amount of rhetoric from me, no matter how passionate, could easily overcome popular perceptions about what a typical classics curriculum has to offer. So, when the opportunity arose several years ago for me to design a classics course that could become part of an academically based service-learning curriculum sponsored by the University of Pennsylvania's Center for Community Partnerships, I immediately saw this as a chance to communicate to students just how false and pernicious the polarization of the "intellectual" and the "practical" can be, especially in humanistic disciplines such as classics.

My challenge, then, was to design a course that would reflect what I had always believed, namely, that classical studies can indeed sharpen our understanding of our world and perhaps even help us solve some of its most pressing problems. It was initially an exhausting task even to contemplate. The world would be rightly bored by yet another pursuit that concluded glibly that "the Greeks and Romans were just like us" or that "everything began with the Greeks." Every classicist knows how incomplete and often simply wrong these attitudes are, and the nonacademic public has little choice but to regard perceived connections with antiquity as novelties at best. I wanted to find a context in which to analyze and integrate the many differences between ourselves and Greco-Roman antiquity as well as the connections, to examine our very discourse about and construction of antiquity as a reflection of how we define ourselves in our society. And I hoped to show that what we can learn from the Greeks and Romans tangibly enriches our understanding of our behavior both as individuals and as political creatures.

First Attempt

The first course I designed was called Community, Neighborhood, and Family in Ancient Athens and Modern Philadelphia. I chose this topic because ancient Athens in particular has been mythologized in modern times in a number of telling ways. We call the fifth century BCE the "Classical period" in Greek history; we speak of the "Greek enlightenment"; we idealize Periclean Athens; we think of "Classical" Athens as the "birthplace of democracy"; we tend to think, in general, of Periclean Athens as a cultural pinnacle, after which "civilization" went into a decline, at least until the Renaissance. What better model, one might suppose, could we find for our own democratic society than fifth-century Athens?

Yet such idealizations reflect only a small part of the whole cultural vista of the time. Many prevailing Athenian practices and ideologies would surely be distasteful to the citizens of a modern democracy: slavery, the oppression of women, intolerance of weakness, a highly restricted political franchise, a culture of male-centered aggression, just to name a few. Part of what I wanted to do in this course, therefore, was to move beyond modern myths about Athens, examine closely how an Athenian polis was organized, how Athenian citizens fostered a sense of community at both local and international levels, and how they framed their questions about the goals of society and the nature of happiness. My aim was not to dwell on whether the Greeks of that time were "good" or "bad" people by our ethical standards, but to show that by studying how an ancient culture quite different from ours wrestled with crucial issues of social organization and interpersonal behavior we might learn something from it about our own formulation of and answers to similar questions.

Classical Athens is practically tailor-made for a course concerned with social organization, the relationship between public and private realms of life, and the diverse, often conflicting, ideologies that control a complex society. Within a mere century, from the end of the sixth to the end of the fifth centuries BCE, Athens developed from a city ruled by autocratic, if sometimes benevolent and impressive, "tyrants" to one that prided itself quite aggressively on its full-blown, participatory democracy. Along the way, we encounter the same sort of controversies that arise whenever one tries to analyze political categories and movements of any kind. Was Cleisthenes, for example, that legendary social reformer at the end of the sixth century, really the great "democratic" patriarch he was made out to be by Athenians of the later fifth century, or was he really an "aristocrat" with his own agenda? How much power did "the people" actually have in Athens by the end of the fifth century? Did a few powerful individuals in fact control Athenian politics? Is a radical democracy a desirable political ideal in the first place, for Athens or anywhere?

While exposing the seminar to the various classical texts (Thucydides, Xenophon, Plato, Aristotle) that bear on such issues, I found it easy to assign parallel readings by modern thinkers on the nature of democracy. More significant, however, the jump to modern Philadelphia proved to be more effortless and profound than I would ever have imagined. When we dipped into the recent history of Philadelphia, trying to see where its current system of government and neighborhood characteristics came from, we saw, along with obvious differences in details, some remarkably analogous trends.

The general development in Classical Athens, for example, from an early democracy controlled essentially by a tightly knit aristocratic elite to a system that attempted, at least, to be more inclusive of the larger citizen population, seems parallel to the shift in 20th-century Philadelphia from a government controlled by an elitist Republican machine to one firmly controlled by Democrats. In each society, one can find proponents and detractors of such developments — some nostalgic for the "good old days" when moral values allegedly were immutable and the term "aristocrat" did not imply repression and the urge for self-aggrandizement; others thrilled that the political franchise was slowly opening up to those who could not claim a distinguished ancestry. Indeed, the reaction of both societies to their aristocratic tendencies even produced two leaders described in their respective times with strikingly similar rhetoric. In Athens in the 420s the "demagogue" Cleon dominated the political scene, a man said by the largely conservative commentators of the time to be violent, boorish, and vulgar, yet brilliant and effective as a general and champion of the *demos*; in recent Philadelphia history, Frank Rizzo cut a similar figure, both in his public persona and in his ability to manipulate public sentiment.

With all the talk about the "exemplary" democracy of Classical Athens, it is easy to overlook the fact that most of the surviving texts from that period remain suspicious of a political system that entrusted too much power to the *demos*. Thucydides's remarks about Pericles summarize the conflict succinctly:

> *Pericles, indeed, by his rank, ability, and known integrity, was enabled to exercise an independent control over the multitude. . . . In short, what was nominally a democracy became in his hands government by the first citizen. With his successors it was different. More on a level with one another, and each grasping at supremacy, they ended by committing even the conduct of state affairs to the whims of the multitude.[2]*

The comic dramatist Aristophanes, too, was uneasy with the way Athenian democracy was developing in the last years of the fifth century, and it is well known that Socrates was executed in 399 BCE after a lifetime spent criticizing the premises of radical democracy. We spent much time in class, therefore, trying to sort out the nature of the evidence about Athenian politics, to transcend the misleading characterizations of the period that are current within modern political discourse, and, most important, debating from practical and philosophical points of view the merits and flaws for a modern urban context of the competing political ideologies that existed within Athens itself.

In focusing on contemporary Philadelphia, class discussion touched on virtually every aspect of urban life, just as it did in the case of Classical Athens, and ancient texts provided an eye-opening set of parallels for the students to contemplate. We looked, for example, at the current state of public education in Philadelphia; the recent history of the School Board; the educational reform movement of the 1960s, its legacies and prospects for the future. Time and again, issues that arose in this pursuit were reminiscent of issues that the students had traced from Aristophanes (in his *Clouds*, a play essentially concerned with educational ideology) and Plato to Benjamin Franklin, John Dewey, E.D. Hirsch, and others. What, for example, should be the role of education in a democracy? Should everyone receive identical training? How should a society balance "technical" educational goals with more theoretical ones? The spirited debates we had in class about education in a democratic society were clearly inspired by our unpredictable and exhilarating combination of ancient and modern theoretical texts, documents published by the Philadelphia School Board, and personal anecdotes provided by the students themselves.

Perhaps the most fruitful avenue of comparison between Athenian and Philadelphian conceptions of "community" emerged from our examination of the elaborate fifth-century organization of the Athenian polis into *demes* and *tribes*. This self-conscious social experiment was the brainchild of the Athenian leader Cleisthenes, who, after the defeat of the tyrants in 510, restructured the social and geographical groupings of Attica (the region surrounding Athens) in an effort to foster cultural and political coherence within a democratic system of government. Cleisthenes divided all of Attica into three geographical areas, City, Coastal, and Inland; and he created 10 new *tribes* of Athenians. He then spread out membership in these *tribes* among the many *demes* (or "villages") of the region by making sure that each of the three geographical areas had some of its *demes* assigned to one of the 10 *tribes*. Whatever Cleisthenes's motives might have been, it is clear that the effect of this social engineering was to unify disparate groups of *demes* into a political whole, and to provide relatively equitable representation of the *demes* and *tribes* in a central democratic government.

Presumably, no one would want to reorganize Philadelphia the way Cleisthenes did Athens; but even though the class did not find a practical blueprint for Philadelphia in studying Cleisthenes's reforms, we were able to articulate a set of problems and questions that concern virtually any group of humans trying to live together cheek by jowl in what some would call a "community." We addressed at some length, for example, the premises about human nature and behavior that evidently underlay Cleisthenes's reforms, and what social problems these reforms set about to resolve. We saw clearly how similar much of the rhetoric about such issues remains today, as when we hear, for example, about how disunity within a polis can only be harmful to individual and city alike, or how democracy can only work with equitable distribution of power, influence, and representation. By contemplating simultaneously Cleisthenic reforms and the recent history of neighborhood development in Philadelphia, the students found themselves asking what distinguishes *community, tribalism,* and *clannishness,* and how our society (locally and nationally) might benefit from sorting out such distinctions for itself. This sort of comparative examination of the rhetoric and ideology of two disparate cultures elicited a level of sophistication and passion in seminar discussion that I rarely find in the undergraduate classroom.

Along with my concern to design a course that demonstrated how well integrated into the modern curriculum the study of classical antiquity can be was my desire to have my students share these discoveries with students at a neighboring high school, University City High School (UCHS). There were several reasons why I thought this would be an exciting and profitable experiment for students at Penn and UCHS alike. To begin with, the curriculum at UCHS had not included much study of any ancient cultures, and so the students did not have many preconceptions about what society has come to regard as "classical." I thought that if Penn students, coming from a traditional academic setting and reading such canonical "classics" as Plato and Thucydides, were to discuss these authors with high school students who had no formal experience with them, the Penn students might succeed in overcoming the stultifying influence of "classicism" that has blunted the power of so many ancient authors. They might instead think about the real-world issues found in these works and, ultimately, understand for themselves how these ancient discussions connect to our own lives.

For the high school students, I was less interested in introducing them to the "great classics of the West" than in showing them how thoughtful writers from a very distant past often addressed profound issues that still resonate in our daily lives. And why might this be important? Hardly because ancient thinkers necessarily had the answers to the big questions that continually plague our species; but rather because it can be highly illuminating to consider how others have already articulated familiar problems. The effort we must make to think cross-culturally and trans-historically also helps us to think abstractly about subjects of the most practical importance; and an ability to think abstractly seems to me to be a prerequisite for framing questions profitably and solving problems most successfully.

I arranged, therefore, with a social studies teacher at UCHS to have my Penn students visit several of his classes every week, in order to lead small discussion groups about some of the texts we were reading in the seminar. I deliberately avoided trying to force the high school students to worry about assimilating facts about a very old and alien culture, as if there were something in the very antiquity of the material that they should admire; I can barely remember even using the term "classical" in any of the high school classes. Rather, with no preparation or fanfare, the students were presented with paragraphs from Greek writers that touched on such issues as the uses of knowledge, the purpose of education, and sexuality and gender.

These visits to the high school were eye-opening for all concerned; for my part, I will certainly never read Plato or Aristotle in quite the same way again. Without fail, our group discussions with the high school students became animated, and often quite raucous, as students with very passionate views about some of these matters wasted no time in articulating them. Even those with the common affect of teenage insouciance could not fail to be drawn into the fray. The result, I think, was dynamic learning at its best: Many of the high school students, their teacher told me, left energized and perhaps a bit confused (in a healthy way) by these classroom debates, and hungry for more.

One subject that we covered in the original course, both in the Penn seminar and in the UCHS classes, was particularly fruitful; namely, the role of the arts in a democratic society. This topic exemplifies strikingly how easy it is to find significant points of contact between different cultures in very unexpected places. In this case, I had the students read selections from Plato, who had little faith that the average human soul can withstand the detrimental effects of poetry, and Aristophanes's *Frogs*, which stages a debate between Aeschylus and Euripides about literature and morality; we then studied and listened to various forms of rap music. Such a juxtaposition of rap and Greek poetry is for some, no doubt, an absurdity; but each art form incited a debate within its own society about remarkably similar issues: whether, for example, art must be socially edifying; whether it should be censored if it is not edifying; who establishes the criteria for aesthetic evaluation; and what responsibilities an artist has to his or her community. Thus, Euripides is taken to task by Aeschylus for corrupting Athenian society, though Euripides himself claims that his motives are deeply noble and socially responsible. Similarly, many rap artists come under fire from critics whose conception of social responsibility does not leave much room for unsettling, sometimes incendiary lyrics.

Classical Studies 240

The success of this topic in the classroom inspired me to design another course, also linked to UCHS, devoted entirely to the question of the arts and society. I decided to concentrate on art that transgresses the boundaries of social acceptability, since those works that clash most directly with tastes and mores are the ones that force citizens to articulate not only the role of art in society but also the nature of aesthetics, and the conflict between cultivation of the self and social responsibility. Such art obviously puts any democratic ideology to the supreme test. We may, for example, endorse freedom of expression in the abstract, but still need to consider whether the people, the *demos*, should ever impose limits on such freedom, and if so, in the name of what. Thus was born Classical Studies 240: Scandalous Arts in Ancient and Modern Communities.

Scandalous art is ideal for a comparative approach for a number of reasons. The first, and perhaps the simplest, is that already in antiquity we find foundational writing on the topic among political and philosophical thinkers (Plato and Aristotle are obvious examples, but there are many others, including Stoic and Cynic philosophers, and Romans such as Cicero and Quintilian). These writers have framed many of the questions we still debate today. Indeed, while the Greeks and Romans were hardly "just like us" in most areas, they did, like us, have concepts of obscenity and pornography, and they did often fret about the power that language, image, and music could have over a society.

Another reason why we can profitably compare the modern dilemma of scandalous art with the same issue in classical antiquity is somewhat more subtle. The very notion of "classicism" in our culture usually bestows on a work a status of authority or legitimacy that indemnifies the work against criticism. Yet the ancient world has left us many works that were scandalous in their time, and which, if composed within our own culture, would be scandalous today. In literature alone, one may think of "shocking" examples from Greek lyric poetry, Aristophanes, and the Roman satirists. Yet these poets are "ancient," and age, coupled with the mere fact of survival, allows us to consider them classics. The result of such classicizing is that a volume of Latin lyric poetry that includes the powerful sexual and scatological obscenities of Catullus, for example, is safer in a school library than is a copy of *The Catcher in the Rye*. Approaching the issue of scandalous art, then, through historical juxtaposition could encourage students to reexamine why some communities turn certain texts and objects into "classics," and why others repudiate them.

Finally, I expected that this subject would be particularly stimulating for an audience of contemporary students in that it has always inspired intense debate among people of all political orientations. The issue of transgression, after all, gets right to the heart of all basic sociopolitical questions, and forces all who address those questions to articulate clearly their very conceptions of, among others things, community, diversity, parenting, and education. Certain recent artistic phenomena, such as gangsta rap, have even created unlikely ideological alliances between conservatives and liberals, and students are excited to see how complex and fluid ideology can sometimes be.

This seminar was first mounted in the spring of 1998, and was affiliated with two humanities classes taught by one teacher at UCHS. I divided the seminar into four groups of five or six students, and we visited the two UCHS classes on Tuesdays and Wednesdays. That is, one group went on Tuesday, first period; a second group went to the second-period class. Then on Wednesday the process was repeated, but with two different groups from Penn. I myself cycled through the groups, visiting a different one each week.

We began the semester by having the UCHS students read a chapter on music from Allan Bloom's *Closing of the American Mind,* and then compare it with Plato's views on art and censorship. We also read with the students some of Aristophanes's *Clouds,* which (like Bloom) deals with the notion of a contemporary society in decline. From there we settled into working through

Aristophanes's Lysistrata, in which the women of Athens band together with Spartan women and decide to withhold sex from their husbands until the men end the war they are engaged in.

In the classes at UCHS, the Penn students worked in pairs with small groups of high school students, and I gave them some guidance previous to each session, suggesting themes to emphasize, strategies, and the like. Sometimes the Penn students would begin by offering some basic information, adding to a time line that the teacher had been constructing during the semester, for example. At other times they would lead the UCHS students in a discussion of the topics or reading at hand. For a few weeks we read aloud Lysistrata, stopping to discuss its content, and compare it with our own times. This led to spirited discussions on any number of topics: the nature of war, the role of women, feminism, obscenity, negotiations. After that, we read with them another Greek play, Euripides's Medea (itself somewhat scandalous in its day), that allowed us to revisit gender politics from a tragic, rather than comic, point of view.

The students at UCHS were uniformly excited by the visits from Penn. Their teacher told me time and again that her students always eagerly looked forward to the visits from the Penn students. She found that even some of the more uninterested students felt drawn out by the experience of having Penn students visit. To my surprise (because this had not been my experience with the first course), she told me that most of the students were actually interested in the antiquarian aspects of the material; that is, they were amazed at the clear connections to be found between ancient society and our own. They got a real charge out of knowing that they were reading something that was more than two millenia old.

The last session we held on Lysistrata illustrates the level of engagement the students experienced. We had decided to act out a scene in class. In the class I visited, we divided into two groups. One group wanted to do a scene more or less straight from the translation. The other group wanted to dispense with the text, but create its own scenes based on its understanding of the original. Before the performance at the end of the class, each group caucused and rehearsed for about 45 minutes. The group that did its scene straight worked hard at modernizing the language and understanding some of the quirks of Aristophanes's style. It chose a director and assigned parts, with Penn students orchestrating and helping out with background and vocabulary.

The group that acted out its own scene tried to extract from the original a basic scheme as follows: "the fight" (between rival gangs, Bloods and Crips), "the return home, and reunion between Lysistrata and her husband," "the negotiation" (between the rival gangs), and "reconciliation." This was an astonishing and stirring performance: It was rehearsed to a point, but the dialogue was largely improvised, and the group worked hard to pull off a coherent narrative. It was, in fact, very difficult for the students playing the rival gang members (not unlike the Athenians and Spartans) to reconcile and establish any reasonable kind of "peace." And when the teacher interrupted the rehearsal to suggest that the peace they had come up with was hardly going to be a lasting one, she was promptly rebuffed with: "Let us work it out ourselves." So she did. But they had actually heard what she was saying, and tried to come up with a more substantive reconciliation, one that got them at least to think about the absurdity of hostile factionalism. The class ended with that group of students asking the teacher whether they could next "write down their dialogue," so they would not forget what they had created in class.

The students in my seminar at Penn were deeply committed to this project from the beginning. Once they had visited UCHS and talked with the teacher, they were very excited about the potential they saw in communicating their enthusiasm for the material, and about seeing whether they could make the ancient texts relevant to their own lives. I began every seminar session by asking them to review their experiences at UCHS and to try to articulate how those experiences affected their interaction with antiquity. They generally responded by saying that working with the high school students allowed them to see just how "alive" these ancient texts still remain for our culture. I think it is not so much the case that they found anything especially unique or timeless about the ancient texts, but that they simply never would have expected that something so distant and old would resonate for them in quite the way it did. I also believe that they experienced a certain comfort (and perhaps frustration!) in seeing that some of our greatest and most intractable philosophical and social problems are nothing new, that they were articulated by great writers of the past, and that placing ourselves in an intellectual tradition that extends to antiquity allows for a deeper perspective on our own real-world problems.

Clearly the two seminars I have described, with their outreach into the UCHS curriculum, represent relatively small-scale experiments in academically based service-learning. But they show, I believe, that the relevance of the classics need not be forced: Classical texts offer us some of the first traces of conversations that have been evolving for millenia, and will no doubt evolve for additional millenia, as long as there are human beings on the planet capable of speech and reason. And frankly, there are few things I can think of that are more essential than is engaging our students, and future generations of students, in conversations such as these — conversations that are directed, even if sometimes only obliquely, toward the improvement of the human condition.

Notes

1. A version of this essay was originally published in *Universities and Community Schools*, Fall-Winter 1994. Portions have been rewritten and new material has been added for the purpose of this volume.

2. From "Thucydides 2.65," translated by Richard Crawley, revised by Richard B. Strassler (ed.), *The Landmark Thucydides: A Comprehensive Guide to the Peloponnesian War*, pp. 127-128, (New York, NY: Free Press, 1996).

COMMUNITY, NEIGHBORHOOD AND FAMILY
IN ANCIENT ATHENS AND MODERN PHILADELPHIA
(Classical Studies 125: Spring 1996)

Dr. Ralph M. Rosen
Williams Hall 720

Weekly Assignments

1) January 17: Introduction

General discussion focusing on: what is the point of studying antiquity? what does it mean to say that we can "learn" from the past? what kind of knowledge can the humanistic disciplines, and Classics in particular, offer us? We will consider the notion of "classical culture" as a construct. How is the term "classical" used and abused in our own discourse? What makes fifth-century Athens an appropriate period to study for comparison to a modern urban culture? What is "interpretation?"

2) January 24: Democracy Ancient and Modern

1) Pseudo-Xenophon's Constitution of Athens ("The Old Oligarch"). [bulkpack]
2) Aristotle, Constitution of Athens (selections). [bulkpack]
3) Sagan, The Honey and the Hemlock: Democracy and Paranoia in Ancient Athens and Modern America, pp. 1-34.
4) Sinclair, Democracy and Participation in Classical Athens pp. 1-23
5) Strauss, "The Melting Pot, the Mosaic, and the Agora," in Athenian Political Thought and the Reconstruction of American Democracy [seminar room]

Short essay topic: Based on the above reading assignments, what, if anything, is familiar to us as Americans and Philadelphians in the Athenian conceptions of democracy? Pay particular attention to practical, day-to-day manifestations of democracy.

3) January 31: The Ideology of Citizenship, Athenian and Modern

1) Thucydides, Pericles' "Funeral Oration" [bulkpack]
2) "Share and Rights: 'Citizenship' Greek Style and American Style," text of lecture by Martin Ostwald. [bulkpack]
3) Tyrrell and Brown, Athenian Myths and Mythmaking, pp. 189-215.
4) Sinclair, Democracy and Participation in Classical Athens pp. 24-48
5) Miscellaneous newspaper clippings on recent War Memorials. [bulkpack]

Short essay topic: What are some of the differences and similarities between Athenian and American forms of commemorating war-dead, and what do they reveal about each culture's concept of citizenship?

---

4) February 7: Demes and Neighborhoods

1) D. Whitehead, The Demes of Attica , pp. 67-120. [bulkpack]
2) Sagan, The Honey and the Hemlock: Democracy and Paranoia in Ancient Athens and Modern America, pp. 320-35.
3) Adams, Bartelt etc., ch. 3, "Housing and Neighborhoods," pp. 66-99. [seminar room]
4) Muller, Meyer and Cybriwsky, Philadelphia: A Study of Conflicts and Social Cleavages, pp. 1-33. [seminar room]
5) Miscellaneous clippings about "Philadelphia Regionalism," including the "Peirce Report" [bulkpack]

Short essay topic: Describe the particular interaction between local and central politics that you have experienced in your own cultural background. Are the issues you have read about this week in the context of Philadelphia and Athens redolent of your own experience in any ways? Be as specific as you can within the framework of a short essay.

5) February 14: "Human Nature," Morality and Politics I

1) Plato, Gorgias, pp. 75-149 (end).
2) Thucydides, "Melian Dialogue" [bulkpack]
3) Sagan, The Honey and the Hemlock: Democracy and Paranoia in Ancient Athens and Modern America, pp. 186-203, 228-47.

Short essay topic: Describe briefly the criticisms both Callicles and Socrates have of democracy, as revealed in the second half of the Gorgias. What do you think "citizenship" means to each of them?

6) February 21: "Human Nature," Morality and Politics II

1) Plato, Republic, pp.227-319; and editor's "Introduction," pp. xi-lxii.
2) Karl R. Popper, The Open Society and its Enemies, ch. 6: "Totalitarian Justice", pp. 86-119. [bulkpack]

Short essay topic: Does Plato's philosopher-king seem to you to be ideal ruler (as Plato would claim), or an uncompromising and dangerous dictator, as Popper would? Try to imagine such a ruler in Philadelphia: the mayor, e.g., as "philosopher-king." What are some of the positive and negative effects this might have?

7) February 28: Interpersonal Relations I

1) Sherry B. Ortner, "Is Female to Male as Nature is to Culture?" [bulkpack]
2) K. J. Dover, "Classical Greek Attitudes to Sexual Behaviour" [seminar room]
3) Fantham, et al., Women in the Classical World, pp. 68-135
4) Xenophon, Oeconomicus (selections) [bulkpack]

5) Wendy Kaminer, "Feminism's Identity Crisis" (from The Atlantic Monthly, October 1993) [seminar room]

Short essay topic: Compare Athenian conceptions of "family" and "household" to our own constructions of such concepts. Does Xenophon's Oeconomicus present a picture of marriage and family life that we recognize in our own society, or is it entirely alien to our sensibilities?

---

8) March 6: Interpersonal Relations II

1) Homeric Hymn to Demeter, ed. Helene Foley, pp. 2-75 (text with commentary), 103-37 (interpretive essay).
2) Essays in back of volume: Marilyn Arthur Katz, "Politics and Pomegranates: An Interpretation of the Homeric Hymn to Demeter", pp. 212-42; Nancy Chodorow, "Family Structure and Feminine Personality," 243-65.

Short essay topic: Why is an essay by Nancy Chodorow included in an edition of a Homeric Hymn?

---

9) March 20: Interpersonal Relations III

1) Plato, Symposium
2) D. Halperin, One Hundred Years of Homosexuality, pp. 1-71. [bulkpack]
3) Interview with David Halperin in Favonius [bulkpack]
4) Miscellaneous newspaper clippings on homosexuality. [bulkpack]

Short essay topic: Compare modern American with ancient Athenian attitudes towards homosexuality (male or female). How "gay" was/is the same-sex experience in Athens/America?

---

10) March 27: Education I

1) Aristophanes: Clouds
2) Weiler (1974), Chapter 5: "Politics and Education" (pp. 77-102) [seminar room]
3 G. B. Kerferd, The Sophistic Movement, 15-58. [bulkpack]
4) Susan C. Jarratt, Rereading the Sophists: Classical Rhetoric Refigured: Ch 4 "Sophistic Pedagogy, Then and Now" pp. 63-117. [bulkpack]

Short essay topic: Is it possible to describe an Athenian "ideology" of education? How about for the Philadelphia public schools?

---

11) April 3: Education II

1) Plato, Republic (sections to be announced)
2) Selections from Benjamin Franklin on education [seminar room]

3) Bellah, Madsen, Sullivan, Swidler, Tipton, The Good Society, Ch. 5: "Education: Technical and Moral", pp. 145-78. [seminar room]

Short essay topic: "On the whole Americans have done better in developing their educational resources for the transmission of specialized knowledge and skills than they have for citizenship." Comment briefly on this quotation. How did Plato address the conflict between "technical" and "moral" knowedge, and its transmission through education?

---

12) April 10: Public Events

[Short abstract of paper topic due today]

The following will be available in the seminar room:
1) R. Rehm, Greek Tragic Theater , pp. 1-30
2) S. G. Davis, Parades and Power: Street Theatre in Nineteenth-Century Philadelphia, 1-48, 155-73.
3) Sophocles, Antigone [seminar room]

Short essay topic: In today's assignment you have seen several manifestations of public events that carried with them, in varying degrees, communitarian ideologies. What analogues to any of these can you find in your own experience? How important are they to your sense of well being as a member of a community?

---

13) April 17: The Arts and Society

1) Aristophanes' Frogs

The following will be available in the Afro-American Seminar Room (4th Floor van Pelt):
2) Houston Baker, Black Studies, Rap and the Academy (1993) (E184.7.B3.1993; also available in Rosengarten Reserve)
3) miscellaneous clippings

---

14) Assignment for April 24, 1996: Presentation of Papers

Return to some of the questions posed during the first class. Students will write a paper on any of the specific issues we studied during the semester, with particular focus on the general question about whether the study of a remote, and in this case ancient, culture can be useful for understanding our own culture, and possibly helpful in effecting social progress. Each student will speak for about 15 minutes about her/his paper topic.

The Unspoken Purposes of Service-Learning:
Teaching the Holocaust

by Steve Hochstadt

As a form of pedagogy, service-learning is among the fastest growing ideas in American education. Applicable to many disciplines, but also completely outside all disciplinary boundaries, service-learning appears to many educators as a perfect union between usually disjunctive territories, the academy and the real world. We encourage students to leave the campus in order to perform service for their community and to further their own knowledge. How to make this connection between service and learning is less obvious in history than in some other disciplines, such as sociology or psychology, where contemporary society is the basis of study. During service, history students must make cognitive leaps from the people they meet and the society they live in to ideas about the past. Often this is most appropriate in thinking about social history. It is much harder to imagine service-learning projects that would connect clearly to diplomatic or military history. Likewise, it is much easier to integrate service-learning into the U.S. history curriculum than into the histories of other continents. For historians, it is much easier to organize service than to promote learning through a particular service closely connected to the curriculum.

Teaching offers a simple way out of this dilemma. Students who teach their subject in local schools can simultaneously serve and learn, performing useful and valued functions for many community members, while deepening their knowledge of a historical subject. It is not easy, however, to find the right opportunity to teach history in local schools. While public school teachers welcome visitors who bring diversity and excitement into their classrooms, history is not usually the favored subject. Apart from particular moments of the year, such as Martin Luther King, Jr.'s birthday or Women's History Month, school systems usually do not seek historical input from outsiders. It is even more difficult to find subjects that can automatically arouse the interest of schoolchildren.

In my opinion, the Holocaust offers an excellent subject for transforming our students into teachers. Public school systems around the country are recognizing the value, and even the obligation, to teach about the Holocaust. Over the past decade, states such as Illinois and New Jersey have mandated the teaching of Holocaust curricula. Few teachers, however, have been sufficiently prepared for this responsibility, so they appreciate offers of assistance from the outside. Public fascination with the Holocaust appears to be at a high point. Lessons about the Holocaust, like the study of African-

American and women's history, can serve the larger purposes of understanding prejudice and teaching tolerance. None of this need result in commercializing, sensationalizing, or popularizing the Holocaust. In fact, teaching the Holocaust requires constant attention to authenticity in every respect.

This is the background of my entry into service-learning through the creation of a Holocaust teaching project in the public schools of the communities around Bates College.[1] I wish to use my experience with this project to examine some of the features of service-learning that might not be obvious at first glance. What I have come to recognize as unspoken purposes in my thinking about this particular service-learning project could be useful in considering more generally how to integrate service and learning into the teaching of history.

The Holocaust Teaching Project

The potentially fruitful connection among Holocaust education, my students, and local public schools developed from my coincidental work as historian, elected representative to the local school board, and board member of the Holocaust Human Rights Center of Maine. As an expression of my commitment to teaching the Holocaust in public schools, I have encouraged my students to offer Holocaust lessons in local elementary, junior high, and high schools since 1992. I initially saw this project totally in terms of its service component, as a way of reaching many elementary and secondary students with a small dose of Holocaust education.

The Holocaust teaching project I have developed depends for its structure on the peculiar calendar of my institution, Bates College. This project coincides with my course on the history of the Holocaust, which I have taught every two years since 1992 during the winter term, ending in the middle of April. Typically about 130 students enroll, an indication of the importance that contemporary students give to Holocaust education. Most students then stay at Bates for a short semester of five weeks, which is intended to be an intensive study in one course, but actually leaves them considerable free time. I ask for volunteers who have taken my course and are willing to donate time during this spring semester to teaching. The volunteers are matched with requests from local school teachers; students offer one- or two-hour lessons on the Holocaust to grades 5 through 12. In the four times this project has been run, there have been an average of 18 student-teachers per year, teaching in about 40 classrooms.

By the end of my course, an average student is certainly knowledgeable enough to teach a lesson about the Holocaust. Few, however, are confident about their pedagogical skills. I offer two 2-hour evening sessions on pedagogical skills. The first is organized around a video in which I give a Holocaust lesson in a local fifth-grade class, which the students and I watch together and then discuss. This example brings up many of the key issues that the prospective Holocaust teacher in Lewiston, Maine, must face: the lack of experience with Jews and Judaism among the predominantly Catholic schoolchildren; the limitations of what can be accomplished in one school period; the inappropriateness of college-style lecturing in a school setting; and the importance of interaction with students at their level of understanding. The second session is led by a former Bates history major, Laurie Sevigny, who has taught the Holocaust in Maine high schools for a decade. She offers much more specific curricular suggestions about the many possibilities of organizing a class session on the Holocaust. She brings in a variety of props that can stimulate understanding for younger pupils, such as paper cutouts representing the many colored badges used by the Nazis to distinguish among concentration camp prisoners (yellow for Jews, pink for homosexuals, green for criminals). These sessions also act as confidence-builders for my inexperienced student-teachers, who come to recognize that they can take their knowledge into an unfamiliar environment and offer interesting lessons. Then the students are given directions to their schools and perform their teaching assignments without any further supervision. In this way about 1,000 local schoolchildren received Holocaust lessons each time this teach-in has been done.

The major goals of this project are obvious. Many students are exposed, even if only briefly, to the Holocaust as a significant historical event. My own students deepen their understanding of the material we covered in my course by preparing for and teaching classroom lessons. The service is widely appreciated and the learning is a direct extension of coursework.

But as I have run this project four times, I understand better that many other purposes can be accomplished. Only gradually did I come to realize what important consequences this service had on my college students' learning about the Holocaust. After nearly a decade of organizing this particular project, I have come to understand some of its less obvious effects in both service and learning. I see more clearly that service-learning is likely to embody a variety of purposes, which are known neither to the students nor to the community members who work with them. There is nothing pernicious about unspoken purposes in teaching; in fact, I believe that good teaching employs many hidden agendas, as teachers pursue multiple effects with particular classroom tasks or assignments. At times it is important that students not know precisely why they are being asked to perform in certain ways.[2] Yet we need to understand fully the less-than-obvious effects of our techniques in order to put them to best use. These implicit goals, as I have increasingly recognized them, can be incorporated into the structure of the project and thereby further emphasized. Their unspoken nature is then called into question, but not always with the result that I would choose explicitly to acknowledge them. An exploration of the unspoken purposes of service-learning, through one example I am familiar with, perhaps will serve to open this topic for further reflection.

Unspoken Purposes

Some of these unspoken purposes come out of my broader pedagogical interests in public education. I believe that teaching about the Holocaust is an important medium through which to offer more-general lessons to American students about prejudice, resistance to oppression, and moral behavior. I belong to an organization, the Holocaust Human Rights Center of Maine, that has promoted Holocaust education in public schools for nearly 20 years as a means to address issues of toleration, prejudice, and diversity. To this end, we have produced curriculum guides for grades K through 8, taped interviews with Maine survivors, and finished a video about the Holocaust based on those interviews.3 Thus I urge my students to teach about the Holocaust in local schools as a means to encourage schoolteachers to see the value of this curriculum, and thus to integrate more Holocaust lessons into their own teaching. This has been moderately successful because I can promise teachers that my students will return to their classrooms, even though only every other year, in this way continually encouraging more integration of the Holocaust into the regular curriculum.

Teaching the Holocaust is, however, only one of my purposes. In this very Catholic city, I also want young students to learn, even briefly, that Jews exist, that they are people with a different culture, and that discrimination against them has had horrible consequences. Many students in Lewiston have never met a Jew, and certainly not heard about them in school. The increasing difficulty of bringing religious issues into the schools means that discussions of the Holocaust may be one of the few acceptable ways of acquainting students with Judaism and Jews. Certainly this is not an ideal linkage, but it can serve as an opening to later, fuller discussions.

I also hope that students will learn from these classroom visitors that history can be exciting. Many students arrive in college already turned off to history by poor high school pedagogy, which stresses names, dates, and memorization. Visitors in public school classrooms often bring specialized scientific knowledge, but rarely are history lessons brought in from the outside. I want my student-teachers to demonstrate that events in the 1930s and 1940s can still be vital in our lives. Because the Holocaust has such an immediate and broad public appeal today, students are eager to participate in this short historical curriculum.

Another effect derives from the interaction between college students and high school students. In the most recent version of this project, one of my best teachers was a first-year student. When she taught in a few high school classrooms, her students could potentially see themselves in her, could imagine themselves able to cross the great divide from student to teacher. The model of a successful student that she embodied can act as a spur to the best of her students, raising aspirations, creating motivation.

Finally, my students are ambassadors of Bates College, a rich, white, upper-middle-class institution, to the overwhelmingly working-class children of French-Canadian heritage in the local public schools. As in many college towns, the divergent social, economic, and intellectual backgrounds of the college population and the local community have created a gulf in understanding, which can border on hostility. Service-learning of all kinds is a means of brightening the education institution's image and of creating positive ties to the community. By offering the service of guest lecturers to local schoolteachers, I can strengthen the natural ties among educators, which can lead to other forms of partnerships around educational issues.

None of these goals is complex or surprising. Yet they are hidden from view as I organize this project. Speaking of them openly might serve no purpose, as in the case of my interest in promoting history as a fascinating study. Or it might even lead to skeptical reactions, if I explicitly referred to my desire to bring Jewishness as an issue into the public classroom or to improve town-gown relations. Because my vision of service likely are broader than the more immediate interests of those who receive these services, some of the purposes of my project will remain unacknowledged.

Learning Outcomes

A second category of outcomes relates to my students who volunteer as teachers, those who are supposed to learn from delivering service. In this particular project, there is no openly addressed pedagogical purpose in the work of my students. Because the project takes place outside the boundaries of my course, is unrelated to credit, and is purely voluntary, my interactions with my students about their teaching are centered on the service activity rather than on their learning. It is important for them to believe that they already know enough about the Holocaust that they can successfully teach it. Yet certainly we all know that their preparation for their lessons involves further learning: making decisions about what elements of the Holocaust they wish to address; refreshing their memories about chronology and causality; thinking most generally about what messages they wish to convey in their teaching; deciding not just what to say, but also how to say it. The students don't realize, nor would it make much difference if I told them beforehand, that the act of teaching itself is one of the most powerful ways we know of learning a subject. They discover this by doing it, and come away from their teaching experience with a much deeper understanding of the Holocaust.

One example of the overlap between a pedagogical technique used in my course and the teaching project that comes afterwards can serve to highlight the interactions between my and my students' teaching and their service. Early in the semester I ask every student to prepare a chronology of the Holocaust limited to about 15 items. This often causes great distress and vocal objection. Events of overwhelming human tragedy must be left out in paring down a list to such dimensions. The pain my students feel in doing this assignment is often transferred to the assignment or to me: I should not have asked them to do this. My explanation — that the highlighting of a selected few historical facts, out of many possible choices, is the normal work of the historian — is only partially convincing. The last time I taught this course, I was taken aback by the strength of the student reaction. Yet my student-teachers, once they begin to prepare their lessons, immediately recognized the necessity of this work. They had automatically begun making such decisions about what they would address and what they would have to leave out. We laughed together about the value of the earlier exercise, but I also realized how I could organize that assignment better. By making the course assignment more realistic by pretending it is preparation for the students' own teaching, I may be able to convince them that it needs to be done, even if the choices are still painful.

As in my thinking about the effects on the recipients of the service, I also have other purposes in mind for my students. I wish to show them that teaching is a wonderful profession, not just because it delivers a service to others, but because it provides rewards for the teacher that are hard to match in other endeavors. Many of my student-teachers have exclaimed afterwards that they had no idea how much fun teaching was. While some of those who volunteer for this project do so because they are already committed to teaching as a career, I hope to convince others to consider that option.

More generally I see this project as offering a kind of reward to some of my best students. Again, this idea would make little sense to most of them were I to mention it at the outset. Yet I can see afterwards that their success has encouraged them, given them confidence in a setting in which they were in charge.

It has taken me years to realize that this teaching project serves as a kind of closure for those students who participate. Teaching the Holocaust presents challenges beyond what is normal in the teaching of history. Anyone who studies the Holocaust is left with a nearly overpowering sense of pessimism and helplessness. I have noted in my students a frustration about their new knowledge: They feel that these historical facts demand a response, more than 50 years later, but they are at a loss about how to imagine or create an appropriate response. Learning of the notoriously weak reaction of the American government to the plight of Jewish refugees before the war frequently impels students toward a more interventionist stance regarding contemporary conflicts where genocide is a possible outcome. But the overwhelming political complications attached to any change in American foreign policy make this unsatisfactory as a personal response to such a course. Students appear to me to need some personal action that they can feel offers an appropriate and immediate confrontation with the unsettling knowledge they have acquired.

The teaching project fills this need very well. At least for this minority of students, teaching about the Holocaust offers a closure to their learning and a sense of satisfaction that they are taking some action oriented toward the future, toward prevention in the largest sense. Teaching allows these students to express themselves about the Holocaust, to take charge of this emotionally difficult historical material. In this case, the timing, directly after the course is over, emphasizes the teaching as a action-oriented response to learning. Teaching is an inherently optimistic enterprise, an antidote to that pessimistic apathy that can result from confrontation with the Holocaust.

Conclusion

I think it has been worth considering the implicit purposes of this particular project because I would argue that every service-learning project has many such unspoken goals, which could reinforce or be independent of its explicit purposes. Once we get beyond the idea of helping others and the value to our students of gaining a particular experience outside of the campus, we must consider fully our own agendas in selecting, organizing, and pursuing service-learning projects. Such agendas might not be clear to us until the project has been in operation for some time, even for several years. However, once our goals are brought to the surface, we can better consider whether they ought to continue to be unspoken, or whether their purposes would be more effectively achieved if they were openly addressed.

The confluence, and perhaps conflict, of intentions in service-learning goes well beyond what we as initiators intend. Every participant in service-learning brings a set of goals to our projects. In 1998 I instituted a postproject meeting among my student-teachers and the public school teachers as a closing event. I wanted this informal gathering to help in evaluating the project as well as in strengthening the ties between Bates and the public schools. At this meeting, however, the multiplicity of others' unspoken agendas came to light. A student-teacher spoke of how successful her quotations from an interview with her Polish grandmother were in riveting her class's attention. It was clear that she wanted to use her teaching opportunity as a forum for discussing her family's Holocaust experiences. Teaching in this way provided some personal form of closure and offered alternative meanings for her family's ordeal. One of the teachers in a rural middle school noted that the presence of college students in her classroom could serve to raise the aspirations of her pupils. She had requested that her school be included in my project because she hoped to widen the horizons of her rural students.

This last example brings up some potential conflicts in the expansion of service-learning. As my project has become better known in the towns around Bates, I have received requests to include more schools. Meeting future requests might expand the project so much that I would lose some control over its management. There could be a point where the increased provision of service begins to interfere with the learning I seek to impart.

I would argue more generally that the full list of purposes of those of us who initiate service-learning projects typically contains some contradictions. Most obviously, my interest in having my students be successful in their teaching conflicts with the complexity of the lessons they deliver. The more I stress the importance of offering clearly developed interpretations of the Holocaust, backed up by intensive pedagogical workshops, the fewer volunteers I will find. More generally, the more I wish to derive from the service, the more of my purposes I explicitly urge my students to consider as their tasks, the less likely it is that they will be able to accomplish them. I need to contain my agendas, both explicit and implicit, concerning the effects on the local schools, in order to achieve my purposes for my own students. Too many goals at cross-purposes from too many sources can interfere with the transmission of the history itself. Goals such as building self-confidence can lead to simplifying complex historical content. Even more troubling, the seriousness of the Holocaust, which can leave learners with unpleasant emotions of helplessness or anger or fear, might be sacrificed to a more feel-good approach to service. There is no simple solution to contradictory goals, but any resolution depends on recognizing how many goals we have and how they interact.

At the most general level, service and learning are not always complementary. Each project mixes these components in a unique way, depending on our purposes, on local conditions, and on the organization of the project. The more we recognize our many agendas, the more likely we are to find success in both service and learning that erases the walls between classroom and community.

Notes

1. I acknowledge here the invaluable help of Peggy Rotundo and Ken Allen from the Bates College Center for Service-Learning, and James Carignan, dean of the College, in making this project work smoothly and in encouraging more generally the integration of service-learning into the Bates curriculum.

2. This is especially true in some classroom simulations used in teaching the Holocaust, which allow underlying tendencies toward group formation and social exclusion to temporarily take over the classroom.

3. Laura R. Petovello, *The Spirit That Moves Us: A Literature-Based Resource Guide on Teaching About the Holocaust and Human Rights,* Vol. 1 (Holocaust Human Rights Center of Maine, 1994), for grades K through 4; Rachel Quenk, *The Spirit That Moves Us: A Literature-Based Resource Guide on Teaching About the Holocaust and Human Rights,* Vol. 2 (Tilbury House, 1997), and "Maine Survivors Remember the Holocaust" (Holocaust Human Rights Center of Maine, 1994).

Annotated Bibliography

by Bill M. Donovan and John Saltmarsh

While the number of publications primarily directed to historians on service-learning remains small, there is a rich historical literature that forms the foundations of much of the current service movement within and outside of higher education. Service-learning as an engaged pedagogy closely linked to education for the purpose of democratic citizenship places its formative traditions within the historical debates and tension over education reform and national service since the late 19th century. John Dewey, William James, and Jane Addams stand out in this regard. A significant body of that literature is referenced in the individual essays in this volume.

The following references are meant as a starting point for historians who seek to gain more information on service-learning's practice and theory.

Books and Articles

Barber, Benjamin R. (1992). *An Aristocracy of Everyone: The Politics of Education and the Future of America*. Oxford: Oxford University Press.
> Barber's concern is citizenship and civic education, and he discusses the current interest in service-learning within the context of debates over the role of education in American society.

———. (1998). *A Place for Us: How to Make Society Civil and Democracy Strong*. New York, NY: Hill and Wang.
> Written by a political philosopher, this book is an important contribution to the calls for civic renewal in America and places service-learning within the context of education that includes, in Tocqueville's words, "apprenticeship for liberty."

———, and Richard Battistoni, eds. (1993). *Education for Democracy*. Dubuque, IA: Kendall-Hunt.
> This anthology contains a rich and diverse collection of writings on citizenship, community, and service.

Benson, Lee, and Ira Harkavy. (1997). "School and Community in the Global Society." *Universities and Community Schools* 5(1-2): 16-71.
> This essay highlights Dewey's contribution to democratic pedagogy and calls for higher education-school-community partnerships as a strategy for improving the American schooling system in particular and American society in general.

Boyer, Ernest. (1990). *Scholarship Reconsidered: Priorities of the Professoriate.* Princeton, NJ: The Carnegie Foundation for the Advancement of Teaching.
> Because service-learning is premised upon a pedagogy that includes experiential education and community outreach, the argument that Boyer makes for a new generation of scholars to enlarge the perspective of scholarship is essential reading.

————. (March 9, 1994). "Creating the New American College." *The Chronicle of Higher Education:* A48.
> This watershed article makes the case that higher education reform at the end of the 20th century should address institutional change toward creating "connected institutions" that connect thought with action and theory with practice in a way that is responsive to community concerns.

Boyte, Harry C., and Nancy N. Kari. (1996). *Building America: The Democratic Promise of Public Work.* Philadelphia, PA: Temple University Press.
> Boyte and Kari offer a populist political theory and history of democracy that they label "commonwealth politics." A commonwealth politics recognizes the fluid and permeable nature of democratic spaces, opening possibilities for citizens to reclaim their civic authority through work and organizations associated with work. They introduce the useful concept of public work as a way to understand and advance the public and democratic contributions of citizens to the commonwealth.

Bringle, Robert G., and Julie A. Hatcher. (1996). "Implementing Service-Learning in Higher Education." *Journal of Higher Education* 67(2): 221-239.
> This is an important essay that examines the ways in which service-learning provides means for reaching educational objectives and examines in a detailed way the process for developing service-learning at the institutional level.

Bringle, Robert G., Richard Games, and Edward A. Malloy, eds. (1999). *Colleges and Universities as Citizens.* Needham, MA: Allyn & Bacon.
This book directly links the vision of an engaged campus with the pedagogy of service-learning, presenting a critical examination of the relationship between campuses and communities and the role of higher education in educating students as responsible citizens.

Council of Chief State School Officers. (1993). *Service-Learning Planning and Resource Guide.* Washington, DC: Council of Chief State School Officers.
This remains a useful guide for finding funding to plan and develop service-learning programs. First, competitive and noncompetitive grants are discussed, followed by an extensive resource guide.

Damon, W. (Oct. 16, 1998). "The Path to a Civil Society Goes Through the University." *The Chronicle of Higher Education:* B4-B5.
Damon makes the case that higher education has a role to play in civic renewal and that service-learning is an important example of a pedagogy of community engagement.

Delve, Cecilia I., Suzanne D. Mintz, and Grieg M. Stewart, eds. (1990). *Community Service as Values Education.* New Directions for Teaching and Learning, no. 50. San Francisco, CA: Jossey-Bass.
These essays provide a good introduction to experiential learning theory and suggest models of program design for service-learning that are based on developmental goals and learning styles.

Ehrenberg, Ronald. G. (1997). *The American University: National Treasure or Endangered Species?* Ithaca, NY: Cornell University Press.
A series of essays written to honor Frank H.T. Rhodes, president emeritus of Cornell University. An important group of essays focusing on the problems confronting American higher education. Although focusing on research institutions, the essays are widely applicable and invite careful reading.

Eyler, Janet, and Dwight E. Giles, Jr. (1999). *Where's the Learning in Service-Learning?* San Francisco, CA: Jossey-Bass.
This is the most comprehensive empirical study done to date on the academic benefits of service-learning, based on two national studies conducted in the mid 1990s funded through the U.S. Department of Education's Fund for the Improvement of Postsecondary Education (FIPSE) and the Corporation for National Service.

Eyler, Janet, Dwight E. Giles, Jr., and Angela Schmiede. (1996). *A Practitioner's Guide to Reflection in Service-Learning: Student Voices and Reflections.* Nashville, TN: Vanderbilt University.
> This highly valuable guide should be consulted by anyone considering service-learning.

Falbo, M.C. (1993). *Serving to Learn: A Faculty Guide to Service-Learning.* Columbus, OH: Ohio Campus Compact.
> Falbo, the director of John Carroll University's community service program, has written a valuable guide to academic service and reflection.

Gamson, Zelda F. (Jan./Feb. 1997). "Higher Education and Rebuilding Civic Life." *Change* 29(1): 10-13.
> A highly important and perceptive essay pointing out higher education's need to rebuild its own civic life if it is truly to engage the wider community.

Goldsmith, Suzanne. (1995). *Journal Reflection: A Resource Guide for Community Service Leaders and Educators Engaged in Service Learning.* Washington, DC: The American Alliance for Rights and Responsibilities.
> This is an important resource for maximizing the use of student journals as a key tool of reflection to connect the students' experiences in the community with their academic study.

Harkavy, Ira, and John Puckett. (September 1994). "Lessons From Hull House for the Contemporary Urban University." *Service* 1: 9-20.
> An excellent article discussing the history of service in modern American research universities. A very useful complement to Harkavy's essay in this volume.

Howard, Jeffrey, ed. (1993). *Praxis I: A Faculty Casebook on Community Service,* and *Praxis II: Service Learning Resources for University Students, Staff and Faculty.* Ann Arbor, MI: Office of Community Service Learning.

> The first volume presents a useful set of service-learning case studies in undergraduate and graduate classes. It includes essential guidelines for faculty on "the principles of good practice in community service pedagogy." The second volume includes institutional considerations and although the curriculum discussions are focused on sociology, this is an important interdisciplinary work for higher education faculty considering service-learning. It presents curricular materials for incorporating service-learning into the classroom. It further discusses evaluation, campus-wide promotion of service-learning, and charts the intellectual and pedagogical rationale for using service.

Jacoby, Barbara, and Associates. (1996). *Service-Learning in Higher Education: Concepts and Practices.* San Francisco, CA: Jossey-Bass.

> The essays in this volume comprehensively cover the challenges that service-learning presents, from the level of curricular design to organizational, administrative, and policy issues.

Kendall, Jane, et al. (1990). *Combining Service and Learning: A Resource Book for Community and Public Service.* 2 vols. Raleigh, NC: National Society for Internships and Experiential Education.

> These volumes compile the seminal writings of a generation of educators who advanced the current movement of service-learning in higher education. While some of the institutional data are somewhat dated, much of the theoretical and conceptual essays are still highly relevant.

Kraft, Richard J., and Marc Swadener, eds. (1994). *Building Community: Service Learning in the Academic Disciplines.* Denver, CO: Colorado Campus Compact.

> This text is aimed at faculty seeking to implement service-learning in their teaching. It contains useful articles ranging from the theory of service-learning to practical advice on effective use.

Lempert, David C. (1996). *Escape From the Ivory Tower.* San Francisco, CA: Jossey-Bass.

> A well-known work that argues the benefits of putting students in the community to complement their classroom education. In addition, Lempert provides course descriptions and problem-solving suggestions.

Mathews, David. (1998). "Creating More Public Space in Higher Education."
Washington, DC: The Council on Public Policy Education.
>   While this essay does not address service-learning directly, it is a sem-
>   inal piece in interpreting the mission of higher education in America
>   and the need for higher education to transform itself to meet needs of
>   a national crisis defined by a crisis in our civic lives.

Morton, Keith, and John Saltmarsh. (Fall 1997). "Addams, Day, and Dewey:
The Emergence of Community Service in American Culture." *Michigan
Journal of Community Service-Learning* 4: 137-149.
>   This essay describes the contours of the history of community service
>   in the United States, arguing that the tensions created over the collision
>   of capitalism and democracy at the turn of the century generated a cri-
>   sis of community and a profound rethinking of the meaning and prac-
>   tice of charity, resulting in three distinct paths of service defined by the
>   thoughts and actions of John Dewey, Jane Addams, and Dorothy Day.

Rhoads, Robert A. (1997). *Community Service and Higher Learning: Explorations
of the Caring Self.* Albany, NY: State University of New York Press.
>   This book is a synthesis of social theory, feminist thought, and experi-
>   ential learning theory that examines the experiences of college stu-
>   dents in their commitment to service.

———— , and Jeffrey P. Howard, eds. (1998). *Academic Service Learning: A
Pedagogy of Action and Reflection.* New Directions for Teaching and Learning,
no. 73. San Francisco, CA: Jossey-Bass.
>   This may well be the most important book for faculty who are inter-
>   ested in a single book that addresses the multiple pedagogical consid-
>   erations of adopting a reflective teaching methodology. The book con-
>   tains short, concise conceptual and practical essays by some of the
>   leading service-learning educators.

Silcox, Harvey C. (1993). *A How-To Guide to Reflection: Adding Cognitive
Learning to Community Service Programs.* Holland, PA: Brighton Press.
>   While not written for college courses per se, and superseded by Giles
>   and Eyler's *A Practitioner's Guide to Reflection in Service-Learning*
>   (Vanderbilt University Press, 1996), this remains a useful work.
>   Reflection is a critical aspect of successful service-learning and Silcox
>   does a very good job on how to use various types of reflection in
>   teaching with a notable lack of jargon.

Stanton, T., D. Giles, Jr., and N. Cruz. (1999). *Service-Learning: A Movement's Pioneers Reflect on Its Origins, Practice, and Future.* San Francisco, CA: Jossey-Bass.

> The importance of this book is its ability to anchor the current service-learning movement solidly within a historical tradition of higher education reform by documenting the stories of those who brought service-learning from the margins of the academy into the mainstream of serious attempts at institutional renewal for civic education.

Zlotkowski, Edward, ed. (1998). *Successful Service-Learning Programs: New Models of Excellence in Higher Education.* Boston, MA: Anker Publishing.

> Accounting for a range of institutional types and sensitive to the nuances of institutional cultures, this book offers a number of institutional examples of successful integration of service-learning into the central academic mission of the campus. Its appendices include syllabi and model tenure and promotion guidelines.

Electronic Resources

www.aacu-edu.org
Association of American Colleges & Universities

> AAC&U's site provides detailed descriptions of its projects, including the Diversity Initiative, in which service-learning and campus-community partnerships play an important role. The site also contains general information about membership, meetings, and publications.

www.aacc.nche.edu/initiatives/SERVICE/SERVICE.HTM
American Association of Community Colleges, Service-Learning Page

> This is the site for AACC's service-learning project. Includes links to model programs at various community college campuses, general information about federal initiatives such as America Reads, and practical information about applying service-learning in the community college curriculum. Also includes a listing of workshops and events and links to service-learning organizations.

www.aahe.org/service/srv-lrn.htm
American Association for Higher Education, Service-Learning Project
A description of AAHE's Service-Learning Project, including coalition-building conferences and the 18-volume *Series on Service-Learning in the Disciplines* of which this volume is one. Also includes links to other service-learning resources and to other AAHE programs and partnerships.

www.fiu.edu/~time4chg/Library/bigdummy.html
The Big Dummy's Guide to Service-Learning
This site is organized around frequently asked questions and divided into faculty and programmatic issues. Includes "101 Ideas for Combining Service & Learning" in various disciplines.

www.compact.org
Campus Compact
This is service-learning's central agency. Campus Compact serves as a resource for finding other faculty engaged in service-learning, syllabi, publications, conference information, grants, and awards. The membership profile indicates Campus Compact's widespread presence in higher education. Historians can download model syllabi from history courses that incorporate service-learning. It is also possible to download the 1999 document by Harry Boyte and Elizabeth Hollander "Wingspread Declaration of the Civic Responsibilities of Research Universities."

www.cool2serve.org
Campus Outreach Opportunity League (COOL)
This website is primarily directed at students to aid their efforts in service. But faculty will find it useful to browse. It contains aids to enhance student leadership, books, and manuals for students, information on meetings, a listserv for questions and to exchange ideas.

www.mc.maricopa.edu/academic/compact/
Campus Compact National Center for Community Colleges
Includes listings of events, awards, and publications (with an on-line order form and a number of on-line versions). Also includes detailed descriptions of CCNCCC's mission and major projects.

http://csf.Colorado.EDU/sl/
The Colorado Service-Learning Home Page
>A comprehensive site with definitions of service-learning; a thorough listing of undergraduate service-learning programs with on-line course lists and syllabi; links to college and university homepages; and a list of links to service-learning organizations, networks, and resources. This site also houses a searchable archive of the Colorado Service-Learning listserv, which most faculty will find more useful for gathering ideas and resources than subscribing to the list itself, and which, on occasion, engages in faculty bashing.

www.studyabroad.com/exp.html
International Partnership for Service-Learning
>This site lists institutions with service-learning study abroad programs. It gives information about programs, lists countries that have established service-learning courses of study, curriculum information together with information on intercultural exchanges, and internship programs.

www.edb.utexas.edu/servicelearning/index.html
Learn, Serve & Surf
>An "Internet resource kit" for service-learning practitioners. A site created as part of a graduate student's work in instructional technology and the University of Texas at Austin. Lists model programs and practices, listservs, discussion sites, links, etc. Also contains a definition and description of service-learning and its various components, with a bibliography.

www.umich.edu/~ocsl/MJCSL/
Michigan Journal of Community Service-Learning
>MJCSL is a peer-reviewed academic journal containing papers written by faculty and service-learning educators on research, theory, pedagogy, and issues pertinent to the service-learning community. The site contains abstracts of MJCSL articles and information on subscribing and submitting manuscripts.

www.nicsl.coled.umn.edu
The National Service-Learning Clearinghouse
>This site contains a searchable database of K-12 and higher education service-learning literature, information about events, listservs, and Learn & Serve America efforts and links to a variety of service-learning information resources.

www.nsee.org
National Society for Experiential Education
> Includes information about various experiential education methods,
> including service-learning. Also includes membership and conference
> information, lists of publications and resources.

Contributors to This Volume

Volume Editors

Bill M. Donovan is associate professor of history at Loyola College in Baltimore, Maryland. He is a specialist in early modern Atlantic history and the history of the Portuguese Empire. He has been a Fulbright Fellow to Brazil and a 1997 Vasco da Gama Lecturer sponsored by the Portuguese Commission on the Discoveries. His publications include the award-winning article "Gypsies in Early Modern Portugal and Changing Conceptions of Social Deviancy" and essays on early modern crime, immigration, and trade.

Ira Harkavy is director of the Center for Community Partnerships and associate vice president at the University of Pennsylvania. He teaches in the departments of history, urban studies, and city and regional planning, and is executive editor of *Universities and Community Schools*. The West Philadelphia Improvement Corps (WEPIC), a 15-year partnership to create university-assisted community schools that connect the University of Pennsylvania and the West Philadelphia community, emerged and developed from seminars and research projects he directs with other colleagues at Penn.

Authors

Albert Camarillo is professor of history and director of the Center for Comparative Studies in Race and Ethnicity at Stanford University. His research and publications focus on the history of ethnic and racial minorities in American cities. His course Poverty and Homelessness in America was one of the first service-learning courses offered at Stanford more than a decade ago. He is the only faculty member in the history of Stanford University to receive the three highest awards for excellence in teaching.

Marshall C. Eakin is associate professor of history and associate director of the Center for Latin American and Iberian Studies at Vanderbilt University. A native Texan, he received his BA and MA in history from the University of Kansas, and his PhD in Latin American history from UCLA. In 1998 he was named to a Chair of Teaching Excellence (1998-2001) by the Vanderbilt University Board of Trust.

Elisa von Joeden-Forgey is an SSRC-MacArthur Fellow for International Peace and Security. She is currently completing her PhD in history at the University of Pennsylvania on race, law, and state violence in Germany as reflected in the experiences of Africans in Germany, 1884-1945. From 1995 through 1997 she worked on academically based community service projects at the University of Pennsylvania as part of her larger commitment to combining scholarship with social justice activism.

J. Matthew Gallman is the Henry R. Luce Professor of Civil War Era Studies at Gettysburg College. Prior to moving to Gettysburg he was in the Department of History at Loyola College in Baltimore, Maryland, where he was heavily involved in the activities of the Center for Public Service. His most recent book is *Receiving Erin's Children: Philadelphia, Liverpool, and the Irish Famine Migration, 1845-1855.*

Steve Hochstadt is professor and chair of History at Bates College in Lewiston, Maine. He teaches a course about the Holocaust and is doing an oral history of Jewish refugees from the Nazis who escaped to Shanghai. He serves on the board of the Holocaust Human Rights Center of Maine.

Beverly W. Jones is professor of history and dean of the University College at North Carolina Central University (NCCU). Prior to her appointment as dean, she served as director of NCCU's Community Service Program. She is participating in the W.K. Kellogg Foundation Initiative Building Bridges Between Practice and Knowledge in Non-Profit Management.

John Puckett is associate professor and associate dean at the University of Pennsylvania Graduate School of Education. His research interests include Progressive education history and the practice of university-assisted community schools. He is currently working on a book on Leonard Covello and the American community school.

Ralph M. Rosen is professor and chair of Classical Studies at the University of Pennsylvania. His research and publications focus primarily on Greek literature and intellectual history. He is currently teaching a new service-learning course in which college and high school students together study Plato's *Republic* in the light of vital contemporary questions.

John Saltmarsh teaches American history at Northeastern University, where he is associate professor of cooperative education and history. He has taught service-learning courses at Northeastern University and at Providence College, where he spent a year as a visiting research fellow in the Feinstein Institute for Public Service. He is currently on leave, directing the Project on Integrating Service With Academic Study at Campus Compact.

Michael Zuckerman is professor of history at the University of Pennsylvania. His current projects — on regionalism, religion, and the history of childhood — may carry him beyond schizophrenia, but teaching community service-learning is surely one of the sanest things he's ever done.

Series Editor

Edward Zlotkowski is professor of English at Bentley College. Founding director of the Bentley Service-Learning Project, he has published and spoken on a wide variety of service-learning topics. Currently, he is also a senior associate at the American Association for Higher Education.